SERMONS
SELDOM HEARD

SERMONS
SELDOM HEARD

Women Proclaim Their Lives

Edited by Annie Lally Milhaven

CROSSROAD • NEW YORK

1991

The Crossroad Publishing Company
370 Lexington Avenue, New York, NY 10017

Copyright © 1991 by Annie Lally Milhaven

Printed in the United States of America
Typesetting output: T_EXSource, Houston

Library of Congress Cataloging-in-Publication Data

Sermons seldom heard : women proclaim their lives / edited by Annie
Lally Milhaven.
    p.   cm.
Includes bibliographical references.
ISBN 0-8245-1066-6
    1. Sermons, American—Women authors. 2. Women—United States—
Social conditions.   I. Milhaven, Annie Lally.
BV4241.S43 1991
252'.0082 — dc20   90-28403
                                                     CIP

Contents

FOREWORD

Elisabeth Schüssler Fiorenza

Sermons Seldom Heard: Women Proclaim Their Lives is a volume
that could not have been envisaged, much less preached, twenty-five
years ago. The book demonstrates in a particular way the strides that
women in religion, theology, and ministry have made in the short
span of a few decades. Women now pour into divinity schools and
seminaries, and many have moved into the official ministry and leadership of churches and synagogues. As a result they are beginning to
change theology and ministry in very specific ways.

Feminist theology begins with the articulation of experience and
the systemic reflection on women's struggles for survival and change.
The sermons in this volume attest not only to the ordeals of suffering and dehumanization but also to the visions and voices, the hopes
and struggles that women today bring to their ministry, opening up
their own experiences and those of their unnamed sisters to public
theological reflection. The experience of women from all walks of
life — white and black, Christian and Jewish, heterosexual and lesbian, free and imprisoned, poor and middle class — comes here to
word. Women claim the Word by reclaiming their power to name divine and human reality, and in so doing they continue to empower
themselves and the Christian community.

The women who give voice in *Sermons Seldom Heard* bring to
the fore their lived experiences of struggle and survival in patriarchal
society and religion. One gets the impression that a more apt title for
a book like this would be *Sermons Never Heard*. For who of us has
heard from the pulpit the life-story of the one woman in three who is
the victim of incest? Who has heard a sermon about family violence
from a woman who was for years battered in a Christian home in the
presence of her two young sons? Have you ever experienced a sermon
on the violence of rape preached by a woman who has suffered rape?
And yet we live in a culture where rape is rampant and women of
all ages are unsafe on the streets of their neighborhoods. How many
of the worshipers in our churches and synagogues have listened to a
homily by an openly lesbian preacher? Who has heard in church from

a homeless mother living with her eight children in a car for fourteen months? Who ever encountered a sermon from a woman in prison for murdering, in a haze of drugs, her small son?

AIDS is a national health crisis, but do congregations come face to face with preachers who are struggling with HIV infection? We hear many clerics railing from the pulpit against homosexual lifestyles and even forbidding any use of condoms in the name of G-d. Have these preachers ever encountered the devastation wrought by AIDS? In this book we hear the sermon preached by a woman minister who is legendary in Boston for her loving ministry to those struggling with HIV infection and their families. Women who have terminated pregnancy are hypocritically condemned in thousands of churches. Yet how many sermons have you heard from women who lived through the experience of having an abortion or have helped other women to make their decisions? How often have you listened to a sermon on anti-Semitism preached by a Jewish woman or on the insidious effects of racism given by an African American woman? What about a homily from a single woman enraged by the exaltation of "blessed singleness" in churches where either marriage or chastity is the norm of respectability? One realizes with surprise that one has never encountered a sermon on depression, considering that many in the pews suffer daily from it.

In this book we read a sermon from a woman who works with "throwaway" children in a society where the focus on unborn life lets us forget that one of every *five* American children lives in poverty. We hear of the old Christian tradition of sanctuary from a woman leading the movement in opposition to United States policy in El Salvador. She speaks of her determination to keep refugees from being deported and of the price she has paid for her witness. These sermons invite us to reflect theologically on retirement, on volunteerism, on doing justice, on the environment, and on turning the process of divorce into a sacrament, an experience of grace and empowerment, by a woman who refused to consign herself to being powerless in a crisis of family upheaval. The multicolored rich tapestry of women's life is spread out before us for critical feminist theological reflection.

This collection of essays, however, does not just contribute to a different way of "doing theology"; it suggests a different model for preaching and proclamation. Women who have been excluded throughout the centuries from ordination and preaching are not simply the silent majority in churches and synagogues. They are the *silenced* majority. The target audience of the sermon is the proverbial "woman in the pew," whereas its rhetoric is fashioned by male clerics. For all practical purposes women of the past and the present are still prohibited from *defining* the role of proclamation in terms of their own experience and feminist theological analysis.

The rhetoric of the homily remains that of the ordained cleric who by law or custom is still male in many religious communities. Even where women have access to the pulpit they are still socialized into a clerical patriarchal model of preaching that does not tolerate any counterargument and focuses on the authority of Scripture or religious doctrine rather than on the lived experience of G-d's people. In such an institutional situation the danger is real that the sermon will not articulate the rich and pluriform experience of G-d's people but merely reflect the experience of those ordained in patriarchal biblical religion. The sermon of the male cleric tends to universalize his own particular and limited experience and to declare it as the experience of the Divine *par excellence*. What is limited and particular to his experience is proclaimed as universal and paradigmatic for everyone.

What this book suggests is that the impoverishment of preaching today is due not to the lack of talented and able preachers but to the structural clericalism that demands that one single group of persons — the ordained — articulate the richness and fullness of the experience of G-d's liberating presence in our struggles today. Instead, this collection proposes that the clerical style of preaching needs to be replaced by a different, more communal communicative praxis of proclamation.

In short, the "silenced majority" must be heard and allowed into speech again if the richness and fullness of G-d's presence with us are to be articulated and proclaimed today. The right of the faithful to proclamation is not just charismatic; it must become the presupposition of all preaching. Women's feminist/womanist/mujerista theological reflection on their experience of G-d's liberating presence in their struggles for survival, justice, and the change of patriarchal structures must be proclaimed as G-d's word for our times. This book takes a creative step in the right direction.

INTRODUCTION

Annie Lally Milhaven

The inspiration for this volume — title and all — dawned on me during a recent New Year Evening's Mass. The pastor of St. Joseph Church in Providence, Rhode Island, preached on "Alcoholism," a sermon that seemed to me well researched and entirely timely. On New Year's Eve, often an "eve" of drinking, a reflection on alcohol and the disease of alcoholism is relevant. One sentence in the sermon stayed with me: "Nine of ten men will leave an alcoholic wife, but nine of ten women will stay with an alcoholic husband."

I had listened to sermons for over fifty years; never until then had I heard a sermon on alcoholism. Yet this disease afflicts millions of Americans, wreaks havoc on family life, and often leaves children maimed emotionally for life. What other sermons, I asked myself, had I never heard? A list of topics began to form: depression, rape, retirement.

Sharing the list with fellow students at Harvard Divinity School not only encouraged the idea for developing a book of such sermons but greatly expanded the list of possible topics. Topics such as incest — experts state one of three women is an incest victim — AIDS, racism, anti-Semitism, throwaway children, abortion, divorce, homelessness, and others were added. Until then, the book was not intended as a volume on women's issues only. At that point I decided to have the book be a *woman's book* as women and children by far endure most in these situations. Simultaneously, I decided that each sermon should be contributed by a woman who herself had experienced what she was preaching, or who consoles patients and their families as in the case of Rev. Jennifer Phillips.

Seeking, finding, selecting, and keeping over twenty contributors was the most difficult work in constructing this volume. The sermons are original writings, and for contributors this work often involved delving deeply into painful experiences that proved psychologically threatening and, in some instances, as in incest, had never fully been admitted to consciousness. In fact, one potential contributor became suicidal in the attempt to write about her defenselessness and suffering

1

as a child victim of incest in a Christian home. Another woman, after first agreeing, later wrote: "I have been struggling this past month with my own healing from sexual abuse. . . . It has taken an enormous amount of my energy and my focus. . . . I will be unable to complete my sermon. . . . "

Another contributor, while doing research and reflecting on her topic, experienced profound and painful feelings of bewilderment. She wrote:

> I do hope you strongly emphasize in your Introduction how painful it has been for women to write these sermons. I have spoken [on . . .] times without number, and rarely had a qualm. Never, however, have I had to write about it theologically or in light of my own story. . . . The process made me anxious and nauseous.

One woman, normally vivacious and energetic, phoned me in the midst of her writing. Full of tears and sorrow she said: "I am crying about my life; it was so sad." Listening to and reflecting on such experiences that some of the contributors described as they wrote their sermons, I questioned my right to be a part of such personal and private distress. I reflected that I, and you, the readers, had no right to be privy to this pain. But the women persisted, and now we are indebted to them for a "first" in these sermons seldom heard with the perspectives they afford.

Here then is a volume that bears *witness* to women's lives; women weaving the personal with the biblical, the practical with the theological. As Rosemary Radford Ruether states:

> The uniqueness of feminist theology lies not in its use of the criterion of experience but rather in its use of women's experience, which has been almost entirely shut out of theological reflection in the past. The use of women's experience in feminist theology, therefore, explodes as a critical force.[1]

The women we meet in this volume are doing theology in a new and different voice as they share with us the testimony and the witness of their unique experiences. Each contribution is divided into sections:

Section One is the *Sermon* proper, often illustrated by the personal story of the contributor.

An *Autobiographical Statement* indicating the experience that compels and enables the contributor to speak or preach comprises Section Two.

Background Information in Section Three, consists of scientific, historical, social and/or cultural data on the topic being presented. This additional data will enrich the reader/preacher on the scope of each issue and should prove an invaluable ready reference for the preacher.

A Bibliography of key books (some annotated) and other references and pamphlets in Section Four provides expert and up-to-date information.

A list of *Resources/Agencies and Organizations* is provided in Section Five. These agencies, organizations, and hot-lines will further enhance a preacher's information but above all will provide help and hope for the hearers of the Word in the pews.

The sermons cluster around issues paramount in social, civil, family, and religious lives. Consisting of twenty-one chapters, the volume seeks new models of expression. The sermons are grouped into six parts: in Part One, "Violence in Women's Lives," Susan Hagood Lee in "Witness to Christ, Witness to Pain: One Woman's Journey through Wife Battering," describes her eleven years of battering in a marriage, which for biblical reasons she felt bound to endure. But she also describes how her liberation came through meditation on biblical passages that helped her move from bondage. Nancy E. Owens and Jayne Rose Brewer in "Shattering the Silence: Family Incest" seek to "shatter the silence" surrounding family incest. They describe incest as the hidden, though common rot in seemingly "model" Christian homes. Beth Gerstein, author of "Rape: Violence against Women," describes how rape changed her life and warns that she may be raped again, and yet again. These women want the churches and synagogues to address this rampant violation of women's lives. It must not be only Phil Donahue and Oprah Winfrey's TV shows that talk about and reflect upon these taboo topics.

Women and children as America's new underclasses are addressed in Part Two, and Jennifer Johnston in "Doing Justice Upstream" describes the need for economic justice for women. She points out that churches have treated the symptoms of poverty for centuries yet have not tried to analyze why the poor have no food nor why the poor are predominantly women and children.

Marion F. Avarista sees six thousand runaway children each year in Providence, Rhode Island. She asks in a moving sermon, "Throwaway Children," if there are so many youngsters in a comparatively small city in the smallest state, what must the numbers be in New York City or Los Angeles? Realizing that these are *our* children, she asks why she must return government money because people — like us in the pews — resist zoning law changes to allow these young people to live under supervision in group homes. One must press further and ask what would be the response of some churches if it were announced today that instead of abandoned children, six thousand fetuses were at risk, about to be aborted at the Travelers Aid shelter of a small city.

Glenda Smith describes two kinds of homelessness: living with her eight children in a car for fourteen months and the family's move into a project where drugs and mice are rampant. The project she graphically records "as hell with a roof over our heads."

The experience of women in prison is poignantly portrayed by Maria Rivera (not her real name), who spent ten years in prison for murdering her four-year-old son while in a haze of drugs and alcohol. The imagery in the first paragraphs of her sermon, "Walls of Ice," is deeply spiritual: the prison as purgatory, the warden as the Virgin Mary, and the psychiatrist as God.

Part Three focuses on "Mental Health: Women Taking Charge of Their Lives." One way to attain and protect good mental health is to have choices and options. In "Depression: When Life Becomes 'Stale, Flat, and Unprofitable,'" Milhaven points out that depression is the greatest major public health problem of the world. It makes no difference, according to the World Health Organization (WHO), if countries are developed or underdeveloped; depression afflicts them equally. She makes clear that women suffer from this disease in greater numbers than men, yet women often have too few choices open to them. Nevertheless, there are alternatives: taking charge of one's life even in small ways is a bulwark against a "stale, flat, and unprofitable" existence. Violet Morin and Mary A. come from another direction in "Alcoholism: I am Powerless Over..." in describing this disease and that of drug dependency. "I am powerless over..." means that with the help of a higher power, people can take charge of their lives...one day at a time.

Retirement has become a major social problem because many retirees, especially men, are unprepared for the void in their lives when they no longer "go to work." This often precipitates a crisis in the home, as Milhaven shows in "Retirement: 'Thus at Time's Humming Loom I Ply.'" She draws attention to the increase in suicide among this group, now almost equal to the fifteen-to-twenty-four age group — the group most at risk for suicide. Finding a new identity and a place in the world of volunteering is described by Betsy Garland. In "Volunteerism: The Gift of Oneself," she makes clear how volunteering is also an ideal way to avoid boredom; by enriching others, one enriches one's own mental, physical, and spiritual life.

"Human Sexuality and Theological Discourse," Part Four, acknowledges female sexuality as a unique area where women's experiences must become a greater force in theology. Karen Keating Ansara's "Throw No Stones" on the issue of abortion is precisely designed toward this end. Showing how we must first hear a woman's story, she indicates how few women volunteer to speak about their decision to have an abortion. Consequently most Americans contemplate abortion in the abstract.

"Overcoming the Fear of Love" is Mary E. Hunt's approach to a sermon on women's love, one for another. "Love," she writes, "is alleged to make all things new...until same-sex ways of loving are broached. Then, as if by magic, the curtain falls...and love that is love is denied, demeaned, destroyed by religiously sanctioned ideology."

"'Blessed Singleness': A Journey in Uncharted Waters" is approached by Frances K. Kissling not only as a woman's choice but also her right and privilege. Against a church background of fear of sex, she demonstrates the basic distrust and blame of women many churchmen exemplify in both word and deed, and how this affects single women.

The five sermons comprising Part Five, "Neglected Issues Women Want Proclaimed," could be expanded greatly.

In "Divorce as Grace, Empowerment, and Sacrament" Janice P. Leary provides an instructive and practical sermon on women's reclaiming their power during a divorce. With a computer she worked out a model settlement of the family estate. Not only that, but she managed to achieve civility in the emotional twists and turns of the separating family crisis. On the day the court finalized her divorce, Janice describes in an empowering fashion how she and her friends held a ritual of celebration to begin her new life.

Helping us move through another fear is Jennifer M. Phillips in "The Hidden Christ" — her call to minister in a time of AIDS. She points out, as Avarista does in "Throwaway Children," that our final judgment will be based not on intention, philosophy, or the state of our inner lives but on an action of the most fundamental kind: "tending the human needs of the least among us."

Kate Penfield in "Declaration of Interdependence: Good News in the Environmental Crisis" exhorts us to reflect on the interconnectedness of earth, air, and water, as well as humankind. She points out that the dualism retained in Christianity requires a new analysis. Similarly, the common comparison between Earth and Woman needs to be evaluated in light of the challenge both pose to the tradition of ages.

A vision of an ancient Christian custom is recast in Darlene Nicgorski's "Sanctuary: Confronting Oppression." Seeing the movement as an opportunity for the conversion of the North American church in assisting persecuted Christians from Central America, she joined in to protect these peoples pouring over the southern border of the United States. For her and her colleagues' pains, they suffered harassment from our federal government and a threat of many years in prison. She quotes Elie Wiesel: "Because of indifference, one dies before one actually dies. To be in the window and watch people being sent to concentration camps... and do nothing, that's being dead."[2]

Part Six, "Dealing with Difference," contains three sermons. Anne Scheibner inverts the coin of racism, to present it from the viewpoint of a white feminist. In "Beyond Inclusivity?: A White Feminist Reflects on Racism," she explores what white women must do to understand racism. She underscores the need for white women to stop colluding in the current racist orientation within "the women's movement," and indeed within the movement toward ordaining women.

Chandra Taylor Smith in "Wonderfully Made: Preaching Physical Self-Affirmation" demonstrates the importance of preaching her message to black women. Racism has taken its toll on these women. Chandra describes the norm of feminine beauty in America: white women who are thin, painted, and perfumed with current creams and potions. The importance of black women seeing what they themselves look like and cherishing that view is crucial to self-esteem. Rather than attempting to pour themselves into white skins, black women must, like Harriet Tubman and Sojourner Truth, claim the reality: they are fearfully and wonderfully made.

The final chapter, "Anti-Semitism: Looking beyond Hostility," by S. Tamar Kamionkowski traces the roots of anti-Semitism from the birth of Christianity through the ages. She delineates the reality of Judaism's long existence as a living and prospering tradition that even today poses problems within the Christian community. "It has become fashionable in our times to speak of a Judeo-Christian tradition. This notion reflects an attempt to look to our shared roots and common beliefs, to make connections and to bond in mutuality. Rather than completely disassociating from Judaism, the parent religion is embraced. On one level, this attempt is admirable; but on a deeper level, it is disturbing." Tamar analyzes the ambivalences and complications posed by her description and looks to a religious reality beyond hostility.

As mentioned previously, the author of each sermon has either personally experienced the issue discussed or worked with or ministered to those who endure the problem. Exceptions have been made in a few sermons as in Maria Rivera's "Walls of Ice." Maria dictated her sermon to Suzanne Schmidt, a friend imprisoned at the same time for her peace work against the Electric Boat Company located in Rhode Island. Suzanne transcribed Maria's words into a moving sermon. Similarly, Elena Natalizia, founder of the Rhode Island Alliance of Justice, prepared the informational background for the chapter. Likewise for "Shattering the Silence: Family Incest" Nancy Owens provided the extensive research and theological framework for this crime against women, and Jayne Rose Brewer wrote the sermon.

In the attempt to find a woman who had had the experience of homelessness, I was led to Glenda Smith by Sister Joan Rokiki of McAuley House, a shelter in the rundown South Side of Providence, Rhode Island. I interviewed this amazing mother of eight young children, who spent fourteen months with them living in a car. I want to acknowledge Jim Tull's invaluable assistance in helping me with background information and the sources for the rest of the chapter that I put together. As co-director of Amos House in South Providence, Tull's twelve years working with the homeless seems to have made him deeply thoughtful: "I use the philosophy of Amos," he says, "but not his methods."

Anne Scheibner, a white feminist, collaborated with Linda C. Powell, who is a black feminist social critic, on the chapter "Beyond Inclusivity: A White Feminist Reflects on Racism." Linda contributed the background information for Anne's sermon on racism as "white peoples' problem."

Many contributors were my recent colleagues at Harvard Divinity School — some of us feeling much of our education was not always at the forefront of the lives we and other women live. In addition, women who have no theological background — save their lived experiences — give voice in this volume to the voiceless in our midst. The mix of women with little or no theological background and of women steeped in theological studies is a characteristic to be noted in the volume. To be noted also some of the sermons have been preached, some have not, and the authors of some sermons are not allowed to preach at all.

The contributors are — or were all at one time — residents in Massachusetts and Rhode Island. But the problems they preach about are countrywide, indeed worldwide, not unique to New England or to the gallant women who persevered at HDS to give us "one more assignment." We are in their debt.

My own indebtedness is multiple. First of all I want to thank Elisabeth Schüssler Fiorenza for her enthusiastic encouragement of this venture. Not only did she think it timely and useful, but she added a couple of sermon suggestions of her own. Elisabeth crowned this assistance by agreeing to write the Foreword and to lead forth the volume to the reading and preaching worlds.

I thank the contributors who worked perseveringly in spite of many obstacles, sadnesses, and even personal resistances, to write down their original work. Each one had to start from her own experiences: there were no models for this series of sermons. I thank especially Nancy E. Owens, my colleague at Harvard Divinity School, for her invaluable help in fitting names, addresses, and phone numbers of students and friends for a specific sermon when needed. She appeared to be a walking warehouse of information on our colleagues in school: who could write what, and failing on one try, whom to call on as replacement.

Early in the construction of this volume Marie Cantlon joined the project. I am in her debt for her unfailing patience as we worked together on the manuscript and her reminder: "Bear in mind this is original material. It cannot be rushed; it will not be easy to pull it all together."

I also want to thank Frank Oveis of Crossroad/Continuum for the encouragement expressed in the magic of his words: "I think the idea of this book is terrific...." I thank Beatrice S. Braun, M.D., for consultation on the sermon on depression. Shelly Martin, our daughter, has provided invaluable services in the preparation and compilation of the volume, and for all the contributors I thank her for helping to see it to the finish.

NOTES

1. Rosemary Radford Ruether, *Sexism and God-Talk: Toward a Feminist Theology* (Boston: Beacon Press, 1983), p. 13.
2. *New York Times*, October 28, 1987.

PART ONE

Violence in Women's Lives

1

Witness to Christ, Witness to Pain: One Woman's Journey through Wife Battering

Susan Hagood Lee

SERMON

In the Name of God the Creator, Nurturer of Life and Love, Source of Compassion and Peace. Amen.

My story is long and painful, hard to tell and hard to hear. But as a Christian called to witness faithfully to the reality of my life, I want to share with you my religious journey through abuse.

From my earliest years, I was a faithful churchgoer, enjoying the religious ambiance, awed by the loving and all-powerful God that I believed watched over me. Then I married a man who, once the wedding ring was safely on my finger, began to abuse me. The crisis was both personal and religious. Where was God when, one month after our wedding, my husband first blackened my eyes? Where was God when he punched me in the stomach when I was pregnant? Where was God when my husband threw me off a kitchen chair because I had talked to a priest? Where was God when he broke my nose because I wanted to see my family? And what did God expect of me, a wife who had vowed at the altar to love and cherish my husband through good times and bad?

The first three years of my marriage were years of confusion. At times my husband was charming and solicitous, as he had been before our wedding, showering me with attention, eager to share his hopes and plans with me. But his mood could change quickly and without warning. Small things would make him irrationally angry; a tea tag that fell into his cup of tea would ruin his day. I tried hard to please him, playing by his rules in an effort to quiet his insecurity, hoping that if only he could come to trust me everything would work out. We had long intellectual discussions about values. As a bright doctoral

---

I plan to preach this sermon to my congregation of the Episcopal Church in Fall River, Massachusetts.

student in psychology, he was an articulate and persuasive advocate for his perspectives. He effectively assaulted my sense of right and wrong and considerably weakened my confidence in my ability to judge the difference. Still there were aspects of his thinking that I could not accept. Why did he want me to cut off all contact with my family? Why did he not want me to work, despite our always precarious finances? Why would he never leave me alone with another adult just for a friendly conversation?

The struggle between us over the values that would govern our life together left me demoralized. I felt as though I were lost at sea with no firm ground under my feet, tossed about by waves beyond my control and with no horizon in sight to give me hope. One evening I sat on the sofa in my living room, my head spinning from the chaos of my life. I realized that I needed some sort of help. But who or what would it be? My trust in my own judgment was destroyed, and I rejected my husband's ways. I had no faith in political belief systems, whether democracy, socialism, or communism, to offer effective guidance for my troubled life. God and Jesus seemed impossibly far away. Glancing around, I saw a dusty Bible on my bookshelf, an unused wedding present. Suddenly I realized that I did trust the Bible; surely the Bible would not lead me astray! The Bible would be the guide I so desperately needed.

Over the next few years, the Bible became my daily bread; I used its precepts as the standard for relating to my husband. I began with the Gospels and was overwhelmed by the vision of Jesus' teachings expressed in the Sermon on the Mount. His vision of a community of justice and trust, where people cared for one another with generosity and selflessness, was so unlike the ethic of my husband, who became enraged if I even suggested saying hello to the neighbors. I was particularly taken with Jesus' approach to enemies: "Love your enemies, bless them that curse you, do good to them that hate you, and pray for them which despitefully use you, and persecute you" (Matt. 5:44, KJV).

This seemed a daring approach to the ordinary ways of relating among nations, neighborhoods, and families. If I was to adopt this radical ethic, though, I had to apply it consistently and continue to try to love my husband despite his abusive treatment. I studied the Bible for instructions about marital problems and found several passages that seemed relevant. The Sermon on the Mount addressed the violence I regularly faced: "Ye have heard that it hath been said, An eye for an eye, and a tooth for a tooth: But I say unto you, That ye resist not evil: but whosoever shall smite thee on thy right cheek, turn to him the other also" (Matt. 5:38–39).

Later on in the Gospels I read Jesus' prohibition of divorce: "What

God hath joined together, let not man put asunder" (Matt. 19:6). I read about the virtue of forgiveness: "Then came Peter to him, and said, Lord, how oft shall my brother sin against me, and I forgive him? til seven times? Jesus saith unto him, I say not unto thee, Until seven times: but, Until seventy times seven" (Matt. 18:21–22). In Paul's letter to the Corinthians, I heard the rationale for not divorcing: "Unto the married I command, yet not I, but the Lord, Let not the wife depart from her husband.... For what knowest thou, O wife, whether thou shalt save thy husband?" (1 Cor. 7:10, 16).

My course of action seemed clear. God's will, as the Bible instructed, was that I stay with my husband, forgiving him when he hurt me, countering his evil behavior with my love, cooperating with God's plan of salvation for him. It all fit into a meaningful program for me and confirmed my deep desire to see my marriage work, as well as to keep my young family together. The only drawback for me in this adjustment was the business about turning the other cheek. When my husband slapped me around, I knew without a doubt that this was *not* good; I never offered him my other cheek. My lived experience of violence conflicted with the Bible-based rationale I had worked out, and this conflict was the seed of my eventual escape from abuse.

I struggled on for an additional three years, trying to change my husband's behavior though patient long-suffering and persuasion, but all to no avail. He became more jealous and intractable than before, enforcing through his unpredictable rages a restrictive set of rules for me. I could not drive or handle money; I could not do the family shopping; I could not take walks in the neighborhood; I could not speak to, or even look at, the neighbors. He arranged our phone line so that our home phone was an extension of his office phone; I could not make a call without the fear of his listening. He censored all my mail. I had no one I could talk to about my life; he would not leave me alone even with his own relatives.

The turning point came when my husband refused to allow the older of our two children to attend kindergarten. I realized that the restrictions my husband applied to my life were being extended to my two sons. To sacrifice my own life for a cause I believed in was one thing, but I was determined not to sacrifice my children's lives. I realized that my biblical plan of overcoming evil with good wasn't working; evil was winning out, and my children's well-being was threatened.

When my husband refused to consider a divorce, I took some money from my children's piggy bank; the boys and I rode the bus to the nearby city, a strictly forbidden activity. We went to Legal Aid for help; the office was closed that day. At a phone booth in a nearby department store, I called Welfare with my last dime; the woman told me there was a three-day waiting period, and besides I was in the wrong city.

"What can I do?" I asked her in despair. "I can't go back to my husband!"

"Sorry, we can't help."

I wandered out on the street in a daze, one small boy in each hand. We stumbled along for a block, when suddenly my husband's car pulled alongside. He pleaded with me to come back, promising desperately he would change. I didn't believe him, I had heard his promises before, but I had nowhere else to go, and I got in the car.

My husband did change his behavior, for a very brief while. Then his violent temper returned, and our lives went back to "normal." I wondered about my lack of success in getting away from him. Was it a sign that God wanted me to stay with him? The possibility confused me. The following spring I tried again to leave, God's will or not. This time Legal Aid *was* open, but the lawyer refused to help me.

"Your husband makes too much money," he said. "You don't come under our guidelines."

"But *I* have *no* money," I pleaded. "I had to take the bus fare from the children's bank again!"

"Sorry, we can't help."

I left his office crying hysterically and made my way home again. This time, I had brought the return bus fare also; I was becoming more realistic about society's — and God's? — lack of support for me.

I didn't try to leave again for several years and became increasingly depressed. I continued to study the Bible and to pray, asking God for guidance about my marriage. I also turned to the *Book of Common Prayer:*

> May thy Holy Spirit guide me in my uncertainty, saving me from self-will, and the placing of desire before the burden of responsibility. Let it be thy will, not mine, that I seek, and show me how I can both serve thee and fulfill my duty towards those dependent upon me. Give me wisdom in this hour, O Lord; and when I see thy way, give me grace to follow in it.   (*Prayers for All Occasions*)

But God was silent. For many months, I heard no answer, no clear path to follow. Where was the God who had promised to be with us? No one was with me! My only companions were my two sweet children, and I refused to burden them, at their tender age, with my inner struggles. Was it God's will that I suffer? I thought of Jesus on the cross; was crucifixion God's will for me? If God had not spared his Son, why should he spare me?

Then one day something happened in my thinking. I was sitting in prayer, meditating on Jesus hanging on the cross. Suddenly, the cross seemed to move! Instead of being in front of me, it shifted over to my side, as if Jesus was hanging on his cross *beside* me. I was crucified and finally knew where God was: God was hanging beside me, crucified also! I was not alone; God was with me in agony also. When I hurt, God hurt; when I was hit, God was hit; when I was bruised, God was bruised; when I could not bear the pain anymore, neither could God. Now this was *not* the God I had hoped for; I was looking for the knight-in-shining-armor God, the God who would gallop in on a white charger, waving a magic wand, and save me! But this rescuer-God had been silent; this savior-God was dead. The God I found, the God in agony, the God with me in my pain, became my new God. This God understood my predicament; this God knew what it was to be crucified. This God did *not* want me to suffer; this God wanted me to be happy. But I had to save myself; God would not do it for me. That was the meaning of the silence. I had to make my own decisions; I was free to make my own decisions; the choice to stay or leave was mine.

Several years after this pivotal event, I finally found the courage to leave. From time to time I would read in the newspaper about a woman's shelter in the area where any woman could go and stay for free. I realized that this was an option I didn't have before; this was a place I could get help at last. The sticking point in leaving was my children, who were now in elementary school. My always-persuasive husband had convinced them that there was something wrong with momma: she couldn't quite be trusted, she had to be guarded, watched out for. The children became efficient little spies, loyally reporting by telephone what momma was doing. I came to realize that the boys would not come with me if I left; and if they knew I was leaving, they would report to their father who would be home in a flash from his office a block away. If I left, it had to be a surreptitious and solitary escape. But how could I leave my children? They were the center of my life. God might accept a wife leaving an abusive husband, but a mother abandoning her children? I knew I could not stay in the family, the pain was too suffocating, but I also knew I could not leave my children. I started to be obsessed by this dilemma, thinking about little else all day long. I felt trapped, and my emotional pain grew heavier and heavier. Late one evening, I sat alone on the floor of the boys' bedroom next to the kitchen. My husband was at his office, the children asleep. I had no more strength to carry on. The aspirin in the cabinet over the refrigerator started to seem like a way out of the unremitting pain. But what would happen to my children? I thought of them waking up in the morning, and finding their mother dead on the kitchen floor. How could I do that to them? Better, I thought, for them to find me gone

one day — but still alive. Suddenly, I breathed a sigh of relief. It was okay for me to leave; life somewhere else could be good; the pain could end.

Over the next months I gathered my courage to walk out. I was too distraught to read the Bible any more, but a phrase from Jeremiah echoed in my mind: "You shall escape with your life, and nothing more" (Jer. 21:9). I would not have my children or my home; I would leave behind my furniture, my silver, and my books. But I would have my life, and that was all that mattered. I had little energy to pray. God had been silent for so long! But the Kyrie Eleison frequently ran through my head: "Lord have mercy, Lord have mercy, Lord have mercy." Have mercy on the violence. Have mercy on the children. Have mercy on my weakness. Have mercy on my broken marriage. Have mercy on me. Then one day it occurred to me that, of course, *God* had mercy on me. God was the Merciful One by definition! The one who had no mercy was me: I refused to forgive myself for marrying my husband, or for staying with him, or for being unable to cope. But how could I blame myself for marrying someone that, at the time, I loved? How could I blame myself for trying to make my marriage work? I had married him in faith and in trust; I had done my best to love him. I had to forgive myself for my marriage's failure; I had to stop being so hard and demanding on myself. I was only human; I was limited in what I could do. I could not change my husband; I could not save him. Other work waited for me. The work I had tried to do, to comfort my husband's insecurities and to help him love himself, was over, incomplete. My new work was to love myself and provide a loving, not a violent, home for my children.

My exodus finally came in the summer. I planned to leave when my husband was with both children, so that I would not be leaving the boys alone. For weeks, he took only one boy at a time, as if he sensed my plan. Then early one afternoon, as I was fixing lunch, he took both boys into our side yard to work on an old car. In the middle of slicing a tomato, I glanced out the kitchen window at the three of them and knew, "This is the moment! Now I'm going to leave." I put down the knife and left the tomato half-sliced. I quietly got my purse — through some mix-up I actually had ten dollars, a small fortune for me. I slipped out the front door, leaving it ajar so as not to alert them by making any noise. I crept around the block and headed through the neighborhood, on streets my husband never used, for a distant bus route, as I knew he would immediately check the bus stops near our house. An hour later, I was on the bus for downtown. Once in the city, I sat trembling in a Burger King, trying to figure out what to do next and decided to call the women's shelter I had read about. They said that, yes, they had a bed available, and, yes, I could come stay.

After taking another bus, I walked the few blocks to the shelter, rang the bell, and the door opened. A woman said, "Come in, Susan, we're expecting you." It was eleven years, thirteen days after my wedding. My long agony was over at last. A new life had begun!

As I have described in this account, my religious beliefs were an important reason I stayed so long in my abusive marriage. I still believe that it is good to care about other people and to extend your life for their sake. But I've learned that God wants me to love myself also, and to balance my love for others with love for myself. I've learned that marriage isn't the ultimate it seemed to be when I was younger; as Myrna and Robert Kysar say in a paraphrase of Jesus, "Marriage was made for humans; not humans for marriage." I've learned that the Epistle to the Ephesians is just plain wrong when it advises, "Wives, be subject to your husbands." My message for women is this: "Wives, leave your husbands, if they abuse you — do it today! God loves you and doesn't want you to suffer." My message for the church is that we need fearlessly to examine the theology that sets women and men up in a power hierarchy that supports violence. We need to reconsider the theology of suffering and self-sacrifice and replace it with a theology of hope and affirmation of human beings. We need to make the church a safe place for women, where pain can be shared and new life found. In this safe place, women and men together may work out nonviolent, nurturing ways to relate to one another. And then God's community of love may come among us.

AUTOBIOGRAPHICAL STATEMENT

My interest in becoming an ordained minister began when I was a little girl, attending a tiny Episcopal church in Saudi Arabia, where my father worked for an oil company. We had services on Saturday night — the larger town, sixty miles away, got the minister on Sundays — and I attended faithfully with my mother and some of my sisters. I remember playing at "wedding" with my sisters early in my life, when I was seven or eight. I never wanted to be the bride or groom; I always wanted to be the minister! We would drape some leftover cloth around my neck to serve as a stole, and I would ceremoniously perform the wedding. When I was a teenager, I remember listening to our real minister say the Holy Communion service, and I thought to myself, "I can read that just as well as he can!"

I soon learned that girls did not become minsters. Although I was allowed to serve on the Junior Altar Guild, I was not permitted past the altar rail once the service had started; only my male classmates could be acolytes. When I was in high school, there were hardly any boys attending the little church near my boarding school in Switzerland, where I was sent once I had finished the school in Saudi Arabia. One young man used to come occasionally, and the English vicar would collar him as soon as he came through the door and press him into duty as crucifer. The young man would charge down the aisle with the cross, clearly in protest. We half-dozen young women watched from the choir, both amused and chagrined that none of us were ever asked to carry the cross.

The situation started to change about the time I was a student at Brown University. I remember our college chaplain, John Crooker, mention the idea of women priests, and I felt immediately drawn to the possibility. My life took an unexpected turn, however, when I married. I drifted away from the Episcopal Church and from any idea of being ordained. When my marriage finally broke up, I felt my life was in too much of a mess even to consider ordination.

Then two years later, I took a course at a nearby parish on Women and the Church. I was astounded to learn that women had been active in the church for many centuries, in roles of great responsibility and authority. I was particularly taken by the abbesses, the monastic women elected to rule their monastery, which in many cases included both men and women, as well as large tracts of land, with its inhabitants. Somehow the idea of women in such positions changed how I felt about being ordained myself. It didn't seem like such a far-fetched idea anymore, or so terribly new and radical. I saw a tradition of women in the church, following Christ and serving their communities in creative and important ways. Suddenly I knew that I wanted to join this tradition, and I decided that if the abbesses could do it, so could I! Within weeks I told my rector that I wanted to become a priest, and I started on the long road to ordination. I was ordained to the priesthood in 1988.

BACKGROUND INFORMATION

Domestic violence against women is a paradox, existing in many homes across the United States, threatening women's well-being and frequently their lives; yet it is often discounted as a private "family" matter. Though a crime in many states, many judges and lawyers still belittle women who seek legal protection. Religious institutions support marriage and family life, frequently frowning on divorce; yet the social structure advocated in the Bible, patriarchy, provides the theological underpinning for violence against women in marriage. Church leaders hesitate to address domestic violence. But such violence is happening in their congregations; millions of women each year, in every socio-economic class and in every ethnic group, are victims. Women are injured and killed on a regular basis, and religion is partly to blame, both for its support of patriarchy and for its silence in the face of human suffering.

A battered woman, as defined by Rita-Lou Clarke in *Pastoral Care of Battered Women*, is a woman who is "repeatedly subjected to any forceful physical or psychological behavior by a man in order to coerce her to do something he wants her to do without any concern for her rights."[1] The FBI estimates that a woman is beaten every fifteen seconds in the United States. More than one million abused women seek medical help for injuries caused by battering each year.[2] At Boston City Hospital, approximately 70 percent of the assault victims received in the emergency room are women who have been attacked in their home.[3] A 1987 report indicated that 29 percent of female homicide victims are killed by family members or boyfriends.[4] A study conducted at a Connecticut hospital revealed that battering accounts for one in four suicide attempts by women.[5] While some women batter their husbands, men commit 95 percent of all assaults on spouses, according to National Crime Survey data from 1973 to 1981.[6] In addition, the severity and extent of injuries incurred by men are insignificant and not comparable to those sustained by women.[7] No social group is exempt from wife battering. Violence against wives will occur at least once in two-thirds of all marriages, estimates researcher Maria Roy.[8] Straus, Gelles, and Steinmetz estimate that 25 percent of wives are severely beaten during the course of their marriage.[9] Montgomery County, Maryland, one of the most affluent areas in the country, reported 650 incidents of wife assault in one year.[10] Such figures may be underreported; a study of Kentucky battered women by Louis Harris Associates reveals that battered women called the police in less that 10 percent of the cases.[11]

These figures are so high because our society inherently believes that violence is acceptable under certain conditions. We also accept that the man is the head of the household, responsible for discipline among family members. When the wife or girlfriend doesn't follow the man's wishes, many men resort to violence, or the threat of violence, as a means of control. The abusive behavior frequently follows a pattern, a three-stage cycle of violence.[12] In the first stage, tension builds between the couple over a period of hours or days or months. In stage two, the tension finally becomes intolerable and a violent explosion occurs, lasting for hours or sometimes days. The third stage is the calm after the storm; the batterer becomes contrite and tries to regain the woman's affection through gifts and attention. This stage is usually brief, but effective: at the time when the woman is most motivated to reach out for help and make changes in her life, her abuser suddenly becomes the partner she always hoped he would be. Then the courtship is over yet another time, the tension starts building, and the cycle starts again. The abuser remains in control of everything except his need to be in control. Massively insecure and paradoxically dependent on the woman, he refuses to accept responsibility for his behavior and blames it all on her provocation.

While domestic violence is perpetrated by individual men, it is not primarily an individual sickness, but rather a societal problem reinforced by beliefs about gender differences. Boys are taught to be strong and dominant in social relationships; girls are taught to be passive, self-denying, and deferential.[13] Only when our society's deeply held beliefs about women and men are addressed, will the epidemic of domestic violence begin to abate.

NOTES

1. Rita-Lou Clarke, *Pastoral Care of Battered Women* (Philadelphia: Westminster Press, 1986), p. 20.

2. Evan Stark and Anne Flitcraft, "Medical Therapy as Repression: The Case of the Battered Woman," *Health and Medicine* (Summer/Fall 1982): 29–32, quoted in "Wife Abuse: The Facts," *Response to Violence in the Family and Sexual Assault* 7, no. 1, Washington, D.C., Center for Women Policy Studies.

3. "Fact Sheet on Family Violence," Center for Women Policy Studies.

4. Federal Bureau of Investigation, *Uniform Crime Reports for the United States 1987, U.S. Department of Justice* (Washington, D.C.: Government Printing Office, 1987), p. 11.

5. Evan Stark, Anne Flitcraft, et al., "Domestic Violence and Female Suicide Attempts," paper presented at the 107th Annual Meeting of the American Public Health Association, New York, November 3–7, 1979, quoted in "Wife Abuse: The Facts."

6. Patsy A. Klaus and Michael R. Rand, "Family Violence," Bureau of Justice Statistics Special Report, U.S. Department of Justice (Washington, D.C.: Government Printing Office, 1984).

7. U.S. Department of Justice, *Report to the Nation on Crime and Justice: The Data* (Washington, D.C.: Government Printing Office, 1983), quoted in "Wife Abuse: The Facts."

8. Maria Roy, ed., *The Abusive Partner* (New York: Van Nostrand Reinhold, 1982), quoted in "Wife Abuse: The Facts."

9. Murray Straus, Richard Gelles, and Susan Steinmetz, *Behind Closed Doors: Violence in the American Family* (Garden City, N.Y.: Anchor Press, 1980), quoted in "Wife Abuse: The Facts."

10. "Fact Sheet on Family Violence."

11. Mark Schulman, "A Survey of Spousal Violence against Women in Kentucky," quoted in "Fact Sheet on Family Violence."
12. Lenore Walker, *The Battered Woman* (New York: Harper & Row, 1979).
13. Clarke, *Pastoral Care of Battered Women*, p. 57.

BIBLIOGRAPHY

The Center for the Prevention of Sexual and Domestic Violence recommends the following:

Bussert, Joy M. K. *Battered Women.* "From a Theology of Suffering to an Ethic of Empowerment." New York: Division for Mission in North America, Lutheran Church in America, 1986. This is the first effort to deal with the theological roots not only of sexism but of violence and punishment within marriage.

Dobash, R. Emerson, and Russell P. Dobash. *Violence against Wives.* New York: Free Press (Macmillan), 1979. An excellent study of wife abuse, which includes a valuable social analysis of this problem.

Fortune, Marie M. *Keeping the Faith: Questions and Answers for Abused Women.* San Francisco: Harper & Row, 1987. This is the first practical guide to address issues of faith for Christian abused women. It is an invaluable resource for victims and for pastors and crisis centers who counsel them.

Horton, Anne L., and Judith A. Williamson, eds. *Abuse and Religion: When Praying Isn't Enough.* Lexington, Mass.: Lexington Books, 1988. This extensive anthology is one of the most comprehensive yet produced that deals with abuse and religious issues. Covering all forms of family violence, its authors include both secular and religious leaders working in this field.

Lobel, Kerry, ed. *Naming the Violence: Speaking Out about Lesbian Battering.* Seattle: Seal Press, 1986. This anthology, a product of the efforts of the Lesbian Task Force of the National Coalition Against Domestic Violence, is the first book to discuss openly the painful reality of abuse in lesbian relationships.

Martin, Del. *Battered Wives.* San Francisco: Glide Publications, 1976. The first book in the U.S. to bring this problem into the open.

Pellauer, Mary D., Barbara Chester, and Jane Boyajian. *Sexual Assault and Abuse: A Manual for Clergy and Religious Professionals.* San Francisco: Harper & Row, 1987. This collection of articles introduces religious professionals to the physical, spiritual, and psychological causes and related issues of abuse.

Schechter, Susan. *Women and Male Violence.* Boston: South End Press, 1982. An analysis of the battered women's movement that provides a valuable historical view and political/social critique.

RESOURCES

Center for the Prevention of Sexual and Domestic Violence
1914 North 34th Street, Suite 105, Seattle, WA 98103
(206) 634-1903
 Publishes a quarterly newsletter, *Working Together to Prevent Sexual and Domestic Violence.*

Center for Women Policy Studies
2000 P Street NW, Suite 508, Washington, DC 20036
(202) 872-1770
 Publishes a bimonthly newsletter, *Response to Violence in the Family and Sexual Assault.*

National Coalition Against Domestic Violence
1500 Massachusetts Avenue NW, Washington, DC 20005
(202) 347-7017
 Operates a toll-free hotline, (800) 333-SAFE, providing counseling and information on local shelters and hotlines.

2

Shattering the Silence: Incest

Jayne Rose Brewer

SERMON

There is an epidemic in our country that is devastating millions of lives. It affects every family. It is prevalent in every culture and socioeconomic group. It is present in the church. It is incest.

The statistics tell us that one in three women have been sexually abused during their childhood by fathers, brothers, sometimes mothers, or other trusted family members or friends. Children are being terrorized by their families. The people they should be able to trust the most are proving to be the most untrustworthy. These are children we are talking about. Defenseless children, at the mercy of the adults around them. The little girl in your Sunday School class. The child who played the angel in the church play. They seem normal enough. You would never suspect they were being subjected to any kind of harm let alone the brutal violence of sexual abuse. They would probably not tell you anything was going on if you were to ask them. They have been taught well to keep the family's horrible secret. To protect those who are harming them. To deny that they are being harmed in any way. They learned to stop asking questions. They were told it was their fault, that they were bad; they were bribed to keep the secret. The "special treatment" from their abuser is sometimes the only affection given by any family member. Perhaps they were threatened with more physical harm to themselves or to someone else in the family. A father will threaten to kill the mother if the child tells. All too often there is no one these defenseless children can turn to for help. And when they do, they are not believed. No one wants to hear that incest, violence against children, is so rampant in our society.

Including the church. The church where all can come for refuge. The church where love is proclaimed as available to all who seek God. The church where the subject of incest is even more taboo than in the rest of society.

After my ordination, I will preach in the First Baptist Church where I am an Associate of Ministry in Newton Centre, Massachusetts.

We, in the church, have created numerous myths about the "happy Christian family." We developed an atmosphere where raising questions about the family's behavior is impossible. The father's position in the family is particularly sacred. No one wants to hear that the deacon, the Sunday school teacher, the preacher sexually abuses their daughter or son. And perhaps neighbors' children as well. Should a child have the courage to tell that she is being sexually abused by her father, she is usually greeted with shocked looks of disbelief. And more often than not the church's protection surrounds the abusive parent, pointing the finger of accusation at the child for making up such lies about her father. No, the church does not have a very good record of listening to the pain of its daughters — a situation in direct contrast to the Scripture in Matthew 7:7–8.

The Scripture says, "Ask, and it shall be given you; seek, and ye shall find; knock, and it shall be opened unto you: For every one that asketh receiveth; and s/he that seeketh findeth; and to them that knocketh it shall be opened." However, the message coming from incestuous families, and supported by the church, is that children, being sexually abused, are not to question their fathers' behavior. They are not to seek help outside the family structure, or in it. They are not to knock on the closed family door, let alone expect it to be opened to let them out. They are expected to live in silence. Keeping the family secret. Forever.

As adults, women are discovering that telling the family secret is still not safe. The family doesn't want to hear the pain any more now than it ever did. The church asks women to be quiet about their pain, not to speak out for fear of embarrassing themselves, their families, or the church. And God forbid that the millions of women who were subjected to terror and abuse as children should knock on the door of the church seeking solace. No, the church is not equipped to handle the pain of its daughters for it is structured in such a way as to hear no evil, speak no evil, and see no evil within the "happy Christian family."

We in the church have developed the ability not to hear what we do not want to hear; to filter out that which does not fit into the way we would like life to be. If we don't want to hear it, we don't hear it. If we don't want to see it, we don't see it. If we don't want to think about it, we don't think about it. We, in effect, have closed our minds to the pain women throughout the country are voicing. To understand how we in the church have been able to shut out the anguish of the women in the church isn't so difficult. To deny reality is something with which incest survivors are all too familiar.

Incest victims are programmed not to feel pain, not to see the destructive behavior around them, not to hear the cries of anguish from their own lips, not to think about what is happening to them. To "see no evil," "hear no evil," "speak no evil" was added "feel no pain" and "do not think about the evil around you." The programming was intense. The victims' parents had a lot at stake. It was vital to their need not to see, hear, speak, think, or feel that their victims accept the programming. And the victims did accept it. They did it to survive.

As we think about what parents have done to the minds and bodies of their children, our minds can't seem to expand quite enough to grasp the horror and terror to which these children were subjected. No wonder their minds rejected reality, denied their feelings, and learned to pretend to live in a world that didn't exist. They learned not to question. They learned it was better not to think. Their minds couldn't even begin to grapple with the discrepancies between how they were experiencing life and what they were told life was all about, both in the family and in the church. Day by day, moment by moment they were programmed to ignore their reality. Instead, they were to see something that was not there, namely, a "happy Christian family." It is a long, slow process for women to break down so many years of firm, sometimes blatant, many times insidious teaching, intent on making them blind and ignorant of the reality around them.

No wonder that when a woman is finally able to break the silence she seems to direct an uncontrolled explosion of anger and hatred toward her abusers. Quickly the church steps in to smother the feelings, for the church has as much trouble handling true feelings as the family does. The church calls on women to love their enemies, to forgive their abusers. It is time the church realizes that love and forgiveness are inappropriate responses, especially when the behavior has never been confessed or repented of. It is time for the church to stop contributing to the silencing of women in pain. It is time that we realize the sexual abuse of our children will not stop until we call the abusers to account for their actions.

How many times does a child have to be molested or raped before she is allowed to be angry? When do those who are abused get to call their abusers to account for the violence against them? Why do the abusers get to be angry, venting their anger in innumerable ways, but those who are being hurt are expected to stifle their anger and hope the abusers will stop hurting them of their own accord? When do the victims get to ask why the abusers behaved as they did? When do they get to seek help, comfort, and protection? When do they get to knock on the doors that have been slammed in their faces with some hope they might be opened?

There is an epidemic in our country that claims thousands of victims each year while infecting still millions more. The time has come to break the code of silence surrounding the presence of incest in our society. The church must take a stand against this reign of terror that destroys so many lives. It is time for the church to listen, to no longer deny the existence of incest in our midst and its devastating effect on millions of lives — including the lives of those in the church.

The victims of incest are asked to live in a damning silence. There is never an appropriate time to tell of the pain, the hurt, the fear, the humiliation they have lived with all their lives. Few people have any problem with being horrified when a child is touched in inappropriate ways or raped by a stranger. Yet, children are subjected to all manner of sexual violence in their homes, and no one wants to hear about it. Victims and survivors need to be free from the damning silence. It is the responsibility of the church, which claims to be a refuge for all who are weary, to take the victims and survivors of incest, who are weary to the point of exhaustion, into their midst.

It is time for the church to allow the Scriptures to live in the lives of incest victims and survivors. Out of the silence voices are beginning to be heard. The church must begin to hear these voices, not silence them. As women tentatively begin to ask why they were subjected to totally unacceptable sexual abuse from their family, we in the church must support them. We must hear their questions and insist they be answered. As women seek to rebuild their lives, to escape the terror of the past, the church must support them in this endeavor. As women knock on the door of the church, asking to be heard, the door must be opened. It is time the church stopped contributing to the silence.

Victims of incest had a right to be loved as children, not neglected and sexually abused. They had a right to have their needs met, to feel safe and nurtured, not always living in fear and giving their hearts' blood to the adults who demanded that they supply their needs. It is time for the church to stand with the victims and call a halt to incestuous behavior. It will not be easy as no one wants to hear the daughters' pain. They want to go on pretending that life is fine, to blame the victim for the abuse. If the church cannot open its doors to these daughters, then the daughters will be forced to seek solace elsewhere. Most do not want to leave the church. Most want the words of Jesus to live for them as well as for others. The church must let these words bring the healing that Jesus intended.

It will take time for victims and survivors of incest to trust the church. The church, in the past, has kept women silent. The daughters are now beginning to call the church to account for its behavior just as they are challenging their abusers. All too often the church is failing the test, continuing to show itself to be untrustworthy. If the daughters are to be reconciled to the church, they must be able to tell their stories and be heard, not condemned. The words of Jesus, ask, seek, knock, must free women to break through the silence that surrounded them in the past and still threatens to smother them in the present. The church must learn to hear the voices of its daughters in new ways, to see the terror in which they live; to speak out against the fathers and brothers, to acknowledge the feelings of fear and bewilderment with which the daughters live, to think about ways to change family systems that are taking a devastating toll on the lives of those who are being sexually abused. It is time the church became an advocate for the abused, not the abuser.

The church is faced with an important decision. It has to decide whether to start believing the daughters when they voice their pain and despair. What the church decides will have an impact on millions of lives. The church can stem the epidemic of incest in our country. Everything it teaches about the love and goodness of God demands that it do so.

AUTOBIOGRAPHICAL STATEMENT

It is the fall of 1991. I will soon be forty-six years old. For the past three years I have been coping with memories from my childhood — memories that reveal I was sexually abused by my father as a child and by two older brothers in my teenage years, memories that reveal a neglect of my emotional needs for love and security, that create an atmosphere that made it necessary to deny all my feelings to survive. I did survive. I am a survivor.

I have discovered many things about my family since the memories began to surface, things I buried deep within myself. These memories have been quite painful to look at. The second daughter in a family of five boys and two girls, I was born after the death of the third son when he was two. I was supposed to be a boy to replace this lost son. I was unwanted, unloved, and sexually abused. I desperately wanted the love of my family. I denied these feelings and experiences and pretended, along with them, that we were a "happy family." In essence, I was silenced. As a child I had no words to express the feelings of hurt and fear, of shame and guilt. My family required my silence. I lived in silence unable to voice the cries of anguish within my soul.

My family has attended church since I was a small child. Quietly I grew with hardly anyone noticing a real person in their midst. I never rebelled. I never questioned my parents or the church's authority. I never sought help outside. I never left home until I was twenty-nine years old, still clinging to the belief that my life was fine. I was active in the church and employed full-time at a local retail store. Despair would often overwhelm me. I would again deny that there was any reason to feel so badly about myself and life and build up the walls of pretense again.

At age thirty-five I decided to attend college. I graduated in 1986 with a B.A. in religion and sociology and from Harvard Divinity School in 1990. I have come face to face with the reality of my past. The feelings of being rejected, unwanted, and unloved, combined with the memories of the abuse, were more than I could handle. I became suicidal. With the help of friends and my therapist I was able to survive the desire to kill myself. This came about partly because, for the first time in my life, I became angry and began to express that anger.

I grew up believing it was somehow my fault that I was being abused and neglected. The adults were telling me there was nothing wrong with their behavior. I felt it must be my fault they abused and neglected me instead of nurturing and loving me. If life was rotten and it wasn't the adults' fault, then it must be mine. Somebody must be to blame. Through therapy, and a growing sense of self, I am learning it was not my fault, that I was not to blame. My parents should never have hurt me the way they did. My healing is slow. The process is long. But I am working at shattering the code of silence imposed on me as a defenseless child.

BACKGROUND INFORMATION (by Nancy E. Owens)

"Conspiracy of Silence," "The Best Kept Secret," "The Unmentionable Sin," "Thou Shalt Not Be Aware" — these are phrases found in titles of books dealing with incest, the sexual abuse of children by family members. The themes of silence and secrecy in these titles attest to the successful denial by our society, our churches, our families, and ourselves of this horrible phenomenon. We have not wanted to know that sexual abuse of children is a common experience, yet as many as one of every three girls and one of every seven boys is sexually abused.[1] As the silence is broken and more people acknowledge they were sexually abused as children, such figures are likely to prove conservative.

Most sexually abused children are victimized by someone they know. Seventy-five to 95 percent of perpetrators of sexual abuse are known by the child they abuse;[2] at least 50 percent of these abusers are relatives of the child.[3] A child is far more likely to be abused in her or his bedroom, a grandparent's bathroom, a neighbor's yard, or in a Sunday School classroom than in a stranger's car.

The vast majority of perpetrators are men, although both women and men sexually abuse children. (In *reported* cases of incest, less than 1 percent of the abusers are women.[4]) While people of every sexual orientation abuse children, most abusers are heterosexual.[5]

Who is a perpetrator of incest? Alcoholics, teetotalers, and social drinkers; ministers, carpenters, teachers, mechanics, secretaries, lawyers, sales clerks, homemakers, scholars, and bank presidents; builders of homes for the homeless, volunteers in soup kitchens, conveners of the Saturday morning prayer breakfast. Abusers attend PTA, go bowling, watch football, play poker, run marathons, take dance classes, make pottery. They are parents, stepparents, siblings, grandparents, uncles, aunts, cousins, family friends. They are of every race, religion, social class, and ethnic background. Perpetrators of incest are the people we deal with every day, the people we live with, the people we respect, the people we love.

Sexual abuse of children comes in many forms, such as vaginal, anal, or oral rape; inappropriate touching, fondling, kissing, or nudity; telling a child sexual stories or "talking dirty"; showing a child pornography; taking suggestive or sexual photographs of a child or in the presence of a child; requiring a child to touch another person's or her or his own body sexually.

Children may be coerced to cooperate in these activities and remain silent about them through bribery, affection, parental or other authority, physical punishment, torture, threats of abandonment, or threats of harm to the child, a pet, or other family members. Using love and attention to coerce a child to participate in sexual activities is as damaging as using threats or physical coercion.

Sexual abuse is beyond a child's comprehension. When such violation is perpetrated by someone upon whom the child is dependent for physical, emotional, intellectual, and spiritual nurture and well-being, the child is forced to find some way to deal with the incredible betrayal of trust such actions entail. Children may decide that they are bad and deserve to be abused, allowing them to retain belief in the goodness of the abuser. They may try to shut out the abuse by closing their eyes, concentrating on a spot on the wall, or pretending they aren't there. Often sexually abused children experience "leaving" their bodies, perceiving themselves as floating on the ceiling, looking down on their bodies as the abuse occurs. And children "forget" — they tell themselves so effectively the abuse didn't happen that they erase conscious memory of the abuse.

Some children try to tell someone explicitly about the abuse. Children do not lie about sexual abuse. Contrary to common popular misunderstandings based on Freud's Oedipal theory, "neither children nor women make up stories that they were abused because they were attracted to their fathers or other adults."[6]

It is more likely, however, that sexually abused children will give oblique signals that something is wrong.[7] They may be reluctant to be left alone with someone, have nightmares, be afraid of the dark, wet their beds, become accident-prone or chronically ill, stop eating or overeat, demonstrate a precocious knowledge of and/or interest in sex, "cause trouble," run away from home, attempt suicide, practice self-mutilation, become scrupulously good, seek escape through reading, fantasizing, or watching television. They may try to keep the time they spend at home to a minimum, or they may avoid leaving the house and become the "caretakers" of their families, trying to anticipate and prevent trouble or fix problems they cannot prevent.

Adults who discover or suspect that a child is being sexually abused are likely to experience confusing and conflicting feelings and thoughts. Many will react with outrage and horror, others with utter disbelief and complete mistrust of their own perceptions and/or the child's story. It is very hard to accept that an adult could so horribly misuse a child, particularly if the perpetrator is personally known and loved or respected. Most people will feel powerless and unsure of what action to take. It is vital that action be taken to protect and help the child, no matter how much doubt one feels about the reality of the situation. The child's welfare is more important than any other considerations.

Unfortunately, most children who survive a childhood of incest grow up without receiving help. As adults, they and the people around them must deal with the negative results of the abuse.[8] Sometimes the consequences are obvious — for example, permanent disabilities resulting from physical injuries sustained during the abuse. Often, however, the consequences are more subtle, though no less damaging. Incest survivors tend to have very poor self-images, with little or no self-esteem. They often consider themselves bad, dirty, inadequate, incompetent, unlovable, crazy, stupid, weird, worthless. Many survivors feel guilt about the abuse and tell themselves that if they had resisted, or told someone, or screamed, or run away, the abuse would not have happened. Such guilt is inappropriate; children are *never* responsible for having been sexually abused by an adult, no matter what the circumstances.

Some incest survivors do not know they have a right to self-protection, or may not recognize when people are acting dangerously or in a threatening manner. They may not realize they have a right to say no, no matter how unreasonable a request might be or how negatively they feel about it. Thus some may be particularly vulnerable to violent assaults and rape. Such survivors are not responsible for the violence directed against them; the perpetrator of the violence is responsible. Their pasts, however, may have deprived them of tools for self-protection that should not have been needed in the first place.

Many incest survivors find it very hard to trust anyone, including themselves. They may find it difficult to enter into and/or maintain intimate relationships and are often unable to distinguish between healthy and unhealthy relationships. They often take the role of caretaker in their relationships to the exclusion of receiving care themselves. They may find it difficult to maintain friendships and business relationships. Sexual dysfunction is common. Some survivors find it impossible to engage in any kind of sexual activity; many are unable to stand any kind of touch. Other survivors become sexually promiscuous, having learned from an early age to equate sex with love. Some find it possible to engage in only certain kinds of sexual activity.

Survivors may find it difficult to recognize, identify, and/or feel emotion. They often feel "different" from everyone else. Many survivors become overachievers in an attempt to hide this "difference" or to justify their right to love. Others are barely able to provide themselves with basic necessities. Survivors often report a sense of emptiness within, as if nothing or no one is there. They may feel unreal. For some, self-mutilation, such as cutting or burning oneself, provides proof that the survivor is real. (Survivors deliberately harm themselves for other reasons too. Steps should be taken to stop self-mutilation as soon as such a pattern is recognized; professional help should be sought from someone who has helped other survivors stop hurting themselves.)

Survivors often see the world in terms of extremes — something is either right or wrong, good or bad; they may find it hard to understand compromise or a middle ground. Survivors also may have a strong need to be in control of their environment and of the people with whom they interact. Many need to always have "a way out," whether that means knowing where the exits to a room are or avoiding committed relationships.

Survivors may find it hard to acknowledge and handle their own anger. They may deny that they are ever angry or explain away harm other people have done to them to avoid anger. Others use anger as a refuge from sadness and pain, frequently exploding in rage at seemingly minor incidents.

Survivors often "space out" — distancing themselves from their surroundings and what is happening. This can lead to accident-proneness; it also tends to be responsible for conversations in which the survivor will suddenly "come to" and realize she or he has no idea what has just been said. Still other survivors develop multiple personality disorders.

A quite common result of childhood sexual abuse is the suppression of some or all memories of the abuse. Some survivors will have "flat" memories of the abuse without emotional content; others emotional memories without visual or physical content; others "body" memories; others bits and pieces of memories. Some survivors will remember one or a few incidents and not others, or one perpetrator and not a second or third (it is not uncommon for a child to be sexually abused by more than one person). Many survivors have a nagging feeling that something happened, but no details with which to flesh out the feeling. Others will completely suppress all memories of the abuse. Survivors may also have few or no memories of other aspects of their childhood.

Survivors often experience flashbacks of the abuse they suffered. Flashbacks involve reliving a particular event, reexperiencing the physical and/or emotional sensations felt as a child. Flashbacks can occur as emotions, images, body sensations, or thoughts. They sometimes become very intrusive in a survivor's life and can be frequent and intense. Because so many survivors have suppressed conscious memories of the abuse, flashbacks can cause a survivor to feel as if she or he is "going crazy." Even survivors who have some memory of the abuse can become terrified if the flashbacks come to dominate their lives. Survivors often have difficulty in distinguishing between old feelings and current reality during flashbacks.

Survivors may become substance abusers. They may use alcohol, drugs, food, work, gambling, sex, and even religion in an attempt to reduce their emotional pain, avoid intimacy, and escape memories. Such addictions, although entered into in an attempt to cope with the abuse and its effects, limit healing and cause new problems.

Many incest survivors attempt to kill themselves one or more times. Some succeed. Others feel suicidal at some point(s) in their lives without actually acting upon the feelings. Suicidal feelings should be acknowledged and dealt with immediately, not minimized or ignored. If you are feeling suicidal, find someone who can be with you during this time, by phone if not in person. If no one is available, go to the emergency ward at your local hospital. You are worth the effort it takes to get help. It is okay to ask for help.

Healing from childhood sexual abuse *is* possible. Incest survivors have much inner strength. Survivors were courageous, clever, and creative in the means they used as children to deal with the incredible trauma of incest, and they bring that courage, wit, and creativity with them into adulthood. Because adults have more options and power than children have, many of the means survivors used as children to protect themselves are not functional for adult living and in fact become the source of disruption and hurt. It is possible, however, to identify those defense mechanisms that once protected and now harm, and to learn new ways of living.

Healing begins with the survivor listening to herself or himself, to an inner voice that speaks the truth. To develop skill at listening to one's self may take a very long time, because most survivors have survived precisely by stifling that inner voice. Healing continues as the survivor names her or his reality as incest, first inwardly, and then out loud. Speaking the truth aloud is a powerful healing tool, and each time another voice breaks the silence, another step is taken toward healing both the individual and society. Speaking the truth aloud is also risky, and survivors must learn when it is safe to speak, when it is not, and when breaking the silence is worth risking the danger that might attend speaking.

Speaking the truth aloud helps us to develop true pictures of the victims and perpetrators of childhood sexual abuse. Many of the stereotypes surrounding sexual violence in the United States are steeped in racism. As Ellen Bass and Laura Davis point out, "Because much of white America holds the stereotype that abuse happens only to 'others,' many women of color are reluctant to disclose their abuse for fear that it will reinforce already existing prejudices."[9] Two examples (among many possible examples including those about people of color other than African Americans) of false and racist stereotypes are that of the black male rapist and the sexually promiscuous black woman. Thus, someone sexually abused by an African American male family member may be concerned that disclosure will play into the hearer's prejudice, paralleling the dilemma of an adult who has been raped by an African American man, but knows that there is an incredibly higher prosecution rate for African American rapists than for white rapists, and numerous instances of false imprisonment of African American males for rapes they did not commit.[10] The disclosure of sexual abuse by a white family member can combat such racist stereotyping. Naming the abuser(s) and abuse to oneself causes one's own inner pictures of rapists to change; telling others raises a serious challenge to their stereotyped images of rapists.

People who love or care about an incest survivor may feel powerless and inadequate because they are unable to take away or "fix" the survivor's pain. They may become angry at the survivor for not feeling better quickly or for dwelling on unpleasant things. Incest survivors may go through periods of withdrawing from intimacy, which can be very painful for significant others. Significant others may feel great rage at the perpetrator and/or other family members who did not protect the survivor. Or they may be torn between loyalty to the survivor and loyalty to the perpetrator. They may urge the survivor to cut all contact with the perpetrator and/or other family members, or counsel the survivor to reestablish relationships that have been broken. When advice is contrary to the survivor's decisions, great tension can arise. The survivor is likely to make varying decisions about relationships with her or his family and the perpetrator at various points in the healing process; the survivor's right to make such decisions should be respected.

Learning more about the impacts on the adult life of incest survivors can be helpful to significant others, as can learning about the healing processes through which survivors may go. People close to an incest survivor should consciously make use of support systems outside their relationship with the survivor, as she or he may be unable to provide needed support, particularly during crisis periods.[11] It is also important for people in helping professions who work with survivors to develop good personal and professional support systems; working with incest survivors places helpers in situations of witnessing much pain, where boundaries are strongly tested.

Healing is a process that involves the survivor's whole being, requiring time, integrity, and commitment. Healing is as much a spiritual journey as an emotional, physical, or intellectual journey. It is often an explicitly religious journey as well. Childhood sexual abuse is often mired in the twisting of religious injunctions to honor and obey parents. Biblical passages such as Exodus 20:12 and Colossians 3:20 may be understood to mean that children should never disobey a parent, even if that parent is telling them to perform a sexual act. If a child is abused by her or his father and then taught that God is Father, that child may come to think that God will act like an abuser. A child may infer from a teaching of God's omnipotence that God could have stopped the abuse, and since God did not stop it then God must have either willed the abuse or not loved the child enough to protect her or him. Such ideas will influence both the understandings of deity that a survivor develops as an adult and the relationship an adult survivor has with God. Just as incest survivors often enter into unhealthy relationships with other people, they can enter into unhealthy relationships with God.

It is vital that survivors learn that they were not created to be abused, that God did not intend nor ordain the suffering they experienced, that God is not an abuser and will not invade the survivor's self nor force the survivor into any relationship the survivor does not want. As the survivor heals, the survivor's understanding of and relationship with God will likely change. Such changes are steps on the path to wholeness and right relationship. Many survivors will go through (sometimes lengthy) periods of distance and/or estrangement from God. Prayer may be difficult or impossible; the survivor may quit believing in God. These occurrences can be part of the movement away from false and unhealthy understandings of deity and toward health, love, and affirmation of life. For some survivors, movement toward wholeness and right relationship involves embracing new images and concepts of deity quite different from traditional ideas; for others, redefining or deepening one's understanding of traditional concepts; for still others, rejection of the very concept of deity.

Friends, clergy, members of the survivor's religious community, or family members may urge the survivor to forgive the perpetrator. To Christians, this may seem to be sound theological advice rooted in doctrines of love and reconciliation.[12] However, problems arise when true forgiveness and reconciliation are confused with patterns of denial that minimize the wrong done and the resulting pain and woundedness. Forgiveness toward the perpetrator is not necessary to the survivor's healing process.

An incest survivor cannot forgive what she or he does not know. Before forgiveness is possible, the survivor must become fully aware of the wrong that has been done and the harm suffered. The survivor must be able to place the responsibility for the abuse with the perpetrator. Survivors were *sinned against* when they were sexually abused; they did not commit sin. The survivor must also come to know, experience, and express the grief, despair, loneliness, bewilderment, terror, and rage that are normal and right responses to the sin of incest. Such inner knowing and outward expression is the result of a long process of healing that may take years. While the healing process can be aided by others, it cannot be hurried; each survivor will heal at the rate that is right for her or him.

Forgiveness does not mean that survivors forget the wrong done; it does mean that they have worked through their experiences and responses to a point of no longer being dominated or controlled by that experience. Reconciliation does not mean that there are no boundaries or restrictions imposed on a relationship; rather, it means that both the survivor and the perpetrator recognize and honor the survivor's right to set and maintain boundaries and limitations within the relationship, even if those limitations result in no further contact.

Clearly, incest causes much pain and suffering for survivors, their families and loved ones, and society in general. But every adult who was incestuously abused as a child is a survivor, someone who as a child found within her or himself the resources, strength, and courage to keep on until she or he grew up and gained the power to step outside the old damaging relationships. Uncovering the pain, experiencing it, and then transforming it into wisdom that can be used to create right relationship makes space for joy, love, happiness, and autonomy, and provides the survivor with the glorious freedom to live.

Nancy E. Owens graduated from Harvard Divinity School in 1989. Herself a victim of incest, she plans to minister to other victims of this silent family violence. Her contribution to this volume is a scholarly section of background information on incest. For years she hid the truth from herself, unable to reconcile her family's sexual abuse with its public image of holy, family-centered, born-again Christian faith. The family read the Bible together and abstained from alcohol, tobacco, cards, movies, make-up, and dancing. Instead they worked in church, preached on street corners, and served on mission fields. This volume owes a large debt to Nancy Owens for her invaluable knowledge on matters relating to many of these sermons. Nancy graduated from Harvard with a master's of divinity in 1989 and is currently a librarian in the Divinity School library.

NOTES

1. Ellen Bass and Laura Davis, *The Courage to Heal: A Guide for Women Survivors of Child Sexual Abuse* (New York: Harper & Row, 1988), p. 20.

2. Mary D. Pellauer, Barbara Chester, and Jane A. Boyajian, eds., *Sexual Assault and Abuse: A Handbook for Clergy and Religious Professionals* (San Francisco: Harper & Row, 1987), p. 7.

3. Marie Marshall Fortune, *Sexual Violence: The Unmentionable Sin* (New York: Pilgrim Press, 1983), p. 164.

4. Ibid., p. 183.

5. Ibid.

6. Bass and Davis, *Courage to Heal*, 347.

7. See Pellauer, Chester, and Boyajian, *Sexual Assault and Abuse*, pp. 21–23, and Bass and Davis, *Courage to Heal*, p. 94, for detailed discussions of symptoms of children who are being or have been sexually abused.

8. See Bass and Davis, *Courage to Heal*, especially part 1, for a very detailed discussion of the long-term consequences of childhood sexual abuse. This book also is an excellent reference and guide to the process of healing from the wounds inflicted by such experiences. The book is written primarily for women survivors but contains much information that will be useful to male survivors and to survivors' significant others.

9. Ibid., p. 373.

10. Angela Davis, "Rape, Racism and the Capitalist Setting," in *Black Scholar* (April 1978): 24.

11. See Bass and Davis, *Courage to Heal*, and Eliana Gil, *Outgrowing the Pain* (Walnut Creek, Calif.: Launch Press, 1983), for discussions about effects on significant others of adult incest survivors.

12. See Fortune, *Sexual Violence*, and Pellauer, Chester, and Boyajian, *Sexual Assault and Abuse*, for in-depth discussions of theological issues. The following discussion of forgiveness and reconciliation is largely influenced by these two works.

BIBLIOGRAPHY

For Adult Survivors, Counselors, Family Members, and Significant Others of Adult Survivors

Bass, Ellen, and Laura Davis. *The Courage to Heal: A Guide for Women Survivors of Child Sexual Abuse.* New York: Harper & Row, 1988. Note: If you read only one book, this is it. An excellent step-by-step guide to healing for survivors, it includes survivors' first-hand accounts, identifies and discusses the major issues, addresses significant others of survivors and helping professionals, and has listings of resources and a comprehensive annotated bibliography at the end.

For Adults Who Know of a Child Presently Being Abused

Byerly, Carolyn. *The Mother's Book: How to Survive the Incest of Your Child.* Dubuque, Iowa: Kendall/Hunt Publishing, 1985.

By Adult Survivors

Bass, Ellen, and Louise Thornton, eds. *I Never Told Anyone: Writings by Women Survivors of Child Sexual Abuse.* New York: Harper & Row, 1983.
Evert, Kathy, and Inie Bijkerk. *When You're Ready: A Woman's Healing from Childhood Physical and Sexual Abuse by Her Mother.* Walnut Creek, Calif.: Launch Press, 1987.
Fraser, Sylvia. *My Father's House: A Memoir of Incest and of Healing.* New York: Ticknor & Fields, 1987.
Janssen, Martha. *Silent Scream: I Am a Victim of Incest.* Philadelphia: Fortress Press, 1983.
McNaron, Toni A. H., and Yarrow Morgan, eds. *Voices in the Night: Women Speaking about Incest.* Pittsburgh: Cleis Press, 1982.
Portwood, Pamela, Michele Gorcey, and Peggy Sanders, eds. *Rebirth of Power: Overcoming the Effects of Sexual Abuse through the Experiences of Others.* Racine, Wis.: Mother Courage Press, 1987.
Randall, Margaret. *This Is about Incest.* Ithaca, N.Y.: Firebrand Books, 1987.
Sisk, Sheila. *Inside Scars: Incest Recovery as Told By a Survivor and Her Therapist.* Gainesville, Fla.: Pandora Press, 1987.

Incest and Child Sexual Abuse

Butler, Sandra. *Conspiracy of Silence: The Trauma of Incest.* San Francisco: Volcano Press, 1985.
Herman, Judith. *Father-Daughter Incest.* Cambridge: Harvard University Press, 1981.
Miller, Alice. *Thou Shalt Not Be Aware: Society's Betrayal of the Child.* New York: New American Library, 1984.
Rush, Florence. *The Best Kept Secret: Sexual Abuse of Children.* Englewood Cliffs, N.J.: Prentice-Hall, 1980.
Russell, Diana E. H. *The Secret Trauma: Incest in the Lives of Girls and Women.* New York: Basic Books, Inc., 1986.

Guides to Healing

Gil, Eliana. *Outgrowing the Pain: A Book for and about Adults Abused as Children.* Walnut Greek, Calif.: Launch Press, 1983.

Maltz, Wendy, and Beverly Holman. *Incest and Sexuality: A Guide to Understanding and Healing.* Lexington, Mass.: Lexington Books, 1987.

Loulan, Jo Ann. *Lesbian Sex.* San Francisco: Spinsters/Aunt Lute, 1984. Excellent resource for all women survivors (including non-lesbian) and their partners.

Racism and Sexual Violence

Davis, Angela Y. "Rape, Racism and the Capitalist Setting." *The Black Scholar* (April 1978): 24–30.

———. *Women, Race and Class.* New York: Vintage Books, 1981.

Friedman, Deb. "Rape, Racism and Reality." *Quest: A Feminist Quarterly* 5 (Summer, 1979): 40–52.

Hood, Elizabeth F. "Black Women, White Women: Separate Paths to Liberation." *Black Scholar* (April 1978): 45–56.

King, Mae C. "The Politics of Sexual Stereotypes." *Black Scholar* (Summer 1982): 2–13.

Lorde, Audre. *Sister Outsider: Essays and Speeches.* Trumansburg, N.Y.: Crossing Press, 1984.

Moraga, Cherrie, and Gloria Anzaldua. *This Bridge Called My Back: Writings by Radical Women of Color.* New York: Kitchen Table: Women of Color Press, 1983.

Pastoral and Theological Perspectives

Fortune, Marie Marshall. *Sexual Violence: The Unmentionable Sin.* New York: Pilgrim Press, 1983.

Pellauer, Mary D., Barbara Chester, and Jane A. Boyajian, eds. *Sexual Assault and Abuse: A Handbook for Clergy and Religious Professionals.* San Francisco: Harper & Row, 1987.

For Those in the Helping Professions

Haugaard, Jeffrey J., and N. Dickon Reppuci. *The Sexual Abuse of Children: A Comprehensive Guide to Current Knowledge and Intervention Strategies.* San Francisco: Jossey-Bass, 1988.

Gil, Eliana. *Treatment of Adult Survivors of Childhood Abuse.* Walnut Creek, Calif.: Launch Press, 1988.

About Perpetrators of Sexual Violence

Carnes, Patrick. *Out of the Shadows: Understanding Sexual Addiction.* Minneapolis: CompCare Publishers, 1983.

RESOURCES

National Child Abuse Hotline, (800) 4A-CHILD (422-4453)

Child Protective Services can be found in state or federal government sections of the phone book.

Twelve Step groups such as Alcoholics Anonymous, Al-Anon, and others. Many areas now have Survivors Anonymous groups.

The Samaritan's local hotline for survivors who feel suicidal.

Individual therapists with training in survivors' needs when seeking counseling.

If you walk in on a child being sexually abused, intervene immediately — stop the abuse and insure the child's safety. If it is unsafe for you to intervene, call the police.

3

Rape: Violence against Women

Beth Gerstein

SERMON

One out of three women will be raped in her lifetime. This means that if there are sixty women in this audience today, then roughly one-third, or twenty women have been or will be raped. Look around you. Who do you see? Friends, neighbors, sisters, daughters, wives, mothers, and lovers. You may already know that some of these women have been raped — they may have told you. I guarantee that there are many more women you know who have been raped. They keep this information to themselves for good reasons. As a society we turn our backs on the women who by no fault of their own have been raped. This, then, is a sermon that affects each one of us in this room, for women are a part of everyone's lives. *And* we are *all* a part of this society that perceives rape survivors as shameful and allows the violence against them to happen.

Men get raped, too, usually by other men. In fact, at least 5–7 percent of all rapes are against men. These rapes are prompted by the same impulses that make men rape women and children. Rape is about power, control, violence, and domination.

In our society men are more powerful than women (in particular, white, wealthy men). This power is based on economic, political, and social reinforcements. On the whole, men get paid more at their jobs; they constitute the majority of politicians and people in other powerful positions; they have greater status and therefore are often more valued. This status sets them apart from those who are perceived to be not as powerful: people of color, women, children, gay men and lesbians, for example. If you are fortunate enough to have been born into a position of power, this sermon will help you to recognize how you can use your position in ways to help those who are perceived to be weaker than you. You can do this by making others aware of all people's equal humanity.

I have never preached a sermon. While writing this piece I envisioned a mixed group in terms of gender, age, race, and sexual orientation.

40

The purpose of violence against women is to point out and enforce the weaker status of women. In rape, women are made to feel less valued and less significant. Men who rape make themselves feel more in control, more important, more alive as they take that control and dignity from the women they are raping. This violence and need to control and dominate is the same violence that has its roots in racism, classism, and every other type of bigotry. At the heart of any type of bigotry we find one person asserting his or her own vision of an "absolute right." That person sees one way to exist and considers all other lifestyles and opinions as not as good. Well, the fact is that people are varied. Differences, be they based on gender, race, class, ethnicity, religion, or sexual orientation, are to be hailed in each person. The multiplicity of differences can only add to the chorus of voices that make up humanity.

We all exist within the system that promotes this bigotry. And we are all affected by the devastations of rape, whether it has happened to us personally, or to our loved ones. We are all affected by living in a society that allows and encourages violence against women.

Rape affects everyone. People of all races, classes, ages, religions, cultural backgrounds are affected. I want to share with you some of what the devastations of rape are like. (For purposes of this sermon, I will refer to women as victims, but keep in mind that children and men can also be survivors of rape.) When a woman gets raped, she has been overpowered. She says the word "no," either verbally or through some kind of resistance, and finds that her words have no meaning. At that point she becomes acutely aware that she no longer has control over her body, and perhaps her life. Her body is violated in the worst way possible. Her sense of security and trust in the world have also been violated. Most women (approximately 60–70 percent) who are raped are raped by people they know. Women are often told to turn to the men they know for security and protection. When a woman is raped by one of these men, she may doubt her own ability to trust and make good judgments. Acquaintance rape causes her to reexamine her life and question her whole concept of trust. It is *not* her fault for trusting someone. There is never a crime in trusting anyone. The crime is the violation of her trust. The crime is rape. Rape can be blamed only on the one who does the raping, and no one else. As a result of this violent intrusion, women experience other feelings: guilt, shame, depression, isolation, fear, anger, loss of control, grief.

Rape is not about sex; it is about violence. Sex, however, is used as a weapon to make women feel humiliated, dominated, and valueless. Among the most devastating aspects of rape is the new view of reality that women gain as a result. This perspective may not jibe with the one that many of us walk around with: that we live in relative safety, in a relatively secure world. Women who have been raped see clearly, sometimes for the first time, that women are valued less and seen as weaker in society, and are thus more vulnerable to sexual assault. One of the most frightening aspects of reality for women is that though they were raped once, they can be raped again. And, there is no real way for women ultimately to safeguard against this crime. The only way rape will ever stop is if men stop raping women.

Being raped brings up numerous theological questions. Some of these questions have to do with living in a world that is not safe. How do we deal with notions of forgiveness for the sins of those who have wronged us by raping us? Can there be forgiveness? How are we supposed to maintain feelings of self-worth and understand that rape is not some sort of divine punishment, but rather an arbitrary human baseness? How are we to love our neighbors when some of our neighbors are raping us? These are the contemporary theological questions that we must continually contemplate and seek to solve.

Rape survivors are shunned in our society. They are stigmatized and seen as blemished. They are considered "bad girls" and "damaged goods." The mere existence of these common stereotypes of rape survivors in our society stresses that we blame women for being victims. Even though no woman asks to be raped, we tell her that she is somehow at fault and even bad because someone else has "defiled" her.

Various systems reinforce this point of view. Rape, as other crimes, is considered a crime against the state. This makes women witnesses during their own court hearings, and thus further underscores the feelings of loss of control and isolation since they have no control over the prosecution. Unlike other crimes, however, the burden of proof is on the woman — to prove that she did not want to be assaulted. When someone's wallet is stolen, no one asks for proof that the victim didn't want the wallet stolen. At the core of making women prove they were not consenting to assault is the misguided perception that equates rape with sexuality. No woman consents to be raped. That our courts ask women to prove this shows that the courts do not automatically believe women, but rather give the benefit of the doubt to the men raping women. Recent statistics show that only three rapists in one thousand serve a prison term and that term on the average is only two to four years. If rape were a crime that our society took more seriously and if we valued women more, our courts and criminal justice system would be more concerned about the victim, not the criminal.

People are scared to talk about rape and to face its startling realities. Whether it be for fear of hurting someone in the process or for fear of facing how vulnerable we are, this reluctance to talk about rape contributes to the ways we make women feel isolated as a result of this trauma. Because rape is so little talked about and understood, many of us who have been raped feel the need to be silent and thus do not share the aches and pains it brings. We as a society need to embrace rape survivors. We need to tell these women that they *are* whole women, although some are telling them otherwise. They are not contaminated or dirty. Physical intrusions cannot contaminate one's soul; only twisted and violent thoughts can. Women who have been raped should not be punished for crimes they hoped would never happen to them; they should be hailed as survivors who have experienced some of the worst kind of aggression imaginable.

What do we do about this problem? How do we live in a world in which this horror exists? One of the ways to start is to begin to understand the problem. We need to educate ourselves about how prevalent rape and sexual assault are in our society. As I mentioned, in the United States, one out of three women will be raped in her lifetime. One out of four girls and one out of seven boys will be raped or sexually assaulted by the time they are eighteen. We need to understand that rape is a direct outgrowth of a structure that values men's rights and ways of being in the world more than women's rights and contributions. It is much the same dynamic that values white people's culture and contributions more than those of people of color.

Because rape is about power and control, we have to start reexamining what these two forces mean and how they function in our society. Since rape is an act of violence that uses sex as a weapon, we need to start reexamining the ways male and female sexuality is played out in our culture.

Rape is one point on a continuum of violence — male violence against women. Rape is on one extreme, and degrading comments and whistles are at the other. The two extremes exist on the same line of aggressive thoughts of power and domination. When a man whistles at a woman, he is telling her that he has the power to judge and value her for her physical appearance only. When a woman is raped, she is being told that her needs and desires are not worthy of respect and that he, the rapist, has licence to do with her body what he will. Whenever people make sexist comments, they are promoting the idea that women can be physically degraded and are providing someone with a licence to rape.

How do we begin to recognize the attitudes that perpetuate sexism and violence against women? Through understanding and education. Know the problem of rape and begin to understand how the terrorizing of women permeates our whole society. And also use your hearts. We are or have the capacity to be empathic, compassionate, sensitive humans.

Think about the last time you were made to feel less than human. When was the last time that you felt as if someone was controlling and dominating you by their decisions about what was right and not right? When was the last time that you felt absolutely powerless to change a situation? Some people (people of color, women, gays and lesbians, people with disabilities) live their lives constantly confronting the feelings of threat, fear, and loss of control. Others, the more privileged, may feel these things only at isolated points in our lives. For those of us who do not feel this way all the time, imagine those isolated events of being made to feel weak and valueless. Consider how it would feel to live years, decades of our lives that way. And consider the forces that are making you feel that way. Not a pleasant thing to imagine!

How can we interrupt this process of violence against women — of power over others? One way is by taking what our hearts and our minds tell us and by using our knowledge as stimulus for action. We *have* to act to combat this problem because it affects *all* of us. It affects our families and friends. We can interrupt that process by being political — through organizing our communities, lobbying, writing letters to editors of our newspapers, writing to our legislators, fund-raising. We can be active by giving support to those who are hurting from this trauma — giving support, nurturing, and care as friends, lovers, family, and counselors. And we can do it through education. We need to teach each other on a daily basis about sexism and the power dynamic in our society, and the connections between racism, classism, and sexism. When people make sexist comments, call them on their bigotry. If you're concerned about offending them, tell them that you are not rejecting them as persons, but rather their sexist behavior. Not to point out the dangers of a sexist joke is to allow sexism and the skewed power dynamics in our society to continue. To allow these dynamics to continue is to take part in the devaluing and dehumanization of integral segments of our society.

For society to proclaim and realize each individual's full humanity we must first acknowledge the ways in which we as a group fail to do this. Then we must individually look inward and uncover the ways we all contribute to the maintenance of this skewed system — either by our active participation in sexist behavior or by not calling others to task when they act sexist. And finally each of us must take it upon ourselves to overturn our ailing system and to work toward building an equitable society that embraces *all* its members. For us to do any less is to further infect the already festering wound in our society.

AUTOBIOGRAPHICAL STATEMENT

August 1, 1983*

Well, I've just been raped. Even as I write that word now it doesn't seem to have the force and the violence that one — I — usually associate with that concept. Whenever I hear that word I have always (or I have in the past) gotten angry — enraged! What an incredible act of violence! What an intrusion! What insanity for that to happen! What a horror! I've said that it's one of the most horrifying and terrible things to happen to a woman.

It happened to me.

I haven't yet internalized all the horror of it. One, it wasn't as horrifying as it could have been. He wasn't at all brutal or violent — other than the fact that he committed a violent act. I'm lucky to get away with my life — and also with being so unscarred. I'm lucky that everyone has been so incredibly supportive, helpful, and caring.

Except for the first five minutes of the episode, the whole ordeal seems so divorced from my life. I unthinkingly forced myself into a strange calm state. I now can't believe I acted the way I did. I almost feel it wasn't really me. I talked, acted incredibly calmly, was witty, sensible, functioned, etc. It's all so unbelievable that I did all that because I never once said to myself: "Okay, Beth, think! Calm down, deal with this situation in the best way you can." It's that part, when he raped me twice and we talked for quite some time, that I haven't really internalized and felt the full impact of.

How could I have let myself feel the full impact of the most terrifying experience of my life right after it happened? I had been raped. I was in shock. No one would deny that rape really does exist in day-to-day life. But I had/have to struggle with the pain of incorporating this nightmare into my realm of realities for life. Real women get raped, not just "bad girls" that exist somewhere out there. I really got raped — it did happen to me. And what is worse, I now know that it could happen to me again, and again.

It was sometime during the very early hours of August 1, maybe one or two o'clock, that I awoke briefly from a very deep sleep. My shade was moving and making noise. When I look back at it now, my shade should not have been moving at all; my window was not left wide open. At that time, however, I wearily thought to myself that the wind was moving the shade, and I returned to sleep. It must have been minutes later that I again awoke, but this time with a start. Immediately I saw the silhouette of a man standing beside my bed. There was a moment where my brain was working furiously to try to figure out whether this was a nightmare or if this was really

*Journal entry written less than twenty-four hours after I had been raped.

happening. I screamed. It was a very deep guttural noise, perhaps a moan, that came from somewhere deep inside me. I never heard that type of sound come from me before. I can only attribute it to being the sound of utter terror. For me, this was the most frightening aspect of the rape.

He quickly clasped his hand over my mouth and laid down, full length, on top of me. He had no clothes on, nor did I, since I always sleep naked during the summer. I am small, reaching 5' 1/2" on my good days. He was a lot bigger than I, and I felt trapped; I was pinned down. At this point, there was no question that what was happening to me was not a dream. It was only much later that the reality of what did happen finally *hit*.

I felt his hot breath on my neck as he talked quickly into my ear, threatening me and promising that if I didn't scream, he wouldn't hurt me. He explained that he thought I was some other woman who had stolen his wallet. He also said that he had been watching me that day. A friend and I had been sitting out on the front porch earlier that afternoon. He started asking me questions about my boyfriend. I was outraged that he assumed that I even had a boyfriend, but I wisely decided that this was not the place to start educating this man about feminism. I lied. My boyfriend was far away in Israel, but I told him that he was due to stop over any time that night. He started caressing my body and said he wanted to fuck me. I was sickened at his touch. I shuddered and turned my head away when he kissed my neck and breasts. Again I was angered to hear the excuse I gave him: "I can't," I said. "My boyfriend will be really pissed." I thought that it was at this level on which I needed to relate to him. I don't think that explaining to him the intense violation and intrusions women feel as a result of rape would have been helpful. For the rest of the time that he spent in my apartment, I tried to gauge and second guess him. I didn't want to do anything that might anger him so that he'd beat or kill me. I wanted him to think that what was happening was perfectly normal: he just happened to break into my apartment and was forcing me to have sex with him (I wasn't allowing myself to call it rape at that point). It happens all the time! There was nothing out of the ordinary about this, right? I thought that if he felt I was nonthreatening he would "just" rape me and leave. I was gambling on my life. I knew rape was about anger and aggression. I didn't want to do anything to tip that level of hostility to the point where he would become the sadistic killer.

Despite my protestations (I even tried to convince him that I had some venereal disease) and resistance, he raped me. I don't remember much of the first time. I know that afterward we talked for what seemed like hours. He said that he knew that he was doing something bad, and even mentioned that if his mother found out, she'd really get him. I had very little sympathy for him. He talked a bit about his brothers, about the submarine base (I was living in New London, right across the river from the Groton sub base), and about his being on leave for the weekend. I didn't want him to know that I was going to Connecticut College. I feared that this type of information might fuel his anger and give him license to get back at the snobby rich kids who go to the beautiful school on the hill that overlooks the depressed city.

Despite his knowledge that he was "being bad," he invited me out for breakfast the next morning (using, no doubt, the money he stole from me) and offered to write letters to me. I declined his offer, envisioning all the while receiving a letter from him at my school mailbox. It seemed bizarre. The whole night was bizarre. There I was, sitting totally nude, feeling incredibly vulnerable, trying to pacify this guy who broke into my apartment and raped me.

After some time, he raped me again. This time I tried to resist more, and he got more forceful. I remember that my head was turned, and I was pretty relaxed. I had totally disengaged my mind from my body. I felt as though I were watching a movie, and that I could see what was happening to me, but from a distance. I wasn't inside my body as it was happening. After the second time, he started getting more brusque. He ordered me to stand in the kitchen facing the wall so that he could leave my apartment without his face being illuminated by the hall light. I felt completely humiliated. He left, finally, taking my wallet, address books, and tape deck with him.

I was scared. He had threatened me and told me not to tell anyone. I was scared to leave my apartment for fear that he was prowling around and would kill me for trying to tell. I had no phone, and thus couldn't call anyone. I was trapped again. I turned on every light in my apartment. I didn't even think about going to the hospital or the police. I was in shock.

I wanted to shower, but being naked made me feel too vulnerable. I had to get dressed. Even though it was the middle of summer and a very hot and humid night, I put on two long-sleeved shirts, pants, wool socks, and hiking boots and lay down on my bed and shivered. At times the shivers intensified and my body shook violently, uncontrollably. I finally decided that I needed to find a safe place and to be with friends. I risked the dark unknown of the night and ran the half block to the 24-hour store. I asked the woman working there if she would call the police for me. I really only wanted them to give me a ride to a friend's house — I didn't know where else to go or what else to do.

I must have looked awful, because the woman asked what had happened to me, and if I was okay. I just stood there, looking at her.

I thought: I can't tell her that some guy just broke into my apartment and made me "do something." I knew that wouldn't make sense to her and that this "something" was a very serious "something." So I said: "I guess I've just been raped." That was it! I had been raped. *That* I knew was serious. I got depressed. The room started spinning and nothing felt real. The woman took my arm, and with the utmost compassion took me to the back room, explaining that she had been raped, too. I was surprised; I had no idea of how frequently women, children, and even men get raped in our society.

When the police came, I panicked. I thought they were going to blame me and say that I had provoked the rapist. Luckily, they were very good and told me that I had done everything right. I was brought to the hospital emergency room and examined. A policewoman met me there and stayed with me. The hospital was yet another trauma. The last thing I wanted to do was to take off my clothes and get into a vulnerable position by putting my feet in the stirrups so that a male doctor could give me a pelvic exam. It was there, at the hospital, that I began to feel so alone. Just two months earlier I had returned from a year abroad in the Middle East where I had traveled and lived thousands of miles from family and friends. Yet I felt more alone and isolated in that hospital room, lying on my back, naked, as evidence of my rape was being collected, than I felt in all of my travels. "No one will ever understand this experience," I thought. "This one is beyond belief and comprehension."

BACKGROUND INFORMATION

That experience happened almost exactly ten years ago. Since that time I've sought counseling and received much support from my friends and family. I am lucky in that respect. Many women can't tell anyone. Many women, when they do tell someone, get negative reactions as a response. There are many myths and misperceptions about rape in our society. These myths and stereotypes about women and about male and female sexuality contribute to and encourage women to remain silent about this horror. Six years ago I started volunteering at the Boston Area Rape Crisis Center. Five years ago I started full time employment there as the day-time counselor. From my first-hand experience as a rape survivor and from counseling hundreds of women, both in person and on the phone, I have learned a great deal about the realities of rape and how it is commonly perceived in our society.

Let me start first by defining rape and then by citing some very basic statistics. Massachusetts law defines rape as any penetration against a person's will of any bodily orifice (mouth, vagina, anus) by any body part (penis, tongue, fingers) or object, using force or the threat of force. A woman is raped every three minutes in the United States. In the fifteen minutes to half hour that it takes you to read this essay, five to ten women will get raped. These statistics are based on FBI Uniform Crime Reports. Think of all the women in your life. Offhand you might not think that any of them have been victims of this crime. I guarantee that at least a handful of them have been. Rape is not a common topic of conversation. Many women feel tremendous shame, guilt, and isolation as a result. Many women try never to think about it.

The reasons for our feelings of shame and guilt are not hard to figure out. Our society does not generally applaud women's sexuality as something positive. Women are supposed to be discreet in their sexuality. We are supposed to look pretty but not "enticing," so that we can get a man. Just recently, for instance, over lunch with my grandparents and their friend I was told that a woman who wears a short skirt and no bra is being promiscuous and is asking to be raped. No woman asks to be raped.

Common opinion holds that if a woman has been raped, then she must have provoked it. Many think that women also like being overpowered, and thus really enjoy being raped. This is simply not the case. At the base of this misperception is the idea that rape is a sexual act. Rape is not sexual. It is an act of violence. It is an act where a man (in the vast majority of cases) overpowers and controls a woman's life and body, using sex as the weapon. It is an act of anger, aggression, and domination. Rape is about power. A woman resists either physically or verbally, and finds that she is not being respected: when a woman is raped she is being told that she is worthless. By taking a woman's control over her body out of her hands, the rapist is increasing his own sense of control in the world and in his life. Rapists control *all* types of women this way. Men rape women of all ages, races, classes, and religions — be they sexy or not. Similarly, men from all races, ages, classes, and religions rape. *No* woman is safe from this crime.

Most women are raped by someone they know (which was not true in my case). According to Massachusetts statistics (compiled from the eighteen rape crisis centers in the state), at least 70 percent of women who are raped were acquainted with the rapist. This means that a woman could have met her rapist that day or knew him because he was the mechanic who fixed her car; they could have been good friends, lovers, married, or related. The vast majority of all rapes do not include any dangerous weapons or brutal beatings. Most people in our society think of rapists as being only the kind who hang around dark alleys waiting for women to walk by. Many women don't realize that acquaintance rape is just as serious and just as real as stranger rape, and far more common. Many women who know their rapist fear that no one will believe that he really did rape her and that she really didn't ask for it. Women often blame themselves for trusting the men they know and who they thought would never do something like this. There are few ways of knowing beforehand that a man is going to rape you. And even if a man seems generally abusive in his behavior before raping a woman, he is still to blame for the attack, not the woman for being with him. This fear of not being believed is one reason most women are reluctant to press charges against their rapists.

Over 90 percent of all rapes occur between people of the same race. There is a common myth of "the black rapist." Many white women are more fearful of black men walking behind them than they are of white men. The reality is that the black man is no more likely to rape her than the white man.

In Massachusetts almost 50 percent of women who are raped are raped in their own homes. Often we hear others warn women not to jog alone and not to walk alone past sunset. But women are in just as much danger sitting at home as walking outside. Saying that women should be the ones to take precautions against rape puts the blame on women for being raped, because it means that they hadn't been careful enough. The only way rape will ever stop is if men stop raping women. Plain and simple.

BIBLIOGRAPHY

Brownmiller, Susan. *Against Our Will*. New York: Bantam, 1975. A historical look at how rape permeates our society and how popular attitudes contribute to its perpetuation. She does not deal well with race issues, though her historical analysis is good.

Burgess, Ann, and Lynda Holstrom. *The Victim of Rape*. New Brunswick, N.J.: Transaction Books, 1983. An excellent in-depth account of how major institutions (such as hospitals, police, and criminal justice systems) respond to rape. The authors also provide a good clinical overview of rape trauma syndrome and the emotional healing process after rape.

Davis, Angela Y. *Violence against Women and the Ongoing Challenge to Racism*. Latham: Kitchen Table: Women of Color Press, 1985. An excellent analysis of the forces that connect rape and racism. Davis looks at rape on a political, social, and economic level and points to the common attitudes that see women and people of color as less valued and thus more open to exploitation.

Fortune, Marie. *Sexual Violence*. New York: Pilgrim Press, 1983. Fortune is an ordained minister in the United Church of Christ. She examines the social and religious roots of sexual violence, as well as the lack of attention to this problem. She also encourages religious communities to develop a just and ethical response to the issue of sexual violence.

Katz, Judy. *No Fairy Godmothers, No Magic Wands: The Healing Process after Rape.* Saratoga: R & E Publishers, 1984. This is the best personal account of a rape survivor's story that I know. Katz describes her rape and gives the readers an in-depth account of her healing process after the event. This includes her descriptions of telling friends and family and how she got the support that she needed. An excellent resource for rape survivors.

Lerner, Gerda. *Black Women in White America.* New York: Vintage Books, 1973. This is a great documentary history of the social, economic, and political position of black women in America. Lerner has sections that focus on the myths and stereotypes of the black rapist as well as of black women's promiscuity that encourages white men to rape them.

RESOURCES

The best resource is a rape crisis center. Each rape crisis center should have lists of information and referrals for legal counsel, medical needs and emergencies, therapists who have expertise in counseling sexual assault survivors, and other pertinent contacts such as battered women's shelters, AIDS information and testing, child sexual abuse hotlines, gay and lesbian hotlines, teen and adult suicide hotlines, etc. Rape crisis centers also provide counseling, both to individuals and in support groups. They can offer counseling over the phone or in person, and their services are confidential. Rape crisis centers also provide public speakers and have resources for educating the public. They can be contacted by looking under the emergency numbers in the phone book or by calling information.

PART TWO

America's New Underclasses: Women and Children

4

Doing Justice Upstream

Jennifer Johnston

SERMON

I will rejoice in Jerusalem, and be glad in my people; no more shall be heard in it the sound of weeping and the cry of distress. No more shall there be in it an infant that lives but a few days, or an old man who does not fill out his days, for the child shall die a hundred years old, and the sinner a hundred years old shall be accursed. They shall build houses and inhabit them; they shall plant vineyards and eat their fruit. They shall not build and another inhabit; they shall not plant and another eat; for like the days of a tree shall the days of my people be, and my chosen shall long enjoy the work of their hands. They shall not labor in vain, or bear children for calamity; for they shall be the offspring of the blessed of the Lord, and their children with them. Before they call I will answer, while they are yet speaking I will hear. The wolf and the lamb shall feed together, the lion shall eat straw like the ox; and dust shall be the serpent's food. They shall not hurt or destroy in all my holy mountain.
—Isaiah 65:19–25, New Oxford Annotated Bible

There once was a peaceful village nestled in the mountains with a river flowing through. All was well with the people. One day, a woman was washing clothes in the river and noticed to her horror there was a dead body floating in the river. She rang the village bell and everyone came to inspect the body and help pull it out of the river. Never had such a disturbing event disrupted the peaceful villagers. The entire village bustled around, arranging for a proper burial of the body. After the funeral, everyone slowly returned to their occupations. The next day another body was discovered in the river. Again everyone busied themselves. The following day, two bodies floated down, and this time they were babies. Each day more bodies came down the river. Months went by; people were completely occupied with funeral and burial arrangements. Finally someone said, "We must go upstream and see

---

This sermon was prepared with the candidates committee of my presbytery in Alabama in mind. The members of the committee are lay and clergy from various churches in the Presbytery of Sheppards and Lapsley.

what is killing all these people." A delegation was sent from the little village.

How often our churches are like the village in this story (passed on to me by oral tradition). We are completely occupied with the bodies in our midst. There is so much suffering right in front of us. However, our job is even bigger. We say we do not have time enough even to stop and wonder what is going on upstream and ask, "Could we stop the suffering?" "Do we know the cause?" In the story of the village that some should go upstream seemed obvious, yet when we are flooded with people coming to food cupboards and shelters, is it as obvious that the church should find out what is happening in the economy to send all these folks to us? Taking care of the suffering in front of us is important. Charity must go on. But we cannot stop there. We must go upstream and ask *why* are people hungry? The task of analysis through the lens of economics cannot be ignored. Just as war is too important to be left to the generals the economy is too important to be left to the economists.

The vision of shalom described in the passage from Isaiah is too important to defer. Shalom is not narrowly defined as the absence of war, but rather includes the well-being of the whole person, the whole community, and the whole world. To emphasize the social and political dimensions of the biblical notion of peace, a theological dictionary states that nowhere in the Hebrew Bible does shalom "denote an attitude of inward peace. Shalom always finds external manifestation and, in its most common use, is a social rather than individual term." For the church, the realm of God is not a utopian ideal only to be attained in an afterlife. For Christians Jesus' words of proclamation are radical because they claim the time is at hand; it is now. Our churches have been criticized, and often rightly so, for having an idealistic dream of all people being free from oppression while the church does too little to make justice visible in our midst. We must put a public face on our faith.

Who will determine what the public agenda of our faith will be? Whose voices have the credibility to us as people of faith? Hebrew Bible scholar Walter Brueggemann points out that in the world in which the prophet Micah spoke the cry for justice, as usual, came from below. The people on top never notice the cost of their prosperity for those on the bottom. The prophet Micah claims in his most familiar passage that God requires us to "do justice, and to love kindness and to walk humbly with your God."

What does it mean to do justice? One place to begin is with accountability for past wrongs. For whites, we must hear the untold pain and injustice that slavery and racism have inflicted. As a nation I do not think we have repented for the sins of the past. The sin of slavery and the sins whites inflicted on the native people living on this land continue to haunt us and continue to destroy the children of slaves and generations of Native Americans who have no work and are plagued with the disease of alcoholism. If we do not feel the pain of racism, it is because of the privilege the color of our skin gives us every day of our lives. We can begin by accepting accountability for past wrongs and as a church confess our corporate sin.

A second step is to begin concretely building the vision of shalom in our midst. Doing justice, as Walter Brueggemann defines it, "is to sort out what belongs to whom and to return it to them." His definition assumes a right distribution of goods and access to the sources of life. When some have unjustly held certain goods and privileges for a long time, it can seem as though they have always belonged to them. To illustrate the importance of figuring out what belongs to whom, and adjusting our behavior accordingly, I share a story of Brueggemann's.

A proper lady went to a tea shop. She sat at a table for two, ordered a pot of tea, and prepared to eat some cookies that she had in her purse. Because the tea shop was crowded, a man took the other chair and ordered tea. As it happened, he was a Jamaican black. The woman prepared for a leisurely time, so she began to read her paper. As she did so, she took a cookie from the package. As she read, she noticed that the man across also took a cookie from the package. This upset her greatly, but she ignored it and kept reading. After a while, she took another cookie. And so did he. This unnerved her and she glared at the man. While she glared, he reached for the fifth and last cookie, smiled and offered her half of it. She was indignant. She paid her money and left in a great hurry, enraged at such a presumptuous man. She hurried to her bus stop just outside. She opened her purse to get a coin for her bus ticket. And then she saw, much to her distress, that in her purse was her package of cookies unopened.

Rarely do we have the opportunity and grace to see the direct costs of our lifestyle on those in other parts of our country or world, as the lady in this story had. She was indignant at the stranger for having what was rightfully his. How often are we aware to whom this land belongs or who paid the cost of building our economic structures? Seldom do we see in our daily lives to whom what we have in fact belongs. It does not mean we can remain in postures of privilege. Doing justice is difficult, especially for those of us who have something to lose or have a debt to repay for benefiting from inequality. There is a shift to be made from charity or helping those we perceive to have had some bad luck, to justice, when the poor or unemployed of our city sit down at the table with our churches and city governments when plans for their welfare are being discussed. In our neighborhoods and local churches changes can be made in the way we make decisions to reflect the vision of shalom, equality, and well-being we yearn for.

We hear so many statistics and numbers in our lives that they sometimes cease to mean anything. There are just two numbers I've read lately that have stuck with me. In 1990, every six seconds in the developing world a child dies and another is disabled by a disease that could have been prevented by immunization. Pause for six seconds; that is not long. That makes ten children every minute and six hundred every hour. The other number refers to our country, one of the wealthiest in the world. Here every fifty-four minutes an American child dies because of the effects of poverty. During the time it takes me to write one page, a child will die. How do we reconcile the death of a child with the priorities of our national and state budgets? New B-2 bombers each cost $1 billion per plane, and the Pentagon wants a total force of 132 of these bombers. Just as Micah was compelled to cry out for justice, we must not increase the burden on those who are poor already. The gap between the rich and the poor is growing. Those below the poverty line are growing even poorer. Two out of every five poor Americans fell into the lowest income category that the Census Bureau measures; their incomes were below one half of the federal poverty line in 1988. At the same time the wealth of the richest Americans increased markedly. The disparity between the rich and the poor is growing wider. One of the most common responses from church folks about issues of justice is that it is too "political." I recently read a definition I found helpful in interpreting what we are doing. The term "political" was derived from the Greek word *polis*, which meant "city," which now we would call "the nation." Therefore "politics" is the science concerned about all the people who live in our nation. In biblical language, it is the love I have toward all those who live with me in the same society.

Protestants and Catholics both have strong traditions encouraging us to move upstream and discover the causes of poverty. Philip Newell reminds us that the Protestant Reformers did not regard the institutions and structures of the world as immutably given or permanent. Human constructs can and must be submitted to reform and change. Political, economic, and ecclesiastical systems alike were regarded by the Reformers as fair game because they are human constructs. John Calvin did not pit the secular against the religious, the worldly against the spiritual order. Calvin's vision took him to Geneva and to nothing less than a reform of the whole human community, including the church and state.

The vision in Isaiah 65 begins to describe the kind of world we want for ourselves, our children, and our world. "No more shall there be an infant that lives but a few days.... They shall build houses and inhabit them, they shall not labor in vain, or bear children for calamity." We can care for those in front of us, in our pews, never underestimating the pain right there. We can move from immersion in the experience of the people we know and those in poverty, to the analysis of the root problem, to theological reflection and return to immersion. Your church can have adult education classes on the economy and its influence on the people in your community. Churches have been involved in coalitions to stop plant closings where thousands of jobs are threatened. Churches can hold hearings in different parts of the city to hear directly from those who are unemployed or from those who work full time and still do not earn enough to be out of poverty. The Council of Churches in West Virginia held a statewide conference on the economy, inviting labor, women's groups, legislators, and business folks into a dialogue that would not have happened without their work. Local churches can find out from the chamber of commerce what kinds of business and industry are being invited into our communities. We can study the underlying values of our economy and become informed about how it functions. We tend to think of the economic forecast as if it were a weather report and forget that it too is a human construct subject to human influences. Margaret Mead once said, "Never doubt that a small group of thoughtful committed citizens can change the world; indeed it's the only thing that ever has." May God's shalom give us our vision and carry each of us lovingly on our journey upstream.

AUTOBIOGRAPHICAL STATEMENT

I am interested in economics first because of knowing Marge Tuite, O.P. Her analysis was clear and her passion and priority were poor women and children. Because of Margie's efforts before her death in 1986, Church Women United adopted an imperative to eliminate the root causes of poverty. As a member of Church Women United I have been active in the effort to dig for and understand the root causes of poverty. My love and respect for her is the reason I write this article.

I learned from economists Pam Sparr and Marjorie Williams that economic literacy is essential for activists, that church folks can understand it, and I am grateful to them for the workshops they have led. I am indebted to Teresa Amott for teaching a course at Harvard Divinity School in 1988 on women and the U.S. economy. She helped me understand the values underlying the free market system and shared her ongoing research documenting the historical differences in the causes for poverty among women. My work in the office of Women for Economic Justice gave me tools for using research in organizing with women in poverty. Program director Barbara Neely's commitment to unite women on welfare with poor working women aided in dispelling the myths that welfare women's issues are separate from poor working women's issues.

Before starting graduate school I was director of the Alabama Prison Project in Montgomery, Alabama, from 1978 to 1982. I graduated from Harvard Divinity School in June 1990 and plan to be ordained in the Presbyterian Church (USA) and continue my commitment to women in poverty.

BACKGROUND INFORMATION

The number of people in poverty is a concern for people of faith. Nearly every faith group or denomination has a policy statement on economic justice. The reality that women and children bear the greatest burden of poverty is not taken seriously enough. From the halls of divinity schools to the halls of Congress, the voices of poor women and children are not heard and represented. The experience of the poorest woman in our society must be what we measure our legislative and theological insights by; for until she is the starting place little can or will be done to challenge the economic structures that keep women at the greatest disadvantage in the global village in which we all live.

To make the connections between women and economics and poverty is overwhelming. There are many entry points to the spiral of connections between sexism, racism, economic justice, and global debt. I want to touch on three major entry places: the local community, the national policy level, and the global economic system. On the local level, in the home, women are abused by men they know well. Most often economic factors keep women in abusive situations. Shelters are vital places to which women can escape and reorganize their lives. Yet money for shelters is being cut back. Violence against women cuts across all countries, classes, races, religions, and cultures. The fostering of women's economic independence is essential to prevent domestic violence.

Job discrimination and pay equity issues affect women in local communities. Worldwide, women still earn only two-thirds of men's pay. The rise of the service sector in our current economy offers less than full-time jobs with no benefits or job security and low pay. Rarely are there employee unions in the service sector jobs, and women primarily work in this service sector. Women are two-thirds of all minimum wage employees. The service sector has been labeled "pink collar," and includes such jobs as social services, sales, clerical workers, teaching, and childcare. Juggling household, children, and jobs restricts many women to part-time employment with low pay, low benefits, and no career prospects. Two out of three poor adults are women. Families with a female head of the household have a poverty rate *six* times that of male-headed families. If wives and female heads of household were paid the wages that similarly qualified men earn, about half the families now in poverty would not be poor. Nearly three-fourths of the over sixty-five-year-olds who are below the poverty level are women. Half of those in poverty are the elderly and children, people whom we do not expect to work. On a local level we must work for quality day care for children and the elderly, for jobs with good pay and opportunities for women and people of color.

On the national level, as we seek to see the broad perspective of women's economic situation, there is a word of caution. Many authors in the field of social science are writing with a note of alarm and urgency about the "new" crises in the rapidly rising number of women and children in poverty. For the past ten years, scholars and activists have called attention to the "feminization of poverty." Poverty, it must be remembered, is not a new phenomenon for women and men of color and white working-class women.

> Like many other working-class women, racial ethnic women were never out of public production. Racial ethnic women diverge from other working-class women in that, as members of colonized minorities, their definition as laborers in production took precedence over their domestic roles. The lack of consideration for their domestic functions is poignantly revealed in the testimony of black domestics, who were expected to leave their children and home cares behind while devoting full-time to the care of the white employer's home and children.[1]

For us to ignore the history of those who have been oppressed by poverty for centuries, as is done with the use of terms like the new "feminization of poverty," is to perpetuate injustice, and it leads to inaccurate conclusions in our analysis of the causes of poverty.

The number of female heads of household has increased significantly since 1960. The number of families maintained by women in the 1970s grew from 5.5 million to 9.4 million in the mid-1980s. There is an unequal distribution of the costs of children between men and women, which is reinforced by public policy. Author Nancy Folbre argues that "mothers, single mothers in particular, pay a disproportionate share of the costs of rearing the next generation."[2]

In the global perspective, the debt crisis is affecting women's lives. Too many of us in the United States, embarrassingly enough, have the privilege of ignorance. Peasants in the Philippines or Peru know all about the World Bank and how it affects their daily lives. The conditions the World Bank places on a country before it will lend money include severe cuts in social spending. Children pay the highest price for Third World debt, according to the United Nations Children's Fund, which estimates that half a million youngsters died in 1989 because of it. In the world's poorest countries during the last few years, health spending has been cut in half, while education declined 25 percent, according to the UNICEF "State of the World's Children 1989." Women's lives and economic contributions are invisible and ignored when it comes to addressing such "macro-economic issues as foreign debt and trade," according to a 1989 UN report on economic development. "Evidence shows that in key respects women are more seriously affected than men by the on-going economic deterioration in scores of countries."[3] The UN report outlines several specific ways women are affected: as poverty rises more women than men are affected, women have greater difficulties countering wage cuts because fewer women are organized in unions than men, foreign investors are invited into a country strapped for external financing and want to employ women, since low wages can be paid and "they are more likely to accept working conditions which would be unacceptable to men."[4] Other problems the UN reports include rising unemployment; more women than men are unemployed, forcing women into the informal employment sector and in some countries into begging and prostitution. The austerity programs have forced women to work even longer hours. With schools closed there are children to watch, and with food prices rising more food must be made from scratch or gone without. Rising food prices have contributed to women's hunger and malnutrition.

During the United Nations' Decade for the Advancement of Women (1975–85) studies found that "with few exceptions women's burdens of work have increased, and their relative and even absolute health, nutrition and educational status has declined."[5] Multinational corporations can move to Third World countries where they find cheaper labor. Third World women work in assembly lines and earn in a day what U.S. women might earn in an hour. "Women are the natural choice for assembly jobs. Multinationals prefer women with no children and no plans to have any. In the Philippines, the Mattel Toy Company offers prizes to workers who undergo sterilization."[6]

Women make up over half the world's population, put in 60 percent of the hours worked, and earn only 10 percent of the world's income. While women are heads of one-third of the world's households, they own only 1 percent of the world's property. Despite the fact the women produce 50–90 percent of the food in developing countries, they are the primary victims of famine and malnutrition. Women and children represent over 75 percent of the world's refugees.[7]

For the past nineteen centuries, the Christian theological task has been performed almost exclusively by educated European men. White Western European men have presumed to represent a universal voice as they described human nature and attempted to define the divine. They have defined even what the theological questions are. In fact, their experience in defining theology has never been a universal experience. Women and people of differing classes and races have had different experiences of God and human relationship than that experienced by those who defined the theological task. Those voices are now beginning to be heard. Economic justice has been largely ignored by traditional theologians and ethicists. Ethicist Katie Cannon says "ethics are written when there is a contestable issue. Black women's issues have not presented the academy with ethical dilemmas."[8]

Women and people of color have challenged the classical theologian's basic premises and asserted that those who have dominated the discourse no longer can speak for everyone. Western, white, middle-class males can write about their experience of God only from their perspective, regardless of their claims of objectivity. Everyone's work is shaped by the historical reality in which they work and by what they know to be normative. The twentieth-century feminist and liberation theologians have changed the face of the theological task. "Liberation theologians have identified ways in which economic imperialism and class, white supremacy, Western Christian cultural and religious imperialism, or male supremacy and compulsory heterosexism have become embedded in Christian teaching."[9] This challenge came in the form of a profound methodological shift. The shift is from a linear model for theology to a praxis model, which radically moves to center spot the experience of those traditionally left out of theological circles, namely women, people of color, and the poor.

As marginalized voices are heard, difference is becoming clear. There was an assumption in the early days of feminist theology that white feminists could represent all women's voices. As Carter Heyward states of feminist theologians, "Few, if any, of us intended to exclude the lives of women of color from our concerns, we simply had not begun to comprehend the extent to which women of different racial/ethnic groups have disparate historical and contemporary experiences of sexism."[10] Our cultural, class, and racial/ethnic group does inform our images and experience of the divine. Feminist theologians have all attempted to replace hierarchical principles that underlie the classical approach to theology.[11] Hispanic feminist theologians Ada Maria Isasi-Diaz and Yolanda Tarango claim that while male Third World theologians have challenged the white/European bias in theology, they have "largely ignored and/or refused to deal with the oppression of women"[12]

We must hear the voices of women in poverty both in this country and around the globe. The economic privilege of the majority of those in the academy has dulled the sense of urgency of the plight of the world's poor, the majority of whom are women and children. The consistently absent issue in theology from the United States is a critique of capitalism. Too many theologians lack the imagination to call attention to those economic relationships that are oppressive. We lack the imagination to describe and call attention to just economic relationships liberating to all. The challenge of poverty and injustice requires and calls from us courage and creativity in finding solutions.

NOTES

1. Evelyn N. Glenn, "Racial Ethnic Women's Labor: The Intersection of Race, Gender, and Class Oppression," *Review of Radical Political Economics* 7, no. 3 (1985): 102.
2. Nancy Folbre, "The Pauperization of Motherhood: Patriarchy and Public Policy in the United States," *Review of Political Economics* 16, no. 4: 72.
3. *United Nations Economic Development Report* (New York, 1989).
4. Ibid.
5. Gita Sen and Caren Grown, *Development, Crises, and Alternative Visions: Third World Women's Perspectives* (New York: Monthly Review Press, 1987), p. 16.
6. Annette Fuentes and Barbara Ehrenreich, *Women in the Global Factory* (Boston: South End Press, 1984), p. 13.
7. Church Women United pamphlet.
8. Dr. Cannon's class lecture, 1989.
9. Beverly Harrison, *Making Connections: Essays in Feminist Social Ethics* (Boston: Beacon Press, 1985), p. 89.
10. Carter Heyward, "An Unfinished Symphony of Liberation: The Radicalization of Christian Feminism among White U.S. Women," *Journal of Feminist Studies in Religion* 1, no. 1 (1985): 101.
11. Ada Maria Isasi-Diaz and Yolanda Tarango, *Hispanic Women: Prophetic Voice in the Church* (New York: Harper & Row, 1988), p. xiii.
12. Ibid.

BIBLIOGRAPHY

Barton, Carol, and Barbara Weaver. *The Global Debt Crisis: A Question of Justice.* Washington, D.C.: Interfaith Foundation, 1989.

Brueggemann, Walter, Sharon Parks, and Tom Groome. *To Act Justly, Love Tenderly, Walk Humbly: An Agenda for Ministers.* New York: Paulist Press, 1986.

Debt Crisis Network. *From Debt to Development: Alternatives to the International Debt Crisis.* Washington, D.C.: Institute for Policy Studies, 1985.

Folbre, Nancy. "The Pauperization of Motherhood: Patriarchy and Public Policy in the United States." *Review of Radical Political Economics* 16, no. 4 (1984).

Fuentes, Annette, and Barbara Ehrenreich. *Women in the Global Factory.* Boston: South End Press, 1984.

Glenn, Evelyn Nakano. "Racial Ethnic Women's Labor: The Intersection of Race, Gender and Class Oppression." *Review of Radical Political Economics* 7, no. 3 (1985).

Harrison, Beverly. *Making the Connections: Essays in Feminist Social Ethics.* Boston: Beacon Press, 1985.

Heyward, Carter. "An Unfinished Symphony of Liberation: The Radicalization of Christian Feminism among White U.S. Women." *Journal of Feminist Studies in Religion* 1 no. 1 (1985).

Isasi-Diaz, Ada Maria, and Yolanda Tarango. *Hispanic Women: Prophetic Voice in the Church.* New York: Harper & Row, 1988.

Lefkowitz, Rochelle, and Ann Withorn, eds. *For Crying Out Loud: Women and Poverty in the United States.* New York: Pilgrim Press, 1986.

Pastoral Letter on Catholic Social Teaching and the U.S. Economy. *Economic Justice for All.* Washington, D.C.: National Conference of Catholic Bishops, 1986.

Schüssler Fiorenza, Elisabeth, and Anne Carr, eds. "Women, Work and Poverty." *Concilium.* Edinburgh: T. & T. Clark, 1987.

Seager, Joni, and Ann Olson. *Women in the World: An International Atlas.* New York: Simon & Schuster, 1986.

Sen, Gita, and Caren Grown. *Development, Crises, and Alternative Visions: Third World Women's Perspectives.* New York: Monthly Review Press, 1987.

RESOURCES AND ORGANIZATIONS

Interfaith Action for Economic Justice
110 Maryland Avenue, NE, Suite 509
Washington, DC 20002
   Interfaith Action for Economic Justice is a coalition of national Protestant, Roman Catholic, Jewish and other religious organizations. It seeks to influence public policy on international debt, foreign aid, and trade among other economic justice issues. It helps to educate through its publications.

Isis International
Via San Saba 5
00153 Rome, Italy
   Isis is a resource and documentation center in the international women's liberation movement with regular publications.

Religious Network for Equality for Women (RNEW)
475 Riverside Drive, Rm. 812A
New York, NY 10115

RNEW is a coalition of Protestant, Catholic, Jewish, and other faith groups whose purpose is to work for justice for women, especially the elimination of poverty and legal inequities. RNEW has published an economic literacy program adaptable to a variety of adult education and action groups.

5

Throwaway Children

Marion F. Avarista

SERMON

*Because you are precious in my eyes
and glorious, and because I love you,...
bring back my sons from afar,
and my daughters from the ends of the earth.*
—Isaiah 43:4, 6

I, a stranger and afraid in a world I never made.
—A. E. Housman

Mary, fifteen, pregnant, sick, and beginning to hemorrhage, had a green plastic garbage bag wrapped around her waist. She was brought to the agency where I work by a known pimp who was concerned for her safety. Mary had been placed in state care at eleven. She confided in a friend's mother that her stepfather had sexually abused her since she was six years old. Mary's mother chose not to believe her daughter, who for the last four years had lived in a series of foster and group homes. Although Mary ran away once or twice a month, she always ran back home to her mother.

Jason, the pimp, age eighteen, came from a family of ten children. When Jason was eleven, his father died, and the mother turned her children over to the state with one exception. She introduced Jason to the world of male prostitution. He spent successive years in foster homes and group homes and finally graduated from reform school. Remembering his own life, he sought assistance for Mary whose health was in critical danger.

God tells us how precious we are, and God loves us. Do you think Jason and Mary felt that love? Do these two faceless, voiceless, and forgotten children feel any sense of dignity and self-worth? I think not. What happens to a society that abandons its children? The price we pay is not only costly in dollars and cents but costly to our very souls.

Although I am not allowed to preach this sermon, I would nevertheless like one day to deliver it at a Sunday morning Mass where families gather for prayer and worship.

I work at the Travelers Aid Society in Providence, Rhode Island, in a small section of the bus terminal. Travelers Aid works with people who fall between the cracks of the systems that are supposed to save them. These people who are in transition or homeless or who have lost their way are of all ages. We served six thousand runaway children in 1988 alone. Of these we opened files on three hundred, to whom we still attempt to provide holistic services. Six thousand runaways in a state with a population less than a million will give you some idea of the magnitude of this problem in cities like New York, Chicago, or Los Angeles.

The frightening part of this terrible uprootedness is that these children are our children, our future, and our Social Security when we are old if viewed from an economic viewpoint. From a Christian viewpoint, how are we to measure, never mind undo, the damage inflicted through all the formative years of these children? Think of the physical and nutritional neglect as their brains are being developed, of the mental and emotional trauma while their personalities are being formed.

Not all the youngsters come from broken homes or from parents whom we call "no good." At Travelers Aid, we see children from affluent homes parallel to those from poorer homes. Both suffer from absentee parents, and both move around easily among accessible drugs, alcohol, and sex. In other words, all children are among these runaways. When we see young people, we don't ever *assume* they have no home to go to.

Recently 225 corporate executive officers and university presidents succinctly stated the nation's self-interest in investing in our children. They wrote:

> This nation cannot continue to compete and prosper in the global arena when more than one-fifth of our children live in poverty and a third grow up in ignorance. And if the nation cannot compete, it cannot lead. If we continue to squander the talents of millions of our children, America will become a nation of limited human potential. It would be tragic if we allow this to happen. America must become a land of opportunity for every child.

Yet what are the realities? National studies show that there are thirteen million poor children in this country. That means that one of every five children lives below the poverty level. What kind of country is this? Is it the kind those of us here this morning want? America has a public policy of compartmentalizing problems. At the moment the problem is drugs, last year the issue was homelessness. But these young people may have both a drug and a homelessness problem, as well as physical and mental health problems. And educational problems. What can we the people in the pews do? How can we help our nation deal *holistically* with these problems?

First we must help our politicians by encouraging them to develop a national family policy. At this moment, politicians know such a policy will cost money. And they are afraid. Why? Mention the word "tax" and politicians run for cover — even though it costs much less per year to care for one of these children — to feed, clothe, educate, and provide physical and mental health care — than to keep one of them in a training school or a prison.

A second change we can support regards zoning for group homes in our neighborhoods. No one now wants a group home next to them; therefore we have coined a new acronym: NIMBY (Not in my backyard). The lowest moment in my professional career came in 1988 when I had to return $500,000 to the federal government. We at Travelers Aid scrounge for money. Yet we could not get a zoning clearance to build a home for ten young people, to help them learn life skills and to provide needed support. Not only did the government have to take back the money, but we lost a matching half-million dollars from the state. So it is well and good to talk or to preach, but we must go further. We, the weak, must act in helpful ways.

A third and most important way — one that all of us can engage in — is to come face to face with these children. Come and visit and talk to these children at Travelers Aid. Put a face on one of them, listen to what he or she says, and you will be convinced that there are too few people to work with so many forgotten children. Drop in at a community room and share a cup of cocoa with a lost kid. Then *you* will be convinced you want to help.

What runaways lack most is an adult who acts as a surrogate parent — a person who cares for them, who will see them through their trials and tribulations. That is what is missing from these children's lives. We cannot write a proposal for this need; we cannot hire people to do it. It must come from faith-filled people. Only they can fill the vacancies in vacant lives.

What a wonderful opportunity especially for retired people. We notice that older people have much more in common with kids than the middle-aged. The elders understand what is really important in life; they are not put off by long hair, overdone make-up, or style of clothes. Two wonderful women over fifty now tutor children trying to get Grade Equivalency Diploma certificates. The women love the children; the children love them. There is no reason for an able retired person to be bored; call us and we will put you in touch with many, many youths. Come face to face with a child and you come face to face with God.

I have come full-circle in my ministry. Initially I was involved in grassroots organizing, which I still believe in. I moved on to mobilizing people, *but* one day I came face to face with children like Mary and Jason. I reflected: "My God we can never do this one on one" — with six thousand runaways in one year alone. Now I believe the *only* way is one on one, because we have to change people's hearts.

I believe further that when we come before God, it is not the sins we committed that we will have to account for, but rather the actions we omitted when we were called. We were too busy; we had our own family. What do we give back for having received so much?

We who are so committed to an anti-abortion position, who spend time, effort, and money supporting legislative action to repeal the Roe v. Wade decision, let us not forget the children who are here who suffer so much. Let us work as hard for them as we do for our unborn children.

The Lord asks us, "Bring back my sons and daughters from afar," those sons and daughters who are strangers and afraid in a world they never made. Amen.

AUTOBIOGRAPHICAL STATEMENT

Travelers Aid Society for Runaway Children has for the past four years provided me the opportunity to practice the message of my faith and of the gospel in the secular world. I feel more involved in ministry now than during the twelve preceding years when I worked for the diocese. I feel that my ministry is more "hands on," that I'm a priest to so many forgotten children.

Children like Lisa who recently sat across from me in my office with tears streaming down her face telling me how she hated her mother. Lisa sobbed, not out of pity for herself, but out of guilt. She felt guilty because she was finally able to say, "I hate my mother." Nothing in my experience as a mother of three grown sons and a grandmother of three had prepared me for this moment. Lisa hated her mother and felt guilty even though her mother hung up the phone when Lisa asked to come home for Christmas. Lisa hated her mother and felt guilt, although at the age of fifteen, Lisa gave birth to her stepfather's child and her mother blamed her and threw her out. Lisa hated her mother but felt guilty although Lisa had spent three years in foster homes, group homes, and reform school.

My Italian family heritage was the foundation of my value system — a close-knit family, a mother image that was very strong and supportive. I grew up in an Italian section of Providence called Federal Hill. My sister and brother and I never knew we were poor until we were in junior high school. After all, didn't all kids live in a tenement house with only cold running water, no bathtub, and oil located in the cellar that your parents brought up in gallon jugs to put in the heating stove? Our poverty was economic, not spiritual or emotional. If nothing else, we knew our parents loved us and protected us and wanted only the best for us. So here I am, at age fifty, working with adolescents and young adults who are described as street youth, those faceless, voiceless, and seemingly hopeless "forgotten children" of our times.

My working with the Travelers Aid program and with street youth is an outgrowth of my faith commitment. I struggle with the knowledge that there are too few people to work with so many forgotten children. I ask when do I acknowledge that I've given all I can and I must pass the torch to someone else? My faith tells me and my heart confirms that someone/everyone must care for and love these children. Without that, not only are they a lost generation, but we will be held accountable for that loss. Right now I feel guided by the Lord. I am living out my faith in caring about people, and that is how I will be judged.

BACKGROUND INFORMATION

The Children's Defense Fund in 1988 published *A Call for Action to Make Our Nation Safe for Children*, a troubling booklet on children, youth, and families.[1] Subtitled *A Briefing Book on the Status of American Children in 1988*, it provides succinct and startling data about our country:

> Our children are not safe. Millions of our homes are not safe. Our streets are not safe. Our national and world economies are not safe. Our environment is not safe....Our national future — where each of us will spend the rest of our lives and which depends on the safety and the healthy development of the young — is not safe.[2]

Just as the public health of a nation is judged by two criteria — neonatal death rate and longevity of women and men — so too is the willingness to protect children a moral litmus test of any decent and compassionate society.

There are two groups of children particularly at risk in America. One group consists of thirteen million poor children: poorly housed, fed, and educated, of mental and physical health often way below average. The second group consists of increasing numbers of privileged youths — the "affluenza" — who suffer from spiritual poverty, boredom, low self-esteem, and lack of sustaining motivation. Both groups suffer from broken homes, absentee parents, and the easy access to drugs, alcohol, and sex.

Between 1.2 million and 1.5 million children run away from home each year. It is estimated that one-third of these youths are running away from physical or sexual abuse at home. At least an estimated 7.5 million children and adolescents are in need of mental health services. Approximately 3 million of them have serious emotional problems. Seventy to 80 percent of these youths with mental health problems do not receive the care they need.

Children cannot vote or lobby for the policies and the investments they need to grow up healthily, safely, and with hopes for a productive future. Susan Champlin Taylor asks: Can America rouse itself to conquer the perils facing its children? One route she suggests is arousing public awareness. Quoting the Children's Defense Fund she writes: "We've got to make a critical mass of Americans understand that the breakdown of the American family is a great threat. It's greater than the Soviet threat, greater than the savings-and-loan crisis."[3]

A few examples of immediate, cost-effective steps to make children physically safe from death, disease, hunger, homelessness, and inadequate day care will describe what is meant.

1. Preventive health coverage especially among blacks and Hispanics will prevent low birth weight and increasing mortality rates. Yet priorities of the 1980s have bequeathed to the U.S. rising rates in infant mortality. For years these mortality rates were on the decline, but now we are below Singapore, Spain, Hong Kong, and Japan. And when it comes to black infant mortality we are *twenty-eighth* in the world, with higher infant death rates in Memphis, the District of Columbia, and Boston than in Jamaica.[4]

2. There is a rising tide of infectious diseases that were long thought to be eradicated. But funding for immunization is missing; an increase of $40 million is needed — less that we spent in 1988 on military bands.

3. Many of the 9.5 million mothers in the work force need better day-care services. Why should a three-year-old in day care be left for three hours in a closed car in Connecticut on a sweltering August day — to die of heat prostration as this child did?

In addition to these small efforts, people in the pews are in an excellent position to reflect on values. The values of a people, a nation, inspire women and men of vision to rise up and see the whole picture of a society. Attacking problems piecemeal has not worked for America. Even the War on Poverty was not successful except for Head Start and the Women, Infants and Children Nutrition Programs.

What seems to be needed is the emergence of a leader who will hold up the vision of an America that can lead credibly and decently in the world. And as the 225 corporate executive officers and presidents for the Committee on Economic Development stated: "This nation cannot continue to compete and prosper in the global arena when more than one-fifth of our children live in poverty, and a third grow up in ignorance. And if the nation cannot compete, it cannot lead."[5]

Runaway children come from all sorts of homes. In 1985, 49,322 juveniles were being held in public juvenile facilities. Fewer than one-fourth of them had been charged with violent acts. About four thousand of them had committed either no offenses or "status offenses" such as running away or truancy. Neither of these would be a crime if committed by an adult. Yet many of these detained youths need multiple services.

What can religious people do? Besides becoming aware of the magnitude of the problems facing America's children, we can ask ourselves how the problems can be solved without leadership and money. Our politicians say, "Money must come from other programs." We must reflect on the importance of spending money to make and keep the country safe and productive.

Street youths have had to endure an enormous amount of disappointment and rejection; often distrustful and angry, they will respond only to genuinely warm, accepting, supporting, and nonjudgmental surrogacy. This demands a one-on-one relationship, and adults with leisure can give these children precisely that. No amount of money can cure the derelict state of so many of our children. But volunteers working with each child can make a difference.

Profiles, which describes a successful treatment program for street youth in Denver, states that volunteers are critical to their success. Most of the youths in this program were envious of others who had normal relationships with non-street youth and adults: "Developing friendships with healthy, well-adjusted adults is particularly important, because quite often the only adults they know well — their parents, pimps, drug pushers, and the like — are abusive and exploitative. At some point...they must learn that some adults can be trusted."[6]

Travelers Aid Society is one of many successful programs working with runaway children. It can put you in touch with these children. If you want to know how many throwaway children there are in your neighborhood, consult *A Call for Action* listed in the bibliography. For example, Massachusetts with 1,364,000 children under eighteen has 228,000 children, or 16.7 percent, living in poverty. Thirty-six percent of black and 69.9 percent of Hispanic children live in poverty in the Bay State. Similarly in Tennessee (1,231,000) there are 323,000 children — 26.2 percent — living in poverty; of these 45.1 percent are black and 47.5 percent are Hispanic.[7] Figures such as these are supplied for every state in the Union.

NOTES

1. *A Call for Action to Make Our Nation Safe for Children: A Briefing Book on the Status of American Children in 1988* (Washington, D.C.: Children's Defense Fund Printing, 1988), p. iii.
2. Ibid., p. 3.
3. Susan Champlin Taylor, "A Promise at Risk: Can America Rouse Itself to Conquer the Perils Facing Its Children?" *Modern Maturity* 32, no. 5 (August–September 1989): 35.
4. *A Call for Action*, p. 3.
5. Ibid., p. iii.
6. *Profiles: Treating Street Youth* (Champaign, Ill., Community Research Associates), p. 7.
7. *A Call for Action*, pp. 16–17.

BIBLIOGRAPHY

A Call for Action to Make Our Nation Safe for Children: A Briefing Book on the Status of American Children in 1988. Washington, D.C.: Children's Defense Fund Printing, 1988. This book is one of the best sources of up-to-date and readily accessible information on America's children.

Profiles: Treating Street Youth: Juvenile Justice and Delinquency Prevention is the report of a community in Denver, the Ogden House, that struggles to find ways to reach street youth. Community Research Associates, 115N Neil Street, Champaign, IL 61820.

Taylor, Susan Champlin. "A Promise at Risk." *Modern Maturity* 32, no. 5 (August–September 1989): 32–41, 84. An excellent and comprehensive view of the plight of thirteen million children in poverty in America. She asks if America can stir itself to conquer the perils facing its children and itself.

RESOURCES

The Children's Defense Fund
122 C Street, NW
Washington, DC 20001
Serves as a kind of mentor for policy makers, politicians, clergy, and all of us who are interested in improving the lot of millions of America's children.

Travelers Aid Society
1001 Connecticut Avenue, NW
Washington, DC 20036
Travelers Aid began in St. Louis in 1851 during the westward expansion. It offers shelter, food, counseling, and other protective services. Consult your telephone directory or write Travelers Aid at the address above.

State agencies for children's services in the various states offer information more specific to local needs.

6

Living in a Project: "Hell with a Roof over Our Heads"

Glenda Smith

DIALOGUE SERMON

You lived on the streets for fourteen months?
When I was on the streets, I cried all the time. I felt heartbroken and began not wanting to pray. I felt as if my family had turned on me and that I was going through all these changes because God was punishing me for having all these children while not being married to their father.

Do you still think God is punishing you in these children?
No. I remember my grandmother telling me that God don't put on us burdens that we cannot bear. That brought me to my senses; it brought me up on my feet. As a child, kids were always coming in our home and we went through a hard time. My father was an alcoholic; my mother took care of us and got us everything we wanted. While doing her housework, she would always kneel down and pray. When I walked these streets, I too started praying, but then I thought: I don't want to hear of prayer, because why should I be going through all of this here, I, who pray every day. We spent our welfare money to stay in a hotel room on very cold nights. I used to go into the supermarket and take my kids with me to get bologna and bread. We walked down the aisles. I flattened a loaf of bread and put it and the bologna right up here in my bra, all under a great big coat of mine.

I then could give my kids something to eat as we sat on a sidewalk somewhere. We did not have a house; we did not have anyone to turn to. People who I thought loved us and cared about us were saying: "You can't stay here with all of those kids." All of those kids were my kids. So I used to sit and talk to God, and then I began to pray again. I lived in the streets fourteen months.

Because I am a Catholic woman, I am prevented from preaching this sermon for Glenda Smith. The sermon is intended for the regular comfortable churchgoer anytime — A.L.M.

Describe what a night on the streets was like.

I was hidden, sleeping in a car with all of my kids. Although we were on top of each other, we were all close together. And I knew they were safe with me. Eight children and myself in a car was very crowded, but that way I could save my little bit of money for food. One time my kids' father found an apartment, and we slept there for a month.

The landlord found out I had all my kids there and he put us out. He padlocked the door. He already set all of the little things, like clothes, out on the sidewalk. No mover would go in there and get the furniture because the kitchen floor was so weak. I now feel that I have never gotten back to what we had in that little place. But I have to believe that everything is for a reason.

So you never lost your faith?

I never lost my faith in God. But I lost my faith in a lot of people. A lot of people turned their backs on me. Most of all, I believe it was my sins turning in on myself from having all of these children out of sin, living with their father in sin.

What does that make you think about God? Do you think that's how God is, a punishing God?

I think that God has a plan for everybody. You either follow God's plan or you make your own plan. You know, I've met the devil. My whole life was in darkness. Nothing was light for me. I was always depressed. The devil was constantly trying to tell me: "Kill yourself, kill your kids," and so on. See, God wants us to live in the path of the righteous.

I was mistreated and felt betrayed by the people out in the world. I call it "out in the world," because I had never seen anything like this in myself. All the people that I wanted to be around, church Christian people, would not take me and my kids in.

But when I got around the drug addicts and the alcoholics, me and my kids could sleep in a room with them. All they wanted was a few dollars to give them a bag of dope or a bottle of wine or alcohol, a shoot-up or pipe-up, or whatever they call it. Then we could sleep with them.

I couldn't get accepted for food stamps if I wasn't begging, begging, begging. As long as they saw me feeding my kids with something, they would drive me crazy. The doctors were outrageous too. I could see that this here was stone evil. I felt nothing. I had become cold and empty and wiped out. All I could do was just take care of these kids. I went to the stores to pick up three pairs of underwear for my girls, and opened a different size pack for each. I did the same for my boys. I began to steal all of it. I wasn't raised to do so. So it was nothing but the devil in the form of a big black snake. With red eyes....

I knew then that I was out in the world with nothing but sin. I went so close to the edge that I couldn't grab a hold and come back. I began to talk to God at night, because the devil was telling me that if I was dead my kids might have this, that, and the other. As a child I went to church five days a week with my grandmother, and all I had learned was to live in the path of righteousness. "Come to me...." I even heard my grandmother talk to me. My grandmother is dead. The doctors think that I had a nervous breakdown.

My grandmother always stroked my hair when I was a little girl. I began to pray and talk to her and think of her. I felt her hand stroke my forehead. The doctors felt that I wanted to feel this thing. I was on the edge; I was going crazy. Then I met St. Jude Thaddeus, the saint of difficult cases. God sent him to me. He introduced himself to me as St. Jude Thaddeus, and nurtured me back to life. He says when all of your sins turn in on yourself, when you don't feel like praying, that's when you pray the most. And I prayed myself back to life. And I end up here.

Here in the Hartford Projects in Providence?

Even so. Thanks to St. Jude, there's God in my life. I heard these voices talking to me after I was here. I know that I broke down again while I was here. When I got to this project and saw all the crack, all the roaches, all the rats and mice that I had not had in my little green house, where the floors caved in...my house was paneled, it was very nice. There was a yard there for my kids.

They never had a chance to mix with other kids because I was living on the street. Then I come to a place that I never wanted to live in, and I became depressed. I had fifteen to twenty mice running around, which I now sometimes catch. Mice in here until the pipes back up and the water comes out in my bedroom and on my floor. When my pipes back up, the whole building does. So we call, and that's when they put the poison out. When those mice start dying, you can't come in my house in the morning because it stinks so. I have to get up and go out, because of the dead mice all through the pipes. I put all of the glue stick down to catch those escaping. I put it down at night, and I get up in the morning and try to get the mice out before my babies get up and start going through. And I've seen a few roaches crawling around.

Why did you decide to come into the project if it's so bad?

I came into this project because I had no roof over my head for my kids. I came into this project because I was living in the street with nowhere to go. I would have to lie, like I didn't have kids, in order to get a house. But my kids are always going to be with me. I knew that the projects were bad, but I never, never in my wildest worlds dreamed that the projects were like this. It's worse than I ever could imagine. I mean this crack and stuff. Like yesterday, when Sister Joan was here. She just missed something. They began shooting and fighting with knives and they were falling up against my door.

A girl was getting stabbed. I opened my back door and another girl cut her thumb off. I was screaming and hollering, and James had to slap me. Another girl was fighting her, cut her thumb off with a butcher knife. What had me hysterical was that my kids were outside.

They thought I was outside and they were looking for me, and I was just screaming, "My kids, my kids," looking for them, and I don't even think I was in my mind. James says: "Glenda, I've got them, I got them. They are all in the house, they are all in the house." And then these neighbors came out with a shot gun, and it's crazy over here.

In a way you're saying this is almost homelessness....

This is homeless to me. The project is homelessness with a roof. This is like when I lived in the street. I'm depressed. I don't know if I could live here if I didn't know how to pray.

I get down on my knees. I teach my kids to pray because the project is hell with a roof over our heads. We got snakes on this side, snakes on that side. They're people who are evil as snakes.

This is like brick walls and the snakes are stuck in the walls. And we're in the middle, and they're trying to get to us. They take my kids' money, they beat my kids up, they take bread from them. I have lived here for three years. Sister Theresa and Father Abbott used to come by to see us and bring food and things. We didn't have anything. All I had worked for was gone, and I started over from scratch, and with the help of God, people, people came to help me.

After living in the street, I didn't even want to say, "Hi." Then I met Sister Theresa and Sister Joan and I felt that they loved me. The way they used to hug me. My mother was in Houston, my sisters and my brothers in Dallas and Houston, and nobody had hugged me, or held me and told me that they loved me. When the nun says, "I love you," I says, "You do?" I didn't know people cared because of the way they treated me and my kids. Then I used to go to the McAuley House with my kids to eat. I used to take them to bus stops where they could still get to school. I'll tell you, my kids can walk a long ways.

I began to cry so much that even now when my kids hug me and tell me not to worry, they say: "God's going to help us, Mommy. What are you worried about now, Mommy? Christmas? We'll just sit around the tree and sing. Sister Joan is gonna bring us something, Mommy." I say: "How do you know?" They say: "That's what you used to tell us, Mommy." They tell me the same thing that I used to tell them. They want me to get a little house because I went to school for fashion designing and interior decorating. I'm a good decorator. I got scholarships to go on, but I didn't.

I often wonder why. My whole life wouldn't have been in chaos. But when I went out in the world, I was an easy person to lead. I hung around the wrong people at the wrong time. I went places at the wrong time. But I went to school up to the twelfth grade. And with only six months left, I didn't finish. I did dumb things like that.

Anyway, my mother wasn't home when we were little for one reason: she was working. She worked two jobs full-time and a part-time job. She went through hell to keep us out of a project, with three brothers and five sisters. I got the same amount of kids, three boys, five girls. We always lived in a house and we always played together. We never had a lot of company over except when we went to school. We were always each other's best friend. Now we all are very close, my mom and brothers. If my mother was short on cash and couldn't send us what we wanted for Christmas, my older sisters would say: "Ma, don't get us nothing this time. Get for Glenda," because I was the youngest girl. My sisters are now all up here in Providence. We hug a lot and touch a lot.

I teach my kids to touch a lot, and when they're real angry at each other to rub noses. I make them stand there and rub noses. That was their father's idea. He says when they are being cruel to each other, make them do it, because that's what he and his sisters had to do. And they say "Ma," until they just burst out laughing and hugging on each other. I love to see them when they do that.

So you feel very tender about the father of your children?

If I had to have these kids over again, I would have them by the same man, but I would be married to him. Just last night, he asked again: "When are we going to get married?" And I constantly tell him: "When we can." I don't want to marry him and come back to a project. He's not a rich man. He helps me out all he can. He just went through that feeling of being a failure, because we were homeless. That green house, the house with the five bedrooms, all my new furniture that I had, came from him. All of it had to go. I had the prettiest velvet living room set. It was lovely. I had my Jesus who stood on the window. He got it for me. And when I turn all my lights off at night, my Jesus lights.

You're a very spiritual woman, a religious woman.

Because you can't do nothing without God. He let me wake up this morning. He let me dream in this simple world. So when you're living in a world like the world today, you got to be on your toes. You got to think. You're not doing what Satan wants and you're not living for Satan, you're living for God. You got to feel good about life. For so long I didn't feel good about life and I went through this lonely stuff. It changed me. It made me a different person. I had become the person that I knew nothing about. I could hardly hear people talk to me after I was treated that way. I tried to keep my kids clean. We used to have to wash up at gas stations, hotels, restaurants. And I could only carry so much with me. Even though I believe in God, I still cry all the time because I live in this project.

I'm happy when my kids are happy. I'm happy when my kids' father is happy. I don't want him to feel that he has failed me because I remember when I wasn't on welfare, he worked to take care of me, but he's had surgery eleven times. This surgery brought him down. He only has 25 percent of his stomach now. When he got shot, he had to have his stomach done, and when he came out of service, he was still being operated on. He's still fighting for his disability, not for himself, but for my kids. I love verses like Psalm 100: "Make a joyful noise unto the Lord." And I love the twenty-third Psalm. My kids know all these Psalms. I sit here, I read the Bible. I just bought this for my kids — the *Precious Moments Bible*. I just ordered me a Bible Dictionary, and I send all types of donations to the people on TV like...

Gerry Falwell?

I sent donations to Robert Tilman, and I send donations to Lynsey and Richard.

And what about keeping it for yourself? For your children?

I think they need to have more about God on the TV, for people who can't get out. My $20 might not keep them on TV, but I just sent $100 to Robert Tilman to help him out. I, who don't even have a Christmas for my kids.

Yes, what about that?

My grandmother said it's better to give than receive. And I believe anything my grandmother said to me. He'll put it to good use to help people out. People that don't have food and stuff.

Here in this project, they strip the car and take our batteries. That's because they're on drugs. You know, I don't even mistreat them because they're drug addicts and alcoholics. I just tell them: "You did your drugs today, but did you pray?" I tell them that I bought those fifty-pound bags of potatoes from the food market and a case of hot dogs with twenty-four packs so when their kids knock on my door, I can give them a pack, and their kids can eat. Around last Christmas I was blessed with extra toys and I gave them some. So I help other people have a Christmas too. My house was loaded, and so the kids could come and eat and have toys.

Sister Joan feels that you're an outstanding woman. How do you feel about yourself?

I feel that I have a long way to go and a short time to get there. And even though my door is not fully open yet, I know that it soon will be open. And it might not be a green house. God is going to bless me. God has already blessed me. I appreciate the blessings that God has given me because I've met with drugs too. It was years ago. So I don't criticize a person who messes with them. Some people are not as blessed as other people. See, I was taught one way, and I went another way. So I don't criticize a person because you don't know why that person is doing what they are doing.

Your children are very relaxed; they are not nervous wrecks.

My kids. I like to be really careful how I talk to them, how I handle them since being homeless. Sister Joan says so too. I like to be very careful how I talk to them, how I handle myself when I'm talking to them. I have to listen when they talk to me because I'm the type of person who has a wandering mind. I can wander and not even be sitting here, not even be in this house. I teach them obedience. What kid won't do right all the time. I teach them: "Yes, ma'am," "No, ma'am," "Excuse me," "Thank you," "You look nice." All those things they say. But when it comes to saying you're sorry, that's a different thing. They're not allowed to say "sorry" in this house unless they mean it. So if you're going to go over to her and tell her you're sorry, and you don't mean it, I tell them to keep it.

My kids follow me everywhere ever since we lived out in the street, ever since we were homeless, when we lived in cars and hallways and empty apartments. Right now my problem is that I was never able to break the habit of staying awake at night, watching them when they were sleeping. Right now when night comes, I can't sleep from staying up all night watching over my kids. I sleep during the afternoon when they're in school. But at night, that year and two months we slept out in cars, I trained myself to stay awake and watch them so they could sleep. That's why I was totally exhausted during the daytime.

You're also sending your children to Catholic schools?

Yes, I will go without to get for my kids. And before I'm done, I'm going to have all eight of them in Catholic schools. I'm going to do it because I have faith in myself. I have my pride back, and I'm never going to lose that again. I'm never going to be without a roof over my head again. I know that I went through my deepest life darkness. I know that God has forgiven me for my sins. I know that I yet have more to ask forgiveness for, but you know the good thing about that? All you got to do is ask.

Today, now my favorite Bible passage is John 14: "Let Not Your Heart Be Troubled": "Ye believe in God, believe also in me. In my Father's house are many mansions if it were not so, I would have told you. I go to prepare a place for you, and if I go and prepare a place for you, I will come again and receive you unto myself. That where I am, there you may be also. And whither I go, you know, and the way you know." When I was going through some of my troubles, James took the Bible and said: "Instead of crying so much read John 14." He said: "God, this is for me and Glenda, help her make it through this. She's a strong woman, and I know she's going to make it." Part of the reason I made it is because he was constantly telling me that. We read verses out of the Bible together and sometimes we hold hands and pray at night. Prayer is so important: "The family that prays together stays together."

AUTOBIOGRAPHICAL STATEMENT

I was the youngest of eight children in a family raised in the South. My father, seldom at home, was an alcoholic. My mother held two full-time jobs, and one part-time, in her struggle to hold the family together. Consequently, she was seldom at home, and I was raised mostly by my grandmother.

My grandmother was the greatest influence on my life. Attending church with her almost daily, I learned the importance of prayer, the Bible, and love of God. In my darkest moments on the street, I could hear grandmother's voice and it helped me to carry on.

I often ask myself why I never finished high school, since I was just months away from receiving my diploma. But I did not, and I fell into the company of people who used drugs. I began to use drugs too, and today I never judge drug addicts harshly. In fact, while we were homeless, it was the alcoholics and drug addicts who in snowstorms would let us share their space.

Space, a place to live, became out of the question in the mid-1980s. Rents in Providence skyrocketed and we could not afford a home. One landlord put all our belongings out on the sidewalk. My eight children and myself became homeless. For fourteen months we lived in a car parked in out-of-the-way places. My children's father tried to find a place for us and to help us out all he could. But rents were impossible — nobody wanted a woman with so many children.

Sister Joan of McAuley House entered my life at this terrible time. Through her we were able to get a hot meal at the shelter and eventually we moved to the Hartford Project. As my sermon shows, the project is "homelessness with a roof." We are surrounded, up to our very door, with drug people. I never feel safe; my children are not safe here. But I still hope to have a better home one day. I pray and get my kids to kneel down on this floor and thank God for bringing us this far. We have a long road yet to travel.

BACKGROUND INFORMATION

There are today more homeless people in America than at any time since the Great Depression. A report by the American Affordable Housing Institute at Rutgers University cites the most recent figures: "Current estimates of the number of persons likely to be homeless on a given night vary from 655,000 to 4 million."[1] Since many of the homeless are "hidden," not just living on the streets but doubled up with relatives or others, we do not see them as homeless. Even when we become aware of this crowding — usually in the event of their eviction — we begin to adapt ourselves to the sufferings of the homeless.

Jim Tull, co-director of Amos House, a shelter and soup kitchen in Providence, puts this capacity of ours to adapt to suffering as follows: "Suffering grows on us over a period of time, and we begin to tolerate it, to adapt to it in small doses." We are like the frog in a beaker that is gradually heated. At the boiling point the frog, without resisting, will die.

But if placed in a beaker of boiling water, the frog will immediately jump out, refusing to adapt to a catastrophic threat to life.[2] So too with us. Because we adapt gradually to people being homeless, we do not clearly see its harmful effects on individuals, on families, and especially on children.

These harmful effects go far beyond the considerable inconvenience of having no home. Homeless families often disintegrate, and with little remaining morale, they slide into substance abuse or mental illness.

Who are the homeless? They can be divided into four groups:

1. The homeless of the 1940s and 1950s who closely resemble the stereotypic image: older men who were alcoholic and chronic street dwellers. We still have such persons, but the stereotype — the image — of the homeless has greatly changed.

2. The homeless in the 1960s expanded when mental health and psychiatric hospitals across the country began to "deinstitutionalize" most of their patients. The government called for better and more humane services for these discharged patients in community health centers and with varying housing options. Unfortunately, the plan was aborted midway, because the funds were directed to the Vietnam War. Many of the discharged patients, without any support services, began to wander the streets.

Beginning also in the 1960s, many veterans returning from Vietnam found themselves incapable of independent self-care due to the trauma of war and drug dependency. These veterans also began to join the homeless, living on the streets of our cities and towns.

3. A third group, which swelled the frightening numbers of homeless persons, appeared in the 1980s. Individuals and families became homeless due to a severe and still growing shortage of medium- and low-income housing. It is this group that, by far, accounts for the largest increase in homelessness since the Great Depression.

The cause of this major social upheaval was a 72 percent cut in 1981 in federal support for such housing. The reason President Reagan gave for cutting funds from $32 billion to $7.5 billion was to make the states responsible for such services. The $25 billion "saved" went to the military buildup.[3]

This cut led to a housing shortage and was immediately felt in inflated rents and home purchase costs. The poorest competitors for housing were squeezed onto the streets, swelling the ranks of the homeless.

To this group, we must, according to the authors of the Rutgers Report, add the following: "4 million to 14 million American families now living on the knife-edge of homelessness; they are doubled and tripled up in the mostly overcrowded and deteriorating apartments of friends and family; they are one paycheck, one argument from the streets."[4]

4. A fourth group considered homeless are the middle-class young families who cannot *afford* to buy a home. Although they can (if both spouses work) afford rents that claim as much as 30–50 percent of their income, still they are unable to afford the costs of what has always been considered part of the American dream. Gentrification of neighborhoods has led to home prices more than quadrupling in recent years, until now an *average* home costs between $120,000 and $150,000. For the single-parent households a recent Harvard study shows that on average they pay 58.4 percent of the household's income on rent alone.[5]

Before proposing "cures" for the homeless, it is important to consider the children. According to a report released by the U.S. Department of Education (DOE) in Spring 1989, there are 222,000 homeless school-aged children in the U.S. The report is a compilation of data from all fifty states. But the National Coalition for the Homeless estimates that there are between 500,000 and 800,000 homeless children among us.[6] What is even more compelling is DOE's finding that a third of homeless children are not regularly attending school.

Solutions for the problem of homelessness in this wealthy nation vary according to people's philosophy and political outlook. *Safety Network* reported in December 1988 that the Miami City Commission introduced a bill to make homelessness a crime. Mayor Suarez was quoted in response: "What are we going to do? Put them [the homeless] in jail where we don't have enough space for hardened criminals?"[7]

On the less extreme side there is need for more transitional shelters and facilities where families and individuals are provided a stable environment with strong support services. These services can help families and individuals to relocate to permanent housing with the skills and income to live independently. Unfortunately, the funds *available* for these kinds of shelters cannot be used because of local neighborhood opposition. This opposition, which has become national, has been labeled "NIMBY," "Not in my backyard."[8]

The mentally ill homeless wandering the streets of American cities and crowding emergency shelters are a special national problem demanding the attention of government, but even more of people in the pews. Because of the 1983 efforts to reform the Social Security Disability Insurance program for 3.8 million disabled workers and their dependents, the rules were changed. The new rules caused 150,000 to 200,000 people to be dropped from the disability rolls before the administration halted its review. Many of these truly disabled people included the mentally ill, who were too disabled in mind to respond to termination notices or to challenge the government.

Ellen L. Bassuk puts it well when she writes of these specially deprived people:

> The question raised by the increasing number of homeless people is a very basic one: Are Americans willing to consign a broad class of disabled people to a life of degradation, or will they make the commitment to give such people the care they need? In a civilized society the answer should be clear.[9]

She further states that there is no mystery about an appropriate solution. The solution calls for carrying out the aborted plans of the 1963 community health law to provide "housing options and related health-care and social services for the mentally ill." We are the voters whose will the politicians carry out. Implementation of this law calls for increased taxes, and if the words "tax increase" cause a politician to lose votes, what recourse do the mentally disabled have? This is a matter of serious reflection for churchgoers: are we willing to love our neighbor as ourselves? Or will we be like the frog in the gradually heated beaker, adjusting to the catastrophe surrounding us?

Another proposed solution to the homeless problem is to replace the money cut from low-income housing in the early 1980s. Indeed, in May 1989 a bill was introduced in the Senate to provide $2 billion in each of the next two years to create 280,000 units of much-needed housing for the homeless and near homeless. Although the bill is only a stop-gap measure by the Senate, still it represents a beginning to relieve the disgrace of homelessness in America.[10]

Finally, an engaging solution is advocated by Jim Tull: "Give the hungry person a fish, and the person lives for a day. But give that person a fishing pole and she or he can live for a lifetime."[11] Even so, that person will still be excluded from many fishing holes. That is why, as people of faith, we must realize, like the prophet Amos, the long-term need to open up our society and to share the goods of our earth equitably. The final goal is to change the forces that keep people chronically poor. This effort deserves the prayers, but much more the active and concrete support, of each of us. Otherwise, we, like the government officials we criticize, participate in the forces that keep people down. Like the Jim Tulls of the world, each one of us must do our part to solve the plight of the homeless, to influence the public policy that tolerates it, and to change the forces that keep people chronically poor.

NOTES

1. John H. Glascock and David C. Schwartz, *Combating Homelessness*, Report from the American Affordable Housing Institute at Rutgers University, reported in the *Providence Journal*, August 10, 1989.

2. Conversation with Jim Tull, Co-Director, Amos House, Providence, R.I., August 11, 1989.

3. Data adapted from "Homelessness," a paper prepared by Jim Tull for Representative Liz Morancy of Rhode Island during the Fall primary, 1988.

4. Glascock and Schwartz, *Combating Homelessness*.

5. *Safety Network: The Newsletter of the Coalition for the Homeless* 8, no. 4 (April 1989): 1.

6. Ibid., p. 2.

7. *Safety Network* 7, no. 9 (December 1988):1.

8. *Report and Recommendations: Task Force on the Homeless*, September 1988, for the Governor of Rhode Island, p. 7.

9. Ellen L. Bassuk, "The Homelessness Problem," *Scientific American* 251, no. 1 (July 1984): 45.

10. *Safety Network* 8, no. 6 (June 1989): 1.

11. Conversation with Jim Tull, August 11, 1989.

BIBLIOGRAPHY

Bassuk, Ellen L. "The Homelessness Problem." *Scientific American* 251, no. 1 (July 1984): 40–45. One of the best analyses of the causes and cures for the many homeless people who are mentally ill and wandering our streets.

Glascock, John H., and David C. Schwartz. *Combating Homelessness*. Newark, N.J.: American Affordable Housing Institute, Rutgers University, 1989. An up-to-date and startling report on the "hidden" four to fourteen million homeless piled up with relatives and friends, often in deteriorating buildings.

RESOURCES

The National Coalition for the Homeless
1439 Rhode Island Avenue, NW
Washington, DC 20005
    The coalition publishes a monthly newsletter called *Safety Network*, acknowledged as the best available source of information on homelessness in America. It covers all aspects: social, environmental, governmental and financial, as well as news of the efforts of various states, organizations, and churches who work with homeless persons.

Habitat for Humanity, Habitat and Church Streets, Americus, GA 31709 (912-924-6935), builds, renovates, and sets a national example for housing the homeless. President and Mrs. Carter and many church people are involved in Habitat.

Shelters and soup kitchens in your own community provide many opportunities to obtain information, as well as to serve the homeless. This service is particularly welcome — at times other than Thanksgiving and Christmas — during the cold winter months. There are, for example, sixteen shelters in Rhode Island alone, a state with a population of 950,000 people.

7

Walls of Ice: A Woman in Prison

Maria Rivera

SERMON

When I entered prison, I thought I was in purgatory. Everything was so white. It must have been the drugs. I kneeled to the captain; I thought she was the Virgin Mary. I was so ashamed that I couldn't look anyone in the eyes. Everyone sounded so far away. When I talked with the psychiatrist, I believed he was God, and I told him what I could remember. But he didn't understand — I was speaking Spanish. I couldn't understand why God couldn't understand what I was saying.

I could always block out the word "prison" any time it was said. I believed I was in purgatory. There's a lot about prison I don't remember — it was so terrible. They put me in the Institute of Mental Health (IMH). I never talked, until one day when I saw visitors coming in, I said, "Why nobody come to see me?" Everyone was excited that I finally spoke. When I asked what I'd done all that time, they said I hadn't slept or eaten much. At first they didn't let my family come in to visit, and when they finally did, I was strip-searched afterward.

Then they took me back to prison from the Institute of Mental Health, where they gave me various medications. They had me on Valium — it takes you down from a high. But at the ACI [Adult Correctional Institute] they won't let anyone have Valium, so they had to give me a different medication, to which I had a bad reaction, and I kept tripping. But I couldn't tell the doctor about it or he'd give me more medication. I couldn't accept where I was or what had happened. It was very painful.

I used to pray every night. I'd cry and ask God for forgiveness, for strength, and for help. Then once I heard the voice: "You didn't hear me before, but now you hear me." It was as if I'd been deaf, and now I could hear God.

Once I heard an inmate refer to our correctional officer: "Lucy never lies." So I asked Lucy: "Is this the place you pay your dues?" She

---

Maria's sermon was taped and transcribed by Suzanne Schmidt, who was imprisoned with Maria for pouring her blood on and battering Trident missile parts in Quonset Point, Rhode Island.

said, "Yeah, you could say that." She didn't say it was purgatory, yet I believed that I was there paying my dues. I felt like I was doing God's work, doing time. Every day I read the Bible; for two years I read Isaiah and Jeremiah. There was one story I remember, about a sick daughter who had no doctor, and someone asking, "Can somebody help her?" I felt it was God talking to me. That story gave me the peace of mind that I was doing God's work in prison. I'd ask, "God, what happened to me?" It was like I was lost and God was looking down, and God thought, "Oh, she needs somebody to help her, she's all alone — *where is everybody?*"

I felt that God was far away too. How can I talk to God? How can God listen to this little person? It was many years later when Sister Julia helped me to find God, to bring God very close to me....

At first, the pain was awful. One day I cut my arms, not to kill myself, but I was hurting so emotionally that I could not bear it. For several months a psychologist came to see me, until he thought I was coping well. It's hard to talk with a prison psychologist — you're always afraid that anything you say might be used against you.

There was one volunteer drug counselor who was very good for me; she became my friend. She made me realize I was an alcoholic, because of what alcohol did to me. I never liked the taste of liquor, but I liked what it did — it let me bear whatever came into my life — and that was a lot of pain. During those years in prison, I saw many beautiful people who had done terrible things under the influence of drugs and alcohol. Very slowly in prison I began to think about my own self-worth. I thought about my life on the outside. Outside I hated myself, so I tried to help others to make me feel better, and I drank to give me courage to bear everything.

I felt very guilty, very depressed. I cried a lot. I did a lot of years with almost no visits from my family. I love my brothers and sisters very much, so they hurt me by staying away.

I made my home and family in prison. The love I felt, I gave to the other inmates. They needed help, a friend to cope with their pain. With love, they can be your sisters. You can make a family wherever you are. There were a few other helpful people during those years who were really concerned and trusting and kind.

People on the outside don't really forget about the ones in prison, the ones in pain and how they suffer. People just neglect them and turn their backs. I was in prison for so long, where one day is a year, unless you can keep busy with work. I often worked in the kitchen for much of the day, and that was hard.

I also took courses in sociology and psychology and learned a lot about myself. I finished my GED and have four college credits. I learned to sew and crochet; I learned to paint, write poems, and touch people's hearts. I took classes in carpentry, art, and refrigeration. When computer classes started in the Maximum unit, I was already in Minimum, so I couldn't take them. All I know now is how to work in a kitchen and sew. There just aren't enough classes or jobs in prison. The women are so unprepared; they are not going to make it on the outside. There should be programs for education and training both inside the prison and after release. Although I'm out only a month, they aren't helping me at all now — no vocational guidance, no job referrals, no training. They just demand that I work, but I feel so unprepared and confused, so hurting and lost in the dark. Yet I have to ask permission for every change of job.

In prison, the warden was sometimes nice to me, then suddenly she'd turn. It's very confusing when someone flips like that. I think it was her problem with power. Those in power know that people will do what they tell them.

Once when I led an AA (Alcoholics Anonymous) meeting in prison, I felt the power of telling others what to do. I even wanted to throw someone out; then I realized what I was doing, and that the other woman needed help, not my bossing or kicking her out. I learned that I can't control others; I am powerless over others, but I could tell my own story. And I could love others.

Punishment worked in my prison. The warden always found something that someone wasn't doing right, and she punished us severely. Prison gave something, like a movie on Saturday, but then one day they'd take it away because someone misbehaved. Everyone feels bad then. In prison you get used to anything. But one thing you know you shouldn't ever get used to is having anything, because they will take it away from you.

The women in prison feel very bad. They are often ice cold; they just don't care because they don't know love. No matter how much they hurt inside, they numb it and go on. They may talk about drugs and sex a lot, as if they had fun. But it's not fun, it's a lot of pain. They just try to numb pain and to cope. I've been able to get through the ice with some of these women. I've felt a lot of times being very loved in there, sometimes by the women who came through here, sometimes even by the officers.

I try to explain how I got to prison, and I think it's the same for the others. Our childhood was messed up. We felt so rotten about ourselves. Then you want to take something to make you feel good, so you drink alcohol, take drugs, and get into bad relationships with men.

My mother gave me a lot, and I love her very much. She's a strong woman and has much faith in God. God is bringing me back somehow. My mother can still smile with big problems. She helps to make me strong.

I learned to say no in prison. I always used to try to help everyone. In prison I'd give things away, until one woman warned me that others were using me. She complained about my looking for the good in others. I began to realize my limits. After years of giving, I felt drained and empty. I gave too much of myself. I did that with the men in my life, and then with the women in prison. Now I want to receive, to fill up the emptiness.

In prison I was lonely, so I kept myself busy. I almost always had someone in my life to care about. Once I was so terribly lonely I prayed to God to send somebody into my life. God sent me that person, a man so handsome, so very good. I was so very happy, being loved, and loving him. And I was in prison! But after six months, he just disappeared, without a word. He never told me why he left — I guess he couldn't bear the prison situation. I cried for a whole year after he left. Two years later, I got a card from him, saying that no matter what he has always loved me. I want to feel that again someday — like it was when he loved me and we were very happy. My mother always says, "If someone is meant to be in your life, they will — don't worry about it." She is right.

I tried to work on my loneliness. I prayed to God to make me feel better, to take the pain of loneliness out of me. I didn't want to depend on others for love or for making me feel good about myself. That's how I started loving me. I have more respect for myself. Sister Julia helped me with that too, loving myself more and being close to God. I find happiness now in other ways — being with my nieces and nephews. I love how they talk and get excited — they make me feel young and warm.

Prison is a dark place. You feel there is no light. When you wake up, you have a routine; others tell you what to do. Without visitors there is nothing to look forward to, except to dream. You want to go to sleep and wake up when your time is up. You can't ever be alone, there is always someone to bother you.

If I were in charge, I would be strict — that helps in a way. Some women need rules and programs to teach them to balance their life. You need something to look forward to, like family gatherings in a pleasant place, with games — not just sitting across a table in a bare room, or no visits at all. For most of us such gatherings would even be worth another strip-search. Prison people are always afraid of drugs being brought in, but drugs get in anyway. They should punish only the inmate caught with drugs, not the whole unit, as they often do.

Prison has deeply affected me. I'm aware of what's going on inside me now. My family tries to control me; they don't have confidence in me. I believe I'm doing what is good for me. Sometimes I feel confused, but I ask God every day for help. I need to numb some of the pain. I feel so lonely. I'm scared and worried about going back to prison.

Having had a life sentence, my parole is for the rest of my life. I'm afraid I'm going to mess up, and they will bring me back. It is very hard to come out into the world, after ten years in prison, and face so many problems all at once. You can't get an apartment or good job. I had to force myself to relax at home and talk with everyone. Then I started working right away, just to keep busy. My sisters think I don't know how to budget money. I'm so happy to be able to buy a few nice things for my daughter or my mother or my nieces — after all those years of no money.

Now I'm living with my mother, and we help each other. But I also know I need to get out on my own, to become independent, to earn something as a grown woman. I want to be free to go where I want to go, but on parole I have to ask permission for everything.

I feel everything deeply. There is much unhappiness in my family, but why? They have a home, food, money, children, yet they don't seem to appreciate it. They worry about little problems, complain, and make themselves crazy. They let problems drag them down rather than accepting responsibility to solve their problems.

Everyone is in a hurry, going with the crowd. They have to learn to slow down, like one does in prison. Now I'm feeling caught up in the rush too; everything happens so fast and I can't slow down. But I have learned to live one day at a time. I've also learned not to be responsible for someone else's life. We each have our own way, and our own choices. Life is not easy and is not always gladness. What I have been through has given me strength.

Prison has built a wall in me. I realized it the other day when my mother tried to hug me and I didn't let her that close. She said, "It's okay." She understood. Then I also realized, and I hugged her tightly.

Prison has not made me insensitive to others. I just feel that I exist and that it is not loneliness so much as emptiness that leaves me very confused and aching.

I've found that people put up their own icy walls, and they can't give. Then I'd rather be alone than in company I can't bear because of those icy walls.

Everyone is trying to tell me how I should be, and I remind them that I've only been out for one month. I can't take everything at once. I have to take it easy. I feel like I'm preparing myself either way — to be in or out. I don't have much, so they can't take much away from me. I'm afraid of getting used to the outside — and being taken away again. My lawyer said that if things don't work out, I might go back to prison. His words stay in my mind.

I've always been concerned about my daughter, Donna. Now she is on her own; she has grown up while I was away. She's sometimes heard others say bad things about me; there is so much to explain and share with her. We lost so much of each other. Soon after I was sent to prison, some teachers went to court to try to adopt Donna, to get her away from the family, and my sister lost custody of her. Then my family sent her to Puerto Rico when she was between the ages of ten and thirteen. She lived with another sister there. On seeing a psychiatrist then, Donna drew a picture explaining: "That's my mother — sick in the hospital; that's me; and that's my brother — he's in heaven." After that they didn't ask her any more questions; they thought she was all right. Maybe later in life if she has problems, she should seek help.

In our lives in some way we will have the chance to receive Christ, to have that experience of peace and love. The experience I had in North Carolina was like that; I went there on my own with two little children. I was newborn in Christ and baptized. I tried to do the right thing, and good things happened to me — like a good job and a beautiful apartment. I felt that I'd been astray, then reborn in Christ, and trying to do God's will.

I don't want to feel that wall of ice in me. I'm an affectionate, loving person. I want to share with others. And I can't bear to feel it in others.

Catching up on the ten years is not easy. Sometimes I feel so confused, I don't know if I'm okay. When you are "free" outside, sometimes you want to die, for something seems not right.

I don't even want to make plans. I feel like this is a big furlough — and furloughs are a kind of torture, being out but knowing you have to phone in to the prison. Even if I try to do the right thing or if I make a little mistake, then I could lose everything.

I started feeling empty when I lost my brother Raf this year. Something was taken from me. I haven't gotten over it. Then I lost my brother José too.... At the funeral, my brother's child said, "My father went to heaven — do you see him? He looks like he's sleeping." The children, so young, yet they teach us.

Now my third brother has AIDS. He's a good man, and he loves kids; he helps my mother take care of our two little nieces. It's hard knowing your brother is dying, that he won't be long with us. He seems healthy, and I try not to think about his death. At home we watch TV, play with the kids, talk, or I go out. I can feel so much pain; then all of a sudden I choke it. Sometimes I wonder if that is all there will ever be.

I want to visit my brothers' graves, to be with them and talk to them. But my family says they are not there, so they won't drive me to the cemetery. But that is where I last left them....

I end with this passage. It sums up the darkness of prison and the light that Christ offers us:

> The people who walk in darkness have seen a great light: night has dawned upon us — dwellers in the land of dark death. You have increased our joy, you have offered us gladness. (Isa. 9:2–3)

> From the time of Christ, the old order of death and sorrow and greed is moving to its end. A sun is risen that knows no setting. An energy was released in Christ that will not rest until all the darkness is made light. (Poster from Jonah House on Isa. 9:2–3)

I have walked in that darkness, and I still feel the iciness of that darkness. But it is that bright light, the love and peace of Christ, that keeps me going. I pray that I keep walking in that light. Amen.

AUTOBIOGRAPHICAL STATEMENT

In my large family in Puerto Rico, I suffered abuse even in good times. During a bad scene at home as a teenager, I left home, and at age sixteen I met an American man who took me to New York. My daughter was born there. Unfortunately, his family made me feel ashamed of being Puerto Rican. Then I left and had my son by another man. I struggled hard to be a good mother and to provide for my two loved children. My dream was of marriage and a solid family.

I sacrificed much to bring my mother to the States, knowing that my father could not beat her anymore. I also brought some of my siblings, yet sadly, when I later needed help they forgot all that. But I found that alcohol and drugs numbed the pains and problems of single-parenthood.

Religion also gave me strength. I ventured with my children to North Carolina to become a born-again Christian, and to follow God's will. Life went well for a time. I worked steadily and set up a beautiful apartment. But the loneliness led me back to drinking and to smoking pot. I lost my job and my apartment.

I moved to Rhode Island and tried to care for my children. In May 1978 came the tragedy. On a very bad trip (LSD or PCP), I had horrifying hallucinations. I sought help in three places, including a mental health center, but I was turned away. The hallucinations continued... and that night I killed my son.

I was locked away in a mental institute and medicated. Later I was sent to prison. Within months I was rushed through trial, convicted of first-degree murder, and sentenced to life in prison. Even during this time I was still drug-tripping from overmedication. I was laden down with grief. Nevertheless, during ten years in prison, I went through deep spiritual and emotional healing and growth in self-esteem.

In prison I reached out to all the people around me, sharing love, joy, pain, struggle, and wisdom. In November 1987 my case was re-opened for reconsideration (on the basis that my attorney had not defended me properly). I then attended several painful court hearings and waited for months. During this time two of my brothers died of AIDS.

Months after these sorrows I was granted parole-for-life. One month after my release — wanting to share the loneliness, pain, and punishment I experienced in prison, and still experience — I prepared this sermon.

BACKGROUND INFORMATION (by Elena Natalizia)

Of the works of mercy Jesus outlined for his followers in Matthew 26, visiting the imprisoned is probably the one with which most people, even people of faith, have the least personal identification. Fed by the media's sensational portrayal of crime such as TV's "Miami Vice," most people would rather forget that prisons exist, taking comfort in the belief that every person locked inside prison walls means one less criminal able to prey upon them, their families, their homes and possessions. Yet the cries of those in prison, and in particular women, compel us to make real our Christian commitment to mercy, forgiveness, and reconciliation.

Women in prison bear a dual burden — they are women in a society that resists giving them full legal equality and they are prisoners in a society in which "lock 'em up and throw away the key" is the prevalent public attitude toward crime. The treatment of women offenders within the criminal justice system reflects the sexism embedded within American culture, the sexism upon which our traditional economic and social systems rest. Law, as administered by a predominantly white male justice system, is often used as an instrument of social control over women and a means of punishing those who have broken with traditional female stereotypes. Because they have violated the moral code defining women's "proper" role in society, female offenders are considered deviant and punished by sanctions often more severe than their offenses would warrant. In addition, because they represent only 5 percent of all prisoners in the United States, women inmates have tended to be ignored by a correctional system that has focused almost entirely on the men under its jurisdiction.

Within the past several years the number of women in prison, though consistently much smaller than the size of the male population, has increased dramatically. Between 1976 and 1985, the number of women inmates rose by 10 percent, while the number of men rose by 80 percent.[1] There were 26,610 women in state and federal prisons in the US at the end of 1986, representing a 15 percent increase over the preceding year; during the same time period, the number of male inmates rose at slightly more than half that rate.[2]

While there is no ironclad theory to explain this rapid increase in women's imprisonment, some would suggest the following explanations: (1) as women move into traditionally male occupations, opportunities for white-collar crime become more frequent; (2) with the increase of drug use and poverty among women, economic crime becomes more prevalent; (3) as women achieve greater equality with men, it has meant the end of the "chivalry factor," which formerly operated to insure greater leniency for women within the criminal justice system. While each of these theories has its merits, one factor is certainly at work in producing higher rates of female imprisonment, and that is the construction of new and much larger prison facilities for women. Rhode Island is a perfect example of the "widening the net" effect of allocating more space for female inmates; since the opening of a larger women's facility in 1984, the population of women inmates in Rhode Island has risen by almost 140 percent, from 48 inmates in 1984 to approximately 120 inmates in 1988.

The table below indicates the differences in types of crimes most often committed by male and female offenders:

Crime	percent of all arrests	
	Male	*Female*
Murder and non-negligent/ manslaughter	88	12
Rape	99	1
Robbery	92	8
Aggravated assault	87	14
Burglary	93	7
Larceny-theft	69	31
Motor vehicle theft	91	9
Arson	87	13

Source: FBI, *Crime in the United States* 1985[3]

All available data supports the contention that women are much less likely than men to commit the more serious crimes (e.g., murder, rape, robbery, or burglary). A much higher proportion of women than of men who are involved in criminal behavior commit property crimes — larceny, forgery, fraud, and embezzlement — drug offenses, and prostitution. In those cases in which a woman is convicted of a violent crime, it is most often against her husband or lover (usually rooted in abuse or jealousy), or her child (usually stemming from drug or alcohol addiction and/or the frustrations of poverty and family disintegration).

Who are the women who populate America's prisons? Whatever may be the details of their personal histories, most of them share a common characteristic: they are caught in a maze of dependency from which they see no way out. From welfare, to abusive husbands, to pimps, to drugs, to illiteracy, these women have tended to spend their lives "hooked" on negative forces that are closely linked to their criminality. The typical female offender, even before going to prison, is among the most victimized segments of society. She is young, comes from a racial or ethnic minority, is poor and in poor health, is likely to have a history of physical abuse, and is the sole supporter of one or more children. She is very likely to be addicted to drugs and alcohol and has inadequate vocational and educational background.[4] And certainly, once she enters the criminal justice system, she is without the skills or the financial resources to make the system work to her benefit.

The following descriptions of women serving time at the Massachusetts women's prison could easily apply to female inmates anywhere in this nation:

> You have to consider the problems women have when they come into prison: 98 percent of them come from poor communities. Most have not held jobs; most are single mothers. They've figured out how to survive on the streets.... The majority of them have the disease of alcoholism or drug addiction....
>
> Women end up in the criminal justice system as a last stop.... There have been problems for a long time, during their teen years and even before. There were problems at school and at home.... Over 90 percent of women in prison are IV drug users.... As a result of the violence and sexual abuse they encountered in their homes, they often run away....
>
> We see women coming in to prison weighing 95 pounds. They have severe health problems, which reflect a combination of poor preventive care, substandard living conditions, and years of drug and alcohol abuse. And they must be able to handle all the things they'll have to deal with after leaving prison.[5]

Like their male counterparts, women inmates face the difficulties of day-to-day survival in a prison environment. But there are some problems unique to women within the correctional system that make doing time all the more difficult for them. Because there are so few compared to men, women inmates are frequently the "forgotten children" within any state's prison system. Rehabilitative programming, meaningful work opportunities, adequate health care, and even privileges such as furloughs may be inferior in quantity and quality to what is offered to male inmates. This type of unequal treatment is often justified in the eyes of prison administrators because it is too expensive to institute full programming for such relatively small numbers of women. Although such discrimination blatantly violates the constitutional principle of equal protection, vestiges of unequal treatment of female and male inmates continue to exist.

Women's prisons tend to stress sex-role socialization, that is, they reinforce and perpetuate the stereotypes of women: childish, passive, and incapable of self-determination. Traditionally, women's prisons have given inmates large doses of "moral" training, intended to transform fallen women into ladies. As one author points out:

> Women's prisons may not be as overtly brutal as male penitentiaries, but they are often institutions where oppression is wholesale. The women are treated like children, and even elderly prisoners are referred to as "girls." They are made to feel even more helpless and childlike than other prisoners. This psychological oppression has worked to such an extent that few women in prison have the sense of political consciousness possessed by their male counterparts, nor do they have confidence in their ability to help themselves legally or socially.[6]

Add to this the fact that women inmates are often helpless in the face of sexual harassment and even sexual assault by correctional officers and other prison personnel. The result is frequently the virtual loss of all self-esteem during a woman's time in prison.

Perhaps the greatest suffering of imprisoned women, however, is the effect of their incarceration on their children. Approximately 70 percent of all women inmates are single parents, with the average mother having two children. Typically, these children are poor, minority, and emotionally scarred.[7] They are often separated from their imprisoned mothers for long periods of time, being cared for by other family members. In some cases, they are placed in foster care and, ultimately, the mother's parental rights are terminated on the basis of her criminal record. In many ways, children become the "other victims" of their mothers' crimes, and the effects in the long term can be devastating:

> For the children of most repeat offenders, the outlook is not very bright. Their dreams of "normal" family life keep crumbling. Angela's mother has been in and out of Minnesota's state prison on drug charges for as long as Angela can remember. Meanwhile, Angela, 14, has had five sets of parents. Now living with her aunt, she

blames her poor academic record on constantly having to change
schools....

Her mother has promised Angela that they will have pets and
a "really nice" house. But now Angela isn't optimistic. She doesn't
want to rejoin her mother. "I don't want to go through getting my
feelings hurt again," she says. "She has made me cry so much for
her that I just don't care anymore...."[8]

Having little exposure to positive influences, constructive coping
skills, or effective rehabilitative programming while in prison, many
women leave the prison system in no better condition than they entered. This makes the transition into free society all the more difficult,
even for the women who have supportive families willing to assist
them during this critical time. The fact that most states have a recidi-
vism rate of over 50 percent is proof that "correctional institutions"
are in reality doing little to correct any of the negative forces that
led people to prison in the first place. One woman who works with
newly released inmates in Massachusetts describes the difficulties of
the readjustment period: "Nearly all the women want to live somewhere other than where they lived before.... At her first meeting with
me after getting out, a woman will be straight. And one week later
she's all strung out. The obstacles are just tremendous."[9]

In the face of all this, what can be done to improve the system
to meet the needs of female offenders? Several steps are necessary to
meet this goal:

1. A cornerstone of equal protection for women in the criminal
justice system would be the adoption of the Equal Rights Amend-
ment. The ERA would require revision of the entire justice process,
eliminating all forms of discriminatory treatment of women. In correctional institutions, women would have to be given equal access not
only to recreation, job training, and other programming within the
walls, but also to furlough programs, work release, and other special
programs outside. Passage of the ERA would provide a strong legal foundation for court actions against any discriminatory practices
within the prison setting.

2. Many nonviolent women offenders should be permitted to
serve their sentences in alternative community-based correctional
programs rather than in the strict confinement of prison. Since they
pose no serious danger to society and since their criminality is often
based in substance abuse, poor job skills, and economic deprivation,
many women guilty of nonviolent crimes could be more effectively
dealt with in alternative programs such as house arrest, intensive probation, or halfway houses. Such programs not only are much less
costly than prison, but they also allow the maintenance of family

unity and the opportunity for offenders to participate in education, counseling, and other social service programs in the community.

3. For those women who must be confined within a prison setting, the quantity and quality of programming must enable the women to acquire the tools for successful reintegration into society upon their release. These types of programs include substance abuse treatment; training in meaningful marketable job skills; educational opportunities; psychological counseling from a feminist perspective; parenting programs that allow as full contact with one's children as possible; conjugal visits; quality gynecological and general medical care; furlough and pre-release programs for those nearing the end of their sentence. In all these programs, the goal must be to empower women by helping them develop the skills and level of self-esteem necessary for success in the free world.

4. Opportunities for extensive post-release follow-up should be provided for all women leaving prison. This would include: more effective counseling by parole officers; formation of support groups for female ex-offenders; linking a woman about to be released with a church or family who would be willing to provide moral and perhaps even some financial support as she makes the transition back into society; establishment of substance abuse and job placement programs geared specifically to the needs of ex-offenders. As much as possible, the entire community should be involved in the process of reintegrating ex-offenders into society, recognizing that all of us are indeed our sister's keepers.

Elena Natalizia is founder and director of Rhode Island Justice Alliance, a citizens' organization established to reduce crime through criminal justice reform. Before working with RIJA she was Catholic chaplain at the Adult Correctional Institute, the only prison in Rhode Island. She holds a master's degree in criminal justice from Northeastern University. She teaches part time at Northeastern and plans to begin doctoral work there.

NOTES

1. U.S. Department of Justice, *Report to the Nation on Crime and Justice*, 2d ed. (Washington, D.C., 1988), p. 46.

2. Bureau of Justice Statistics, *Prisoners in 1986*, Washington, D.C., 1987, p. 2.

3. U.S. Department of Justice, *Report to the Nation*, p. 46.

4. Nicole Hahn Rafter and Elena M. Natalizia, "Marxist Feminism: Implications for Criminal Justice, *Crime and Delinquency* (January 1981): 94.

5. Comprehensive Offender Employment Resource System (COERS), 1987 Annual Report, Boston, 1987, pp. 23–25.

6. Marilyn G. Haft, "Women in Prison," in Michelle G. Hermann and Marilyn G. Haft, *Prisoners' Rights Sourcebook* (New York: Clark Boardman Company, 1973), p. 349.

7. Alix M. Freedman, "Children of a Woman in Prison Are, in Effect, Victims of Her Crime," *Wall Street Journal*, March 26, 1985.

8. Ibid.

9. COERS, p. 24.

BIBLIOGRAPHY

Bureau of Justice Statistics. *Prisoners in 1986*. Washington, D.C.

Comprehensive Offender Employment Resource Systems (COERS). Annual Report. Boston, 1987.

Datesman, Susan K., and Frank R. Scarpitti. *Women, Crime, and Justice.* New York: Oxford University Press, 1980.

Freedman, Alix M. "Children of a Woman in Prison Are, in Effect, Victims of Her Crime." *Wall Street Journal*, March 26, 1985.

Haft, Marilyn G. "Women in Prison." In Michelle G. Hermann and Marilyn G. Haft. *Prisoners' Rights Sourcebook*. New York: Clark Boardman Company, 1973.

Price, Barbara R., and Natalia J. Sokoloff. *The Criminal Justice System and Women*. New York: Clark Boardman Company, 1982.

Rafter, Nicole H., and Elizabeth A. Stanko. *Judge, Lawyer, Victim, Thief: Women, Gender Roles and Criminal Justice*. Boston: Northeastern University Press, 1982.

U.S. Department of Justice. *Report to the Nation on Crime and Justice*, 2d ed. Washington, D.C., 1988.

RESOURCES AND ORGANIZATIONS

Institute of Women Today
1307 South Wabash Avenue
Chicago, IL 60605

Aid to Incarcerated Mothers
138 Tremont Street
Boston, MA 02111

ACLU National Prison Project
1616 P Street, NW
Washington, DC 20006

Women Free Women in Prison
P.O. Box 90
Brooklyn, NY 11215

Justice for Women
National Council of Churches
475 Riverside Drive
New York, NY 10115

Bay Area Women's Resource Center
318 Leavenworth Street
San Francisco, CA 94102

PART THREE

Mental Health: Women Taking Charge of Their Lives

8

Depression: When Life Becomes "Stale, Flat, and Unprofitable"

Annie Lally Milhaven

SERMON

Why are you cast down, O my soul, and why are you disquieted within me? Hope in God; for I shall again praise him my help, and my God.
—Psalm 42:5

The *New York Times* recently reported a remarkable story. The story was incorporated into a lengthy obituary for one of this century's best-known producers: Joshua Logan. The piece noted that this prolific artist of some of Broadway and the screen's most enduring and prestigious hits like *South Pacific* and *Mister Roberts* was notable for his candor in discussing manic depression. He suffered from the disease for years before lithium was discovered, and his moods, known to be excessive, required hospitalization.

In January 1969, when he learned about lithium and began to take the drug, he also began to talk publicly about his condition. "I had been ignorant all my life about such things," he said. "At least I could tell others so they would never be as ignorant as I was."

Depression is not new to the human race. Even though it dates back to the remote recordings of human history, we rarely preach on this subject. The Bible in 1 Samuel 16:14–23 provides a graphic picture of this disease. We read a touching account of what today is described by psychiatrists as one of the most common and treatable of all mental illnesses — depression: "Now the Spirit of the Lord departed from Saul, and an evil spirit from the Lord tormented him." The servants, realizing their king was disturbed, asked Saul to advise them when he felt the evil spirit from God upon him, so that they would find someone skillful in playing the lyre to soothe and settle his troubled emotions. They located David, a young handsome man,

---

As a Catholic woman, I am not permitted to preach this sermon. For those who can, I suggest that the sermon be preached at any time, in any church, synagogue, or mosque. Depression is universal.

who, whenever the evil spirit was upon Saul, played the lyre until the older man achieved calm and serenity.

Notice that the biblical writer addressed Saul's depression as the entry of an "evil spirit from the Lord." This event took place around 1000 B.C.E. This tie between depression and religion persisted until Hippocrates sometime in the fourth century B.C.E. He was among the first to separate illness from magic and superstition and place it on a human scale. Known as the Father of Medicine, Hippocrates described depression as "melancholia" or "black bile on the brain." Interestingly, Freud in 1917 retained the word "melancholia" when he wrote a book on depression called *Mourning and Melancholia*. Despite the many changes over the years in the classification of depressive disorders, the term "melancholia" has been retained.

In the centuries between King Saul and Sigmund Freud, depression was accounted for in curious ways. During the Christian Middle Ages depression was called *accedia* by spiritual writers. It ranged from a certain sluggishness of spirit to the dark night of the soul. Great saints like John of the Cross in *Dark Night of the Soul* and Teresa of Avila in her *Autobiography* have supplied us with classic writings on this phenomenon.

Depression in the thirteenth to the fifteenth centuries was equally and unfortunately attributed to demons, or to witches who were mostly women. Attempts were made to exorcise the demons, but the witches — figures vary from thirty thousand to eight million women — were burned at the stake.

Today, we know and understand much more about the causes, kinds, and treatment of depression. The fact that the World Health Organization (WHO) found in the 1970s that depression was *the* major world health problem shows the importance of addressing this often hidden killer of the emotions of human beings.

In this sermon let us consider two questions: (1) Who are these people who suffer from depression? (2) What can be done to lessen their suffering?

Depression does not respect person, class, or culture. Nevertheless there are several groups of people more susceptible than others. Women are overrepresented, as Maggie Scarf points out: "It is the female's inherently interpersonal, inter dependent, affiliative nature — her affectionateness and orientation toward other people — that underlies her far greater vulnerability."

The kind of women most vulnerable to depression are poor, single, working mothers of young children. They live with loneliness, severe financial stress, and the unabated pressure of rearing children alone. But there is more: the reality for these women is that there is no way out. There are few if any options to choose from, thus increasing the burden of their lives.

This description does not apply solely to women in the teeming slums of India and in the dreadful barrios of South America. This grip of hopelessness hangs over the women in the ghettoes of the cities of the United States. A Mercy nun who works in one such ghetto tells us that the poor with whom she worked in Central America were in no way as "ground down" as the women in South Providence, Rhode Island, where she now teaches in literacy programs. This does not mean that other women, middle- or upper-class women are not depressed, and we must also examine their experiences. While some middle-class women are only too glad to be homemakers for a few years, many others express great frustration at the routineness of their lives. The daily repetition of child care, cleaning, cooking, purchasing can become oppressive and depressive.

Another group suffering from depression are the children of poverty, often from the homes of single parents described above. These little ones often fail to thrive and may show a lack of responsiveness, have a weak cry, or sleep excessively. Senator Patrick Moynihan, who specializes in studying, writing, and legislating about America's poor, states: "40% of the poor in the US are children."

A third group susceptible to depression are school-age children who experience wide mood fluctuations. But it is adolescents most of all who mask their depression by acting-out behavior with drugs, sex, and suicide pacts. Unprecedented bodily growth and developmental changes bewilder many of these adolescents. Consider the recent rash of teen suicides reported in the newspapers: these youths come from both poor and rich families. Suicide, the *tenth* leading cause of death in the U.S., is the third leading cause among the fifteen-to-twenty-four age group.

Another group increasingly susceptible to depression are older men, especially after retirement. Retirement, far from being the long rest they hoped for, tends to leave their lives void and empty. This is particularly true of men who equate "work" with "self-worth" and when they no longer work tend to lose their identity. On July 19, 1989, the *New York Times* reported an alarming increase in suicides among those over sixty-five. The increase to 21.6 percent undoubtedly reflects the underlying effects of depression and loneliness among older persons.

These then are some of the persons who suffer most from depression. We now proceed to the second point: What can be done to alleviate the sufferings of these people?

Looking out over the congregation, Sunday after Sunday, one sees more women than men in church. In preparing this sermon and being struck by women's faithful presence, it is most appropriate to address a problem that afflicts them in greater numbers than men. Experts state that depression is a threat to and a loss of *self-esteem*. Self-worth comes to those who have a feeling of control over their lives and actions. Self-worth or self-love is one of the great commandments: "You shall love your neighbor as yourself." Still if you look for the term "self-love" in Nelson's Biblical Concordance, you will find not one reference under this heading. Depression, on the other hand, is often described as self-hate and rage turned in on oneself.

Miriam Greenspan describes very clearly what *first* of all helped her to become undepressed: "anger, power, and other women." What especially helped her was the "terrifying and exhilarating process" of getting good and angry. She is talking about *good* anger, energizing anger, not the sort that keeps one immobilized and embittered. And this kind of anger shared with other women gave her a sense of power, which is a great help in improving one's self-image, one's self-esteem. Incidentally this therapist is very cautious of medications, using instead "large doses of respect and support."

A *second* help for depression consists of the sufferers' having access to an extensive range of "possible actions with which to encounter difficult situations in life." In other words, it is important that people have choices, and that these choices exist in both the social and psychological spheres. Here again this kind of solution may be well and good for middle-class people. But access to alternatives and choices is precisely what is denied to most women.

What alternatives are open to a poor woman with children living in today's slums? Living in cramped, yet expensive, run-down buildings, can she safely let her children out to play while she takes a breather? Both she and the children are surrounded with drugs, which is making life dangerous for all. And yet persons who work with these families find that small steps make a big difference in women's lives. For example, a mother who cannot read enrolls in a literacy program. There she meets other women and by degrees bonds with them. One step leads to another and some of these women are known to enroll in high school or college. The importance of taking *one* step to alter a life situation cannot be overestimated. This one step can lead to an infusion of hope. With hope, despair drops off.

How about more fortunate women who, on the other hand, often have not the open access men have to jobs, promotion, and upper echelon leadership. In fact, the great tragedy of human life is that the talents of women are denied in public life. Not only that, but roadblocks are set in their paths in the churches as well. Women cannot be altar servers or ordained ministers in some churches, nor be equally represented on the boards of their churches, hospitals, banks, and unions.

In spite of the hurdles women still face, there is no doubt that the role of women in the world is changing. One thing churches and synagogues can do is not pressure women to return to the domestic role as their sole salvation. Why not encourage them to seek choices and alternatives? Choices and alternatives are ways women can conquer depression.

Finally, a *third* way to help the depressed is to encourage people, including ourselves in this assembly, to feel our feelings. Every day we ask and are asked many times: "How are you feeling?" How do I *truly* feel? It is helpful to reflect prayerfully on this question during the days ahead. Awareness of one's true feelings enables a person to understand her actions and behavior. It helps us understand the actions and behavior of our children, our friends, and the people we meet each day. It helps us to feel our feelings.

In this sermon on depression we have considered a great human problem. We reflected on those who suffer from depression and how they can be helped. We know the importance of self-esteem and good anger and of the value of choices in our lives. We can also remember Joshua Logan who said: "Without my illness [manic-depression], active or dormant, I'm sure I would have lived only half of the life I've lived, and that would be as a safe and sane Fourth of July. I would have missed the sharpest, the rarest, and, yes, the sweetest moments of my existence." Here was a person who used depression and a better knowledge of how to cope with it to help him become a creative artist and to speak publicly to help others who suffer from depression.

So too let it be with each of us "who hope in God...[and] praise him, my help and my God." Amen.

AUTOBIOGRAPHICAL STATEMENT

Only when half my life was over did I recognize that I had lived a partly half-life. The insight was gradual: gaining control over my own life enabled feelings of well-being to become a curiously new and sustained experience. Prior to these experiences, my life, outwardly seemingly serene, was in reality in inner tumult.

There were plenty of reasons for turmoil, because after twenty years in religious life, I decided to leave and seek "self-fulfillment." My decision caused chaos among both the superiors and the nuns, as well as intense disappointment, even rupture, in my family relationships. Frequently, I was unsure of my own decision: self-fulfillment seemed selfish and far from the sacrificial spirit that good nuns had set as the goal of perfection in those pre–Vatican II days.

The decision was not taken lightly, simply because it took years to muster the courage to ask for a dispensation from vows. These were the difficult and depressing years; I attempted to carry on without giving *anyone* a notion of my true intentions.

Informing superiors was most difficult, resulting in wide fluctuations in my own decision: one day deciding to remain a nun, the next to leave the convent. The toll on my inner self was considerable, and I became an insomniac for long stretches of the night.

But the greatest turmoil arose informing my parents and family. My mother, initially angry and accusatory, later fell silent. For a couple of years all the mail I received from her was a Christmas card and one postcard.

Settling into "the world" in New York City was a risky venture. By degrees and through experience I learned how as a "secular" things were done. But it was the world of work that began to enhance my sense of self-worth. I had choices of excellent jobs and chose one of managing a Women and Infants Department of Nursing.

Success on the job enhanced my self-esteem and building new relationships significantly reduced inner tension and anxiety. In time all parties to my decision came around to accepting the inevitable. Yet the remnants of my depression clung, and after a couple of years I sought therapy. Therapy enabled me to sift through unresolved conflicts, to understand better my feelings, and to come to believe I *do* have a right to choices in life.

My own experience and the startling discovery of the World Health Organization findings of worldwide depression as *the* major health problem of humankind convinced me that a sermon on depression was overdue.

BACKGROUND INFORMATION

Teachers are often perplexed by the chronically sad child in the classroom, pastoral counselors by the despair of some of the parishioners, and social workers by the profound feelings of hopelessness and helplessness that seize so many families as they become increasingly defeated by circumstances.[1]

The World Health Organization studies health problems of the world with a ten-year focus on the major illnesses that afflict human beings. Through the efforts of *WHO* smallpox has been eradicated from our planet, and malaria significantly reduced.

The finding in the 1970s that depression was the world's major health problem caused great surprise and concern. The research showed this condition was no respecter of person or place, afflicting all countries, classes, and cultures, regardless of the stage of economic development. The study also estimated that one hundred million people suffer from "clinical" depression, and the expectation is of increasingly affected numbers because of rising longevity, the stress of life, fear of war, and the worldwide drug epidemic.[2]

Modern medical science has luckily uncovered many layers of the human psyche and in so doing has enriched human experience and understanding. Religious experience also has greatly benefited from the new insights of psychiatry and psychology, especially the attempt to understand depression: the most ubiquitous malignancy of our time.

Freud describes this illness: "In grief the world has become poor and empty; in melancholia it is the ego itself."[3] As guilt and self-derogation become pervasive for the depressed one, a sense of immobility often takes over. Loss of appetite, sleeplessness, and general apathy ensue. Often poets and artists describe these feelings best. Thus Shakespeare wrote of life becoming "stale, flat and unprofitable." Samuel Beckett in *Waiting for Godot* wrote: "Nothing happens, nobody comes, nobody goes, it's awful."

Although depression is a universal problem, still it is overrepresented in the disadvantaged: the poor, blacks, and other minorities, and especially among women. Greenspan gives a ratio of three women to each depressed white man.[4] Many doctors feel that depression underlies the vast majority of suicides in our country.

Clinicians describe two kinds of depression:

1. *Dysthymia*, or depressive neurosis, which may or may not have an identifiable precipitating stressful life event: death, retirement, loss of country, livelihood, or even an unrealized ideal of life.

2. *Major depressive episode* or *bipolar disorders* in which in addition to depression there can be alternating manic mood swings.[5] The American Psychiatric Association (APA) notes that researchers have found "genetic markers" for susceptibility to manic-depressive disorders. The possibility of a gene is speculated upon because among manic-depressive persons, some are also color blind. The genes for both diseases are closely aligned on the genetic chain. In this category are found persons who at times are deeply despondent and apathetic; at other times they may be highly anxious and agitated.

According to Maggie Scarf bipolar disorder with both manic and depressive episodes affects men and women equally.[6] It is the *unipolar disorder* — depression without manic episodes — that affects more women than men.

Now that we have seen who are the people suffering from this disease, let us go the second point. What can be done to lessen their suffering? People do get well and may never again experience another bout of depression. Proper medical supervision is essential and cannot be stressed enough. Religion by itself cannot cure depression, but it should be emphasized that the tricyclic antidepressants and Monoamine Oxidase Inhibitors (MAOI's) are not called "wonder drugs" for no reason. These medications together with lithium carbonate have provided significant relief for patients and have alleviated severe depression,[7] so that psychotherapy or counseling is then possible. If all else fails, electric shock therapy (EST) usually will be effective. It can turn the tide in an overwhelming depression and literally be life-saving.

Since to be human is to have the capacity for depression, it is important to raise up this subject for reflection and to enable people to understand how widespread the affliction is. Especially noteworthy is the fact that, according to the American Psychiatric Association, nearly 80 percent of depressed people fail to recognize the beginning of their illness. It is equally true that families fail to recognize one of its own struggling with depression. This is especially true when the depressed one becomes manic and often overachieving — families may fail to put these contrasting behaviors in focus.

Preachers of God's word are in a favorable position to enrich the members of the community with a clearer understanding of this major world health problem. Addressing this disease can bring comfort and solace to silent sufferers and give hope and renewed courage to bewildered families. It is a worthy ministry for our time.

NOTES

1. James E. Anthony and Therese Benedek, eds., *Depression and Human Existence* (New York: Little, Brown & Co., 1975), p. xviii.

2. N. Sarlorius et al., *Depressive Disorders in Different Cultures* (Geneva: World Health Organization, 1983), pp. 3–7.

3. Sigmund Freud, "Mourning and Melancholia," in *General Psychological Theory*, ed. Philip Rieff (New York: Collier Books, 1963), p. 167.

4. Miriam Greenspan, *A New Approach to Women and Therapy* (New York: McGraw-Hill Book Co., 1983), pp. 3–9.

5. *Diagnostic and Statistical Manual of Mental Disorders*, 3d ed. (Washington, D.C.: American Psychiatric Association, 1987), pp. 213–33.

6. Maggie Scarf, *Unfinished Business: Pressure Points in the Lives of Women* (New York: Doubleday & Co., 1980), p. 530.

7. American Psychiatric Association, *Facts About: Depression* (Washington, D.C., 1987).

BIBLIOGRAPHY

American Psychiatric Association. *Facts About: Depression.* Washington, D.C., 1987.

Anthony, James E., and Therese Benedek, eds. *Depression and Human Existence.* New York: Little, Brown & Co., 1975.

Daly, Mary. *After God the Father.* Boston: Beacon Press, 1973.

Diagnostic and Statistical Manual of Mental Disorders (DMS). 3d ed. Washington, D.C.: American Psychiatric Association, 1987.

Fredán, Lars. *Psychosocial Aspects of Depression: No Way Out?* New York: John Wiley & Sons, 1982.

Freud, Sigmund. "Mourning and Melancholia." In *General Psychological Theory.* Philip Rieff, ed. New York: Collier Books, 1963.

Greenspan, Miriam. *A New Approach to Women and Therapy.* New York: McGraw-Hill, 1983.

E. Allison Peers, ed. and trans. *Dark Night of the Soul by Saint John of the Cross.* New York: Image, Doubleday & Co., 1959.

———. *The Autobiography of St. Teresa of Avila.* New York: Image, Doubleday & Co., 1960.

Sarlorius, N., et al. *Depressive Disorders in Different Cultures.* Geneva: World Health Organization, 1983.

Scarf, Maggie. *Unfinished Business: Pressure Points in the Lives of Women.* New York: Doubleday & Co., 1980.

RESOURCES

American Psychiatric Association. *Facts About: Depression.* 1400 K Street NW, Washington, DC 20005. Publications in the *Facts About* series are available on other mental and emotional conditions.

County Medical Society: To locate your local psychiatric society of the American Psychiatric Association call (202) 682-6000.

Mental Health Association: Call for operator assistance or look in your local telephone directory.

County Department of Mental Health: Call your local library for the directory of medical specialists. Board-certified psychiatrists are listed by locality.

9

Alcoholism: "I Am Powerless Over..."

Mary A.

SERMON

Although I never said so consciously, I was determined not to be like my mother or to marry a man like my father. At age forty, an alcoholic, married to a man I no longer respected or really even liked, I was repeating my mother's life. The irony was not lost on me. What had gone wrong? What had happened to all those lovely 1950s dreams of suburban living with the perfect husband and the clean, obedient children? Nothing had turned out right and I was mad as hell. I was also without hope that things would get better. This was a new twist. Most of my life had been based on "next year," and suddenly, at forty, there seemed to be no "next year."

AA has a format in which our "experience, strength, and hope" are shared with another alcoholic. We tell "what it was like, what happened, and what it's like now." This is the format I will follow now as I tell what alcohol did to me, first as a child and then as an adult.

I was the second child and first girl of a family of five children. My mother was of French extraction, and my father of Irish-French extraction. My mother's father, a mill superintendent, was an alcoholic. My father's mother died in childbirth. His father, a working alcoholic, left town shortly afterward. He was raised by two maiden aunts and his grandmother. A spoiled, indulged child, he became a self-indulgent man. He and my mother were nineteen when they married; he died at fifty from the use and abuse of alcohol and drugs.

In this sermon, I want to avoid placing the blame for my character defects or failures on my parents and early childhood. However, the children of alcoholics learn at an early age a variety of coping skills, not all of them healthy or productive. We carry those skills into adult life, yet, for most of us, daily living is a difficult proposition. I have always wondered what part a chaotic home life played in my inability

---

This sermon is intended for any season of the year and it is especially appropriate around New Year's Eve.

to succeed in school. From first grade I hated school and was always on the edge of failure. My most vivid memory is of an endless string of teachers telling me to "stop daydreaming" and "pay attention." At home I retreated into books, and to this day I am a voracious reader of biographies, history, current affairs, and the newspaper.

After a mediocre high school career, I went to a state college for one year. The courses were either too hard (chemistry) or too boring (home economics), and I didn't return. The following fall, I went to Katharine Gibbs Secretarial School so that I would be able to earn a living. I certainly didn't want to be there, but I did certify and went out into the world as a Gibbs girl.

The drinking had begun on a regular basis. As a college freshman a pattern of abuse developed, which was a forecast of trouble to come. When I took the first drink, I could never predict when I would end up drinking too much. I lost time from school and work due to hangovers, and, surprisingly, in spite of my family background, I never faced the fact that I was having a problem with alcohol. Denial was very much a part of the problem. I was also having a problem with authority and lost two jobs because of what I now know to be the typical alcoholic personality. Everybody else was wrong and I was right. However, also in typical alcoholic fashion, I usually went on to a better job. I was bright, attractive, and had ability.

During those years, my father died and my mother's alcoholism accelerated — a problem I chose to ignore. I was in my mid-twenties, bored and restless. Marriage seemed the way out of a dull life. The next man who came along happened to be from a wealthy, influential family and seemed to like me, so I set about convincing him that it was time to settle down.

We met in October and married in May. Our courtship consisted of daily drinking and dining, usually too much, and yet we never viewed it as a problem. We were very much people of the 1950s. We went to church together on Sunday morning after being drunk and disorderly on Saturday night. It went without saying that I was to stay at home and have children; he was to work and "bring home the bacon." His own family background, in spite of wealth, had been as chaotic as mine, and here we were, two of the walking wounded, trying to establish a family and a normal home life, when neither of us knew the norm. For me, marriage meant a lovely home in the suburbs, a charge card, and freedom to drink and entertain in that lovely home. It also meant three pregnancies in four years, and a husband who was never home because children bored and bothered him. During those years I continued my pattern of unpredictable drinking and was sick and hung over many mornings as I took care of the children. I was angry and impatient and created a confused and unhappy life. I cannot forgive myself. In AA we are told that our emotional maturity stops the day we pick up that first drink. That is certainly the case with me. When I look back on my marriage, I realize that my immaturity and sick self-will running riot ruined whatever chance I had to make it work.

By the time the children were teenagers, all our lives were a mess. From the outside everything looked quite lovely. A beautiful home, four handsome kids, a Jag and station wagon in the garage, an apartment in Florida, and country club memberships. The works. I was very involved as a civic volunteer and doing everything to avoid confronting the chaos at home. My kids were failing in school and in trouble outside. My husband and I were fighting, sometimes physically, over everything. We were in counseling with our eldest son and I was drinking very heavily every evening at home. More honestly, I was getting drunk every night. I wish I could somehow convey the feelings of desperation and frustration that filled my being.

In AA we are cautioned against finding fault or "taking another person's inventory," and, therefore, I have purposefully avoided speaking of my former husband. But we were married for twenty-one years, and perhaps some clarification is called for. This man was, and is, a deeply disturbed person. During our marriage he was prone to verbal and, sometimes, physical violence. At times I have referred to it as "aggravated assault." I aggravated and he assaulted. But the one who bore the brunt of his anger and frustration was our eldest son. He was hyperactive, certainly not an easy child, but he was hit far too hard and too often. He grew up with deep anger and, like his father, is prone to physical violence. Because he was a behavior problem at school and was a diagnosed dyslexic, we took him to many top-notch doctors and schools over a ten-year period. He was tested and evaluated by the famous Dr. Robert Coles in Boston. However, no one ever questioned our behavior as parents or the stability of the marriage. In our handsome clothes and fine cars we took this boy from place to place and never found an answer. He just got worse. To this day, while his sisters and brother have their lives in good order, he continues to have profound problems.

About this time, a close friend entered rehab for alcoholism and made a remarkable physical and mental recovery. For a few years I watched her life change, and when she suggested I attend an AA meeting, I agreed. As I walked up the stairs of a decrepit former school, I was filled with sadness. Poor me, and all I did was drink just a little bit too much every night. That was in 1976, and the years since have been an incredible journey of discovery and growth.

At that first meeting I spoke up (naturally) and tried in a subtle way to let them know exactly who they had visiting them for the first time. No one seemed too interested, but I figured they'd come to when they really realized how gracious I was to come into their midst. After some months, they still seemed to want to concentrate on my sobriety (or lack of it) and not on the fact that I only drank because of people, places, and things! Anybody would drink if they had four kids who behaved like mine behaved! Anybody would drink, etc., etc., etc. Several years went by and I could never put more than six months of sobriety together. Interestingly enough, I never stopped going to AA meetings. Somehow I knew it was where I belonged. At the meetings I heard people speak of the feelings of desperation I so much identified with. But I couldn't believe that if I put down the drink, everything would get better. I couldn't imagine not taking a drink to dull the pain when life was so painful.

During these years my marriage ended, much to my relief. I was sure that with my husband out of the house, my life would be great and I wouldn't drink to excess. It didn't work that way and I still couldn't predict when I picked up that first drink that I wouldn't drink excessively. My psychiatrist (a member of AA) posed the question, "If you are so happy, Mary, why are you continuing to drink?" Since I admitted I "had a problem with alcohol," I agreed to seek professional help and went to Hazelden Rehabilitation Center in Minnesota for one month. It was the worst and best of times. For the first time there was no alcohol to rely on as I squarely faced my problems. It was also the first time in my life that I submitted to authority for any length of time. I rebelled, cried, ranted, and schemed, but I stayed put and grew up — albeit slightly.

The years since Hazelden have been exciting, painful, but wonderful. Growing up and accepting responsibility for my actions has been painful. The realization of my adulthood has been wonderful. I am not daddy's little girl or one man's wife. I am a mature, responsible, loving, and capable woman. Living the AA program "A Day at a Time" has taught me living skills never learned as a child. Trusting in the power of sobriety and in the caring of my fellow alcoholics, I have turned my life and will over to the care of a higher power. As I sit with my fellow alcoholics and share my experience, strength, and hope, I am confident no problem will come into my life that a drink will solve.

I have seen many miracles during my years in AA, and I guess I'm one of them. I have remarried and our relationship is one of love, humor, and great companionship. For several years life was extremely difficult and sad for my children as they bore the brunt of my divorce. The craziness of an alcoholic home was normal for them and they did not want a change. They "went down fighting." It took a few years for them to understand and accept that I could no longer be manipulated.

(They had learned their own set of coping skills!) When I was drinking, the demons of guilt, remorse, and shame were big factors in our relationship. Those three demons are gone and have been replaced with sobriety, love, and tolerance. I realize I cannot control or change anyone. I can only change myself and be a power of example. So far it is working. My two oldest children have abuse problems. One of them has found AA. The other continues on a downward path, and my heart is filled with sadness. Again the program steps in to remind me that I am powerless not only over my own alcoholism, but over another person's as well. I detach with love. My two youngest children are keenly aware of the dangers of alcoholism. They are all very proud of me and, what is more important, they really like me.

I have come to an understanding and acceptance of my childhood. I believe my parents did their best, just as I did my best at the time. The wonderful miracle of my life is that when I became a member of AA, I broke the rope that tied me to generations of alcoholic families and guaranteed that my children and their children will not have to be bound to that sad legacy.

AUTOBIOGRAPHICAL STATEMENT

The story of my life focuses on sick families and well families. My childhood was spent living with an alcoholic father and a silent, depressed mother. Childhood was a chaotic and unhappy time, and we, my brother and sisters, bear the marks of those dreadful years. My father died when I was in my late teens, and my mother's alcoholism went into high gear. She was a problem drinker from age fifty to sixty-two when, after a minor stroke, she abruptly stopped. She was an unhappy, unfulfilled woman and my relationship with her was an uneasy one. I viewed her silent acceptance with disdain, bordering on contempt, and I was determined not to imitate it.

We were a dysfunctional family and when I married, my role models for life as a wife and mother were those two very sick people. It can be argued that many children overcome great odds and successfully mature into productive, happy adults. Perhaps I would have had a chance at learning and growing, but by the time I noticed that my own marriage didn't compare too favorably with many around me, my dependency on alcohol precluded any emotional stability or consistent behavior.

And so I went about creating another sick family. Reflecting on my siblings, they too have serious human problems and difficult family situations. I am the only one who has sought help for addictive behavior. Alcoholism is insidious. It is the disease of denial. I can honestly say that in all those years it never occurred to me that alcohol was my problem. And as it turns out, it was my only problem. When I took the alcohol out of my life and began to try to live based on AA's Twelve Steps of Recovery, I was reborn — physically, emotionally, and spiritually.

Alcoholics Anonymous is a simple way of life that demands rigorous honesty in all our affairs. It is not as easy as it sounds! Besides myself, the greatest beneficiaries of my recovery are my four children. As we gather for family parties and I look at these young adults with their own families, I am thrilled and grateful. They tease and laugh when I get "carried away" when speaking of the dangers of alcohol, but many times their own words reflect the spiritual and moral values of the program. Very recently my oldest son faced his problem and is in the recovery program. Sobriety has given me the physical and mental stamina to help run a successful business and play a tolerable game of golf. Most of all it has enabled me to become a better friend, a more involved mother, and a loving mate. Life is great!

BACKGROUND INFORMATION (by Violet Morin)

The word "drugs" conveys different meanings to various listeners. Some think of drugs as the new pestilence in the streets of big cities. They think of gangs, deals, guns, quick money, and quick death. But there are others who think of drugs in other ways. Many think of alcohol as especially devastating not only to the addicted drinker but also to the family. One out of three American adults reports that alcohol abuse has brought trouble into his or her family. About sixty-five out of every hundred persons in the U.S. will be in an alcohol-related automobile crash in their lifetime.[1]

On the other hand, 9.5 percent of adults over the age of twenty-six have tried cocaine at least once. Further, there were approximately 5.8 million users of cocaine in 1985. In 1987, 15.2 percent of high school seniors reported using cocaine in the previous month. Of that 15.2 percent, 5.6 percent used cocaine in the form of "crack." The remainder used cocaine in powder form.[2] In 1986, the Drug Abuse Warning Network (DAWN, operated by the National Institute on Drug Abuse), received reports of 4,138 deaths related to drug abuse, of which 27.4 percent were classified as suicide.[3]

In contemporary society one need not give statistics to prove that this century is buffeted as an age of too many choices. Further, with these many choices comes the disease of addiction, the only disease that keeps telling the victims that they are not sick. It is the only disease that people choose to get stuck with.

One just has to look around at the "No Smoking" and the "Just Say No" signs, the health warning labels, the diet fads and condom ads to get the picture. Society is screaming out at us to curb our overindulgence. Why are there so many members of our society not heeding all the warnings? The mystery of addiction remains an unsolved puzzle.

To understand better the addictive state overtaking our society, one needs first to define the word "addiction." Zinberg and Shaffer, at Harvard Medical School's Center for Addiction Studies, give us this model of addiction: "In order to understand an individual's decision to use a drug and his response to the experience at any effective dose below toxic levels, one must consider the drug-set-setting interaction since these factors affect the drug experience directly."[4]

Milkman and Sunderwirth have defined addiction as "self-induced changes in neurotransmission that result in social problem behavior."[5] Addiction is no longer considered a moral problem, a personality disorder, a physiological disorder, but a bio-psycho-social disease that requires treatment.

The above definitions leave one to ponder the bio-psycho-social phenomenon of addiction. Is it the drug, the set, that is, the personality structure of the user, or is it the setting (environment) that contributes to the addiction? Or could all three factors, drug-set-setting, be unified causations for use and abuse?

Some theorists believe strongly in the individual's environmental factors as causing addiction. The theory of becoming "hooked" on drugs starts with the availability of them, especially in low socioeconomic environments. Yet what about all the people in these environments who do not get hooked on addictive drugs? And what about the people in the upper social strata, not around the so-called overwhelming availability of drugs, who also get hooked? The theory gives us no answers. Today, drugs are everywhere and all socioeconomic levels are choosing to use and abuse them.

If environment is not the single cause then it must be an individual factor. Many theorists, therapists, researchers, counselors, ex-addicts, recovering addicts all ponder the genetic factors of addiction. Believers of the disease model, namely, those who view alcoholism as a disease like diabetes, look at alcoholism as a chemically-based allergy to alcohol.

In a series of letters between Bill W., the founder of AA, and C. G. Jung, Bill W. discusses Dr. William D. Silkworth's theory of alcoholism: "Alcoholism has two components: an obsession that compelled the sufferer to drink against his will and interest, and some sort of metabolism difficulty which he then called an allergy."[6]

This theory provides the basis for the psychobiological factors of the disease of alcoholism. It kills! And even though it kills, one still cannot stop choosing to drink again, again, and again. Research shows that there have been many experiments with control groups of abstinent drinkers who do not get cravings when given drinks with alcohol if they are told that the drinks are nonalcoholic. The same holds true for active drinkers given drinks with double shots and told they are nonalcoholic drinks. They keep craving more, thinking the drink was free of alcohol. The confusion of genetics, sociological, or psychological factors goes on unabated.

Recent studies in genetics have revealed the father/son factors of alcoholism. A link has been made between sons of alcoholic fathers and the disease of alcoholism. Henri Begleiter, M.D., of the State University of New York showed that both male alcoholics and some of their (nondrinking) young sons have nearly identical and abnormal brainwaves. Much more research is being conducted looking at brain chemicals and the correlations to the disease of alcoholism. To date, nothing is conclusive. There is evidence for the connection, but it is still an unsolved mystery.

There is no unified theory of addiction. The field is gathering data from all biological, sociological, and psychological areas of expertise. Researchers use their laboratories to study the reactions of animals to alcohol and drugs. Getting a rat addicted to alcohol is more difficult than to cocaine or heroin. Studying how animals become addicted to substances leaves one to question their efficacy for people. The research field has allowed for human subjects to be used in the study of desensitization, but without drug inducement. Theorists and therapists struggle with the biological model and look to the psychology of addiction as "healer" to the wounded ego.

The term "self-esteem" is still resonating in most treatment facilities and therapy sessions. It has always been considered the primary factor in answering the "why" of addiction. If someone feels a low self-esteem, then that person is more prone to overcompensate for this low self-esteem. Drugs offer a respite, a fix, a false high self-esteem. But what comes first? The drugs or the low self-esteem? Many of my colleagues would argue for low self-esteem. Some would even state that it was the combination of low self-esteem and an addictive personality.

What is an addictive personality? In *A Physician's Journey*, Richard S. Sandor states:

> there is no such thing as an addictive personality, it is true that the inability to satisfy a physical craving or psychological compulsion will produce all kinds of unusual behavior, but this is true for natural drives and appetites as well as for created ones.
>
> What might one do to avoid starvation? Such behavior alone cannot be used as evidence for a pathological personality type.[7]

In clinical practice, clinicians observe the common thread of emotional pain and addictive behavior patterns. Most of the acting-out behaviors exhibited by addicts are linked to society's banning illegal drugs. It is a criminal act to use an illegal drug, and if the only way to use it is to behave antisocially, does the addictive personality then create itself? Or does society create the addictive personality?

Today, most researchers and theorists reject the addictive personality concept. Edward J. Khantzian, M.D., of Harvard Medical School believes that "people who become, and remain, addicted are looking for relief from emotional suffering."[8] He theorizes that addicts choose their drugs depending on the emotional state they want to relieve. Heroin, codeine, and narcotics relieve tensions related to violence, rage, and aggression. On the other hand, a depressed person will seek drugs that stimulate. The emotional state defines the drug of choice. The appeal of the drug is greatly linked to the relief it brings to the painful emotion.

The mystery remains. The complexity of the biological, sociological, and psychological factors of addiction needs much further study and research. The drug-set-setting relationship needs to be considered as primary for the abuse. The addictive relationship remains a difficult one to understand and personality clues still need assessment.

Violet Morin, a principal psychologist for the Massachusetts Department of Corrections, graduated from Harvard University with a degree in counseling and consulting psychology. She treats and coordinates a special abuse program for the addicted in Walpole State Prison. Working in the world of addicted youth since the early 1970s, she is committed to the study and research of addiction. Recalling the brown glass quart bottles from which her parents drank funny smelling liquid, she, however, is satisfied with orange soda pop. She had no idea that the content of the brown bottle was the cause of her parents arguments, nor that she would spend her life studying why she liked soda and not the other liquid. A single parent with four grown children, she struggled to raise and educate them. Violet believes that *stopping* drugs is easier for the addicted person than the continuing struggle *not to use drugs again.*

NOTES

1. National Council on Alcoholism, Inc., *Facts on Alcoholism and Alcohol-Related Problems* (New York, 1986).

2. National Highway Traffic Safety Administration.

3. National Institute on Drug Abuse, 1988.

4. N. E. Zinberg and H. J. Shaffer, "The Social Psychology of Intoxicant Use: The Interaction of Personality and Social Setting," in H. Milkman and

H. Shaffer, eds., *The Addictions* (Lexington, Mass.: Lexington Books, 1985), 57–74.

5. H. Milkman and S. Sunderwirth, "The Chemistry of Craving," *Psychology Today* (October 1983): 36–44.

6. C. G. Jung, *Letters*, ed. G. Adler, and A. Jaffe, trans. R. F. C. Hull, Bollingen Series 95, vol. 2 (Princeton, N.J.: Princeton University Press, 1951–61), pp. 623–25. Also in *Parabola*, Addiction, 12, no. 2, pp. 50–90.

7. R. S. Sandor, "Physician's Journey," *Parabola*, Addiction, 12, no. 2, pp. 30–50.

8. Class notes, 1987.

BIBLIOGRAPHY

Khantzian, E. J. "Self-selection and Progression in Drug Dependence." *Psychiatry Digest* 36 (1975): 19–22.

Milkman, H. B., and H. J. Shaffer, eds. *The Addictions*. Lexington, Mass.: Lexington Books, 1985.

National Council on Alcoholism, Inc. *Facts on Alcoholism and Alcohol-Related Problems*. New York, 1985.

National Institute on Drug Abuse. *Annual Data. 1986*. Data From the Drug Abuse Warning Network (DAWN). 1987.

———. *Cocaine: A Capsule Overview*. Prevention Branch, September 1985.

———. *Cocaine Addiction*. U.S. Department of Health and Human Services: Alcohol, Drug Abuse and Mental Health Administration, 1985.

———. *Drug Use among American High School Students, College Students and Other Young Adults*. Rockville, Md., 1988.

———. *Drug Use by High School Seniors, Class of 1987*. U.S. Department of Health and Human Services: Alcohol, Drug Abuse and Mental Health Administration, January 1988.

———. *NIDA Capsules*. U.S. Department of Health and Human Services: Alcohol, Drug Abuse and Mental Health Administration, August 1986.

Shaffer, H. J., and M. E. Burglass, eds. *Classic Contributions in the Addictions*. New York: Brunner/Maze, 1981.

RESOURCES

American Council for Drug Education
204 Monroe Street., Suite 110
Rockville, MD 20850
(301) 294-0600

National Institute on Drug Abuse (NIDA)
U.S. Dept. of Health & Human Services
5600 Fisher Lane (Parklawn Bldg)
Rockville, MD 20857
(800) 662-HELP

National Clearinghouse for Alcohol and Drug Abuse Information
P.O. Box 2345
Rockville, MD 20852
(301) 468-2600

Hotlines

AIDS Hotline/Public Health Service . . . . (800) 342-2437
Alcohol 24-Hour Helpline . . . . (800) 252-6465
Alcoholics Anonymous . . . . . . *local listings in telephone book*
Bulimia/Anorexia Self-Help . . . . (800) 227-4785
Cocaine Helpline . . . . (800) COCAINE
Gamblers Anonymous . . . . *local listings in telephone book*
Narcotics Anonymous . . . . *local listings in telephone book*
National Institute on Drug Abuse . . . . (800) 662-HELP
Runaways — National Runaway Switchboard . . . . (800) 621-4000

10

Retirement:
"Thus at Time's Humming Loom I Ply"

Annie Lally Milhaven

SERMON

And he said to them, "Come away by yourselves to a lonely place, and rest awhile." For many were coming and going, and they had no leisure even to eat.
— Mark 6:31

> *The years of our life are threescore and ten,*
> *or even by reason of strength fourscore;*
> *yet their span is but toil and trouble;*
> *they are soon gone, and we fly away.*
> — Psalm 90:10

In June 1988, *CBS Evening News* profiled three workers among scores dismissed by new owners of the Jordan Marsh department stores. These dismissed people had three characteristics: they were long-time employees; they were more women than men; and all showed signs of significant stress and emotional loss.

One of the three, a vice-president, described how he had given his life for Jordan Marsh. He worked twelve to fifteen hours six days a week. For twenty-five years he gave the company more time than he ever gave his family. Pausing to find words to describe the loss experienced by forced and unexpected retirement, the man began unabashedly to cry.

This vignette presents a compelling picture of what we, in God's presence will reflect on this morning. Although it does not describe everyone's experience with *retirement*, still it demonstrates a common dilemma of modern urban life. The dilemma is: who am I — following thirty to forty or more years on a job — when I no longer work? Who am I when I can no longer answer everyone's second question: "What

---

As a Catholic woman, I am not allowed to preach this sermon. I suggest for those who are that it be preached in the winter or early spring months, in any church, synagogue, or mosque.

work do you do?" Who am I when I no longer teach, preach, paint, nurse, clean offices, drive a bus or cab? In other words who am I when I retire?

Clearly, the identity of our vice-president was vested in his long-term position at the department store. Clearly also, his identity had become completely outer-directed, away from his inner self. The question for all of us is: do we have an inner identity when our life's chosen job is finished? For retirement is a fact of modern life, and unlike other phases of living — childhood, young adulthood, marriage and family — we have few models to show us how to live these years.

Before we examine retirement, let us reflect first on *work:* our job or profession, and the functions it serves in our lives.

A job, be it president of the United States or the janitor in a hospital or a teller in a bank, be it to our liking or not, serves many purposes. Work fulfills many often unnoticed goals and aspects of our lives. It gives us a sense of *belonging* to a group. It gives a focus that keeps us stable and provides a fence that keeps our lives from flowing over, as it were, without the boundary of work.

Socialization with co-workers who have common interests and with whom we can share ideas is a part of work on any job.

We develop *plans, goals, and purposes* that have to be achieved if our job is to be done. In this way we then achieve other personal goals of earning a living, buying a house, raising and educating a family, or planning for retirement.

No matter what one's vocation or profession, it enables one to perform certain tasks. Thus a worker achieves *self-esteem*, and self-esteem in turn keeps one achieving even more self-actualization, which becomes a great assist in living a vibrant life.

Another aspect of our work is that it provides us — even if we do not reflect on the fact — with a *sense of affirmation*. It gives us a sense that we are doing "the work of the world" and so affirms our own person. This sense of affirmation, which was a crucial part of our childhood, is an equally important part of our adult achievements. Like oil on a machine, affirmation helps us over the creaky aspects of work, the difficult days on the job.

While at work we have a *place*, a *territory* or a *turf* of our own. Be it a title, a desk, a closet for supplies, a telephone, or maybe a paging system, each worker has a place from which she or he functions. Workers are able to retreat to this "turf" to recoup a sense of direction during frustrating times on the job. In retirement, this sense of turf is lost, and one often begins to take over the spouse's "home turf." This then becomes one of the major issues after retirement.

Role image is another gift that work gives a person. One becomes identified as a competent supervisor, a good head nurse, a dependable maintenance person. Frequently, this role image flows over into other community interests. Thus one becomes the "nurse" who is active in improving the school curriculum or providing daycare for women with children who also work.

Work provides people with a *sense of power*. Power means control of one's life, and the ability and money to raise a family, to write, to invent, to be creative. Work also supplies us with *support systems*, because we make friends, join clubs, and on occasion socialize on the job. Co-workers come to know us, become concerned with our sorrows, and rejoice with us on happy occasions.

Moreover, we gain *wisdom* and *experience* at work and become mentors to other workers. As the years pass, we are respected for our knowledge, looked up to for our example, and sought out for advice and counsel. Although all these outcomes of work cannot be measured, they add to our self-esteem and self-actualization.

Routine and *structure* are built into a life of work. We arise at stated hours, travel, work, eat, and return home. These routines become part of our lives, using up our energy efficiently in the daily effort to make a living.

Finally, work takes *time*. Time passes on the job. Carl Sandburg said: "Time is a sandpile we run our fingers in." People spend thirty, forty, maybe fifty years "at work"; what an expanse of time we pour into the work of the world.

When we consider all these functions of work in a person's life, we can see that companies and unions have some obligation to prepare people for retirement. Yet very few do. Retirees will spend from fifteen to twenty-five years *after work* in a life that they have frequently thought very little about, for which they have few models to imitate, and which without preparation can be void and empty.

Let us consider now what it is like to retire. Usually someone from the company benefits department will spend a couple of hours explaining Social Security and Medicare; a party is held; often a gift (a watch of all things!) is given in farewell. The employee empties out an office, desk, or drawer and says good-bye.

Experts identify three stages that the newly retired experience. One is the *honeymoon* stage wherein workers, manual laborers especially, cannot wait for the day to come on which they can forget about work. For those who love their jobs on the other hand the opposite is true. Their feelings become unreal, they expect to be back at work shortly, or they visit the work-site only to find friends too busy to socialize. This second stage is *disenchantment*. Many people grope for years to find a new identity. The feeling is not unlike that of the new college graduate who, while awaiting the first job, experiences a time of uncertainty and unreality. Similarly, even people who could not wait to retire find in due time that there is a void in their lives.

The third stage is *reorientation* in which one eventually finds a new path in life. The benefit of preparing years in advance for this span of life is to get a start on how to use our time in satisfying ways. Waiting to plan until after retirement prolongs an uncertain future; many merely begin a slow decline, and suicide, especially among men, rises.

People at sixty-five today are young. There is another lifespan ahead. Rather than thinking of this span of fifteen, twenty, or twenty-five years as uninterrupted leisure, why not view it in a different and new way. Ours is the first generation of retirees on the large scale we see all around — healthy, vibrant people with *time* on their hands. How might we look at this gift of time? Fifty hours are added to each week, leaving the retiree with 168 "free" hours. What are the possibilities for these hours? And what are the ways to avoid boredom, tedium, sitting around watching a numbing TV, and, even worse, drinking beer as we do so?

One thing retirees can do is to ask ourselves: what do I really *want* to do? What would I really *like* to do? What did I always dream of doing, but because my life turned out as it did, I had no *time* for my dreams. Reflect on these questions and begin to make a list. Include your undeveloped talents. Think of the needs of your neighborhood, your state, your church and other groups, and of the nation. Our country is full of unmet needs. And as the sermon on volunteerism shows (see p. 134), there are thousands of unmet needs and no money to meet them. For example, one of every five children (another sermon shows), lives below the poverty level in the United States. That means that every fifth child is underfed, undereducated, and has poor health care available. That child will have a much poorer chance for a decent life and family.

On the other hand, prisons are overcrowded, parolees need mentors and friends. The aged — although only 5 percent are in nursing homes — need companionship. Three of four retirees are women who complain that their major problem is loneliness. In other words, society is full of needs that retirees can help meet and match. I cite this example of practical and wonderful help of a retiree:

> My friend in class with me at Harvard Divinity School was notified that her aged father was killed in an automobile accident. Traveling fifty miles we were met at the hospital by a woman volunteer from Betsy's church, who at once took us into a small room, explained that the old man must have either fallen asleep or had a heart attack at the wheel of his car, which careened ahead until it struck a tree.

The woman explained that the family had come to the hospital, and in which funeral home the body of Betsy's father reposed.

I have often reflected on the incident. Without this volunteer, we may have been sent from one office to another seeking information. As it was, the humaneness of the encounter was impressive and dignified. The volunteer gave freely of her loving service; she too must have felt the rewards of the sad but rich encounter.

Retirement also provides people with time for reflection and meditation, which help one to become serene. Time can be set aside to learn new skills or experiences, such as a long-sought college degree. Other considerations that *enrich* and extend life after sixty-five have been published by Yale University. For example:

Being a woman extends the lifespan as much as six to eight years, and being married extends a man's but not necessarily a woman's life.

Having a child living within fifty miles enriches older years, as does being free of psychological depression.

Possessing a concept of self as a religious person is another sustaining force in older life, as is having two confidants — one preferably outside the home — with whom to share one's thoughts.

Having social supports and networks of friends, such as people who will visit us in hospital and encourage us, for instance, to obtain a second opinion is of great benefit.

Retaining memory and thought processes is an enormous help in enriching and extending lives. This gift, not always under our control, is enhanced if we remain vibrant, interested in life while continuing to learn.

Finally, let us again recall the words of the Psalmist: "The days of our life are soon gone and we fly away." Although the twentieth century has seen our lives greatly lengthened, still our days will end. Death is part of life, and reflecting in a prayerful way on retirement enables us to live while we are alive, and so to enjoy life fully and faithfully, while preparing ourselves by meditation and reflection for our last end.

AUTOBIOGRAPHICAL STATEMENT

Following thirty absorbing years in nursing education and administration, I decided to change my career. Together with associates I set about constructing a Pre-Retirement Preparation Program. The program was designed to prepare people while still in their working years to begin to think about and plan for retirement. An added role for me was to market this package to corporations, colleges, unions, and health agencies.

Creating a career change, I discovered, was in itself like retirement.

During the early years time hung heavily for me. Waiting for growth left unfilled hours that seemed void and empty. Sudden severance from absorbing work and the companionship of co-workers and the loss of income, benefits, and planned paid vacations was, in fact, jolting.

Settling eventually into the more solid dimensions of my new career, I had an additional opportunity to identify with the losses many people encounter when they reach retirement years. My associations with hundreds of people in programs of retirement preparation proved invaluable in demonstrating the importance for all persons to prepare for those years of "leisure."

Persons whose corporations prepare them for retirement are the lucky ones. But they are few. One authority states that only 2 percent of the work force is prepared in a formal way for the fifteen to twenty-five years of retirement. For the others "retirement is becoming one of the major social problems of our culture."

How, one may ask, can living fifteen to twenty-five years *after* retirement be any problem at all? Why should one of the boons of this century — longevity — be dreaded and be a cause for people to pull down blinders around their lives? Psychologists who study life's difficult periods place a figure of forty-five stress points (of a possible hundred) on retirement.

For retirement is a phenomenon new to the developed Western world. Unlike other phases of life, like schooling, work, marriage and family, there are very few role models for successfully achieving the fullness in the additional years. On the other hand, with the numbers of older people increasing in the United States, it is appropriate to meditate on ways in which people can be happy, engaged, and vitally involved in life while they are alive.

BACKGROUND INFORMATION

In 1903 men and women in the United States lived on average between thirty-five and forty-eight years of age. Some few lucky persons lived to fifty or sixty but only 4 percent of the population lived to reach sixty-five.[1] Most Americans at the turn of the century, like the people who now live in the developing world, worked until they dropped dead or were forced by poor health to give up work. Consequently, ninety years ago in the U.S., as now in the Third World, there was no such phenomenon as retirement on the mass scale we experience today.

In 1986, there were 29.2 million Americans sixty-five years of age and older. They represented 12.1 percent of the population or about one in every eight Americans.[2] Women live an average of 78.4 years;

men 72.2 years. Many of these older persons are in our families, churches, synagogues, and neighborhoods. In fact, one of the most serious concerns of many of these older people is that *their* parents are still living, but in frail or failing health. The reason for this is also new — the fastest growing segment of the population is eighty-five-year-olds, in a ratio of four women to one man.

Aging on such a vast scale has taken the developed West by surprise. But what has not yet sunk in is that by 2010 — a mere twenty years from now — one in five Americans will be sixty-five or over. Therefore it is timely to examine what retirement is and what it means to an individual, a family, and a community. It is especially important that people prepare for it years before it is upon them: "Oftentimes retirement is unplanned. People who worked hard all their lives suddenly reach compulsory retirement age and find nothing but a void in their lives. They are unable to cope with their leisure time."[3]

While compulsory retirement is at present almost eliminated, "forced" retirement becomes the new threat. The takeover business often results in the new company's management laying-off hundreds of workers, usually older persons. This disruption of life work at an older age is particularly poignant, especially if the worker has given no thought to preparation for retirement.

Preparation for later life should be well under way by age fifty-five. What does preparation mean? Many people think only of *finances* when they refer to retirement. Finances are, of course, very important, but they are only one of the investments needed for a successful future. Equally important is the state of one's mental *and* physical health and knowledge of ways to keep oneself fit and healthy.

But the most important investment of all is *time:* how do I use the fifty newly freed hours each week? How can the time be used in a satisfying, gainful, and meaningful manner? Research shows that corporate America, too, thinks more of money than meaning when it comes to retirement. For the five thousand or more persons who retire daily, most of them consider money as their number one need, but on the day *after* retirement, *meaning* becomes the most important issue, and money moves to fourth place.

This is particularly true for workers who enjoy great satisfaction or "ego involvement" in their jobs or professions. Persons whose work provides a sense of self-actualization dread the thought of retiring. Unless they have a plan of action for their lives after work, they will experience significant stress and trouble with their new leisure.

People on the other hand who could scarcely wait for the next coffee-break to relieve the dull boredom of their jobs will likely find in retirement initially an expansion of their lives. Persons in these "society maintaining" jobs, on the other hand, may (or may not) be in poor or failing health. For them too, as the days pass, boredom can become a new stress.

According to Stanley Parker, "Retirement never offers adequate compensation or reward for the loss of work."[4] This intuition keeps many people on the job and makes forced and unplanned retirement such a personal and social problem. Still, by thinking and planning, people can reduce the anxiety surrounding retirement and begin to consider more inner direction in their lives.

NOTES

1. Stanley Parker, *Work and Retirement* (London: George Allen and Unwin, 1982), p. 104.
2. *A Profile of Older Americans 1987*, American Association of Retired Persons, 1909 K Street, NW, Washington, DC 20049.
3. George and Marian Fair Daluger, *Human Development: The Span of Life*, 2d ed. (St. Louis: C. V. Mosby Co., 1979), p. 380.
4. Parker, *Work and Retirement*, 138.

BIBLIOGRAPHY

A Profile of Older Americans 1987. American Association of Retired Persons, 1909 K Street, NW, Washington, DC 20049.
Bradford, Leland P. and Martha S. *Retirement: Coping with Emotional Upheavals*. Chicago: Nelson Hall Publishers, 1979. One of the best books on work and the losses experienced by the worker, as well as on the turf intrusions inherent in retirement.
Butler, Robert M. *Why Survive?: Being Old in America*. New York: Harper & Row, 1975. A critical study of old age in the United States before government intervention to reduce the numbers of elderly living in poverty.
Daluger, George and Marian. *Human Development: The Span of Life*. 2d ed. St. Louis: C. V. Mosby Co, 1979. A good study of each of the developmental stages of our lives.
Erikson, Erik and Joan, and Helen Q. Kivnick. *Vital Involvement in Old Age*. New York: W. W. Norton and Co, 1976. A wonderful volume on older years by the couple (now in their eighties), who researched and developed the psychological development of children and young adults.

RESOURCES

The Department or Division of Aging in each state is a source of written materials, and often provides senior centers where the elderly meet and socialize.

RSVP (Retired Senior Volunteer Program) is one of the best sources to help older volunteers use their time and talents. Listed in the telephone directory in each state.

Your local library is a source for reading, music, records, paintings, etc.

AARP (American Association of Retired Persons, 1909 K Street, NW Washington, DC 20049) is a source of multiple services: health insurance, lifestyle, use of time, up-to-date information on legislation. Membership is inexpensive.

Continuing Education like Elderhostel (80 Boylston St, Boston, MA 02116), which uses college campuses, in summer especially, to offer courses in the U.S. and abroad. State colleges and universities often grant senior citizens free tuition if there is classroom space available.

Peace Corps (P-301, Washington, DC 20526) is always looking for skilled seniors to volunteer for overseas work.

An excellent way for a congregation to consider retirement is to sponsor Ingmar Bergman's film *Wild Strawberries*, as is demonstrated in the book *Vital Involvement in Old Age*, by Erik and Joan Erikson and Helen Kivnick. The film is a splendid review of the eight stages of human beings, relived by an old man returning to his childhood home en route to the capital to receive a national award.

11

Volunteerism: The Gift of Oneself

Betsy Aldrich Garland

SERMON

Each one as a manager of God's different gifts, must use for the good of others the special gifts she has received from God.
—1 Peter 4:10, TEV

Last weekend I flew up to Toronto to see my friend Lynda. We had been classmates at Harvard until she graduated last year and moved back to Canada with her husband and three boys.

Two days before I went, Lynda celebrated her forty-sixth birthday, so I bought her a puzzle of the Boston waterfront and wrapped it in wonderful red paper with whiskered cat faces all over. Although I had planned to take the puzzle in my suitcase, at the last minute there wasn't room, so I simply carried it in my hand, not thinking to hide the gift in a bag.

Well, people started smiling at me as soon as I arrived at Logan airport in Boston. When I checked my suitcase, the ticket agent thanked me for bringing her a present. When I boarded the plane, the other passengers watched me inch my way down the aisle, studied those silly tiger and calico and black and white cats, and then looked up and met my eyes. I felt a little foolish and stowed the gift under my seat as soon as I could.

But the truth was out. Wrapping paper and bows recall some of our fondest memories — of birthdays and Christmases and special surprises — of the joys of giving and receiving, of some of our most treasured human experiences.

I took Lynda another gift as well, a much more important and valuable gift, the gift of myself. Over coffee we talked about our lives, our children, our studies, papers written and papers overdue. I made my famous hot fudge sundaes and she made her clam chowder. We compared notes on good books and went for a long walk with her

Preached at Washington Park United Methodist Church, Providence, Rhode Island, August 6, 1989, at a typical Sunday morning service. The congregation is a cross-section of age, ethnic, and socioeconomic groups.

next door neighbor Muriel, who is having chemotherapy, and talked about God and life and death.

I could have stayed home that weekend. I had a lot to do. I could have scraped the peeling paint on my house and used the ticket money to pay my bills. But I chose to go, to spend the gift of myself in the world. Lynda and I gave each other the most precious gift anyone can give another — oneself. And we were just what we each needed for the weekend. In a simple, informal way, we were volunteers.

We are not alone. In more organized ways, almost one out of every two adult Americans — eighty million people — volunteer. They are giving the "gift of oneself," their time, skills, and experience, without financial reward, to others — and discovering in return that they are twice blessed. Let me share some stories:

• A woman named Terry travels into the city every week to visit the child, a ward of the state, to whom she has been assigned. In her first year as a volunteer court-appointed special advocate, all the officials involved in the case changed — the social worker, the supervisor, the judge. Only Terry knows the child well enough to represent her interests in court. She is giving the gift of security while she learns about the state's legal justice system and finds an outlet for her nurturing now that her children have left home.

• Two residents of a group home for retarded adults, Christine and Mary, also are active as volunteers. In spite of their disabilities, they help at a neighborhood soup kitchen, assist with janitorial tasks at a nearby church, and visit with lonely elderly people. Chris and Mary are taking on important work that often goes begging and have made a place for themselves in the community.

• In the same spirit, a fourteen-year-old named Susan has started going after school several days a week to a youth shelter for troubled teens to teach them how to dance. Through Susan, the teens are gaining enough self-confidence and social skills to attend youth activities at the town recreation department.

• Senior volunteer Becky goes to the Blood Center every Monday where she schedules appointments, helps with mailings, and serves juice and cookies to donors. Even though she retired six years ago, she is up and out every morning, bursting with energy and enthusiasm for life.

• And volunteering need not be limited to direct service. Doris chairs the Public Information Committee of an organization that touches the lives of hundreds of people yearly. Caring for institutions and assisting in their able administration can be a greater good.

In the wave of feminism that swept over the nation in the early 1970s, the word "volunteer" became synonymous with exploitation. If work was worth doing, it was worth money. Women should stop frittering their time away stuffing envelopes and hone their job skills, advocates said. Self-development was the goal and the career track the means. Volunteering was viewed as a dead-end street.

Today, the case of volunteering versus paid work is no longer being debated. That volunteering has career-related benefits is widely accepted. People volunteer to gain self-esteem and experience, build a portfolio, develop credentials, and "try on" a career. Those who are employed volunteer to round out their lives, extend the realm of their personal influence, find satisfaction, and gain prestige for themselves and their company. If one becomes "burned out," it is more often seen as a time for a change, for an assessment of the quality of personal support, or even as an indication that a more challenging assignment is in order.

Major corporations encourage employees to volunteer, realizing that they become better workers for the exposure. Teens volunteer in order to discover what life is all about, and retirees to remain active and vital. No one questions that each of us needs a means of adequate support, but beyond material needs, each of us also needs to become involved in the larger world. Volunteering has come to be understood as broadening, empowering, and a valuable way to spend discretionary time.

Has volunteering changed? To an extent, yes. It has become more sophisticated. The growth of the voluntary sector and in the number of agencies that depend upon hundreds of volunteers to carry out vital services — what some of us would view as ministries — has brought increased competition for volunteers and professional administrators who match them with assignments that are rewarding, challenging, and growth producing. It is a "consumers" market. Women are choosing volunteer work that meets their particular needs, suits their schedules, and enriches their lives.

But beyond a social analysis of the value of volunteering, there is a growing awareness of its theological dimensions. Volunteering has significance for us as religious beings, as women who seek to live faithful lives, responsible *for* ourselves and *to* others. I would suggest that we all need to volunteer, that we all have a right to volunteer to our fullest potential, and that we all have a responsibility to volunteer — to spend the gift of ourselves in the world.

We are, you and I, social, interdependent beings. Intrinsically we know that a life lived for oneself alone is no life at all. Much of the spiritual hunger in our society is caused by too much attention to "self" and not enough to the "other." We spend more and more on material goods in an attempt to fill up the gnawing emptiness and grow only more lonely and desolate. In contrast, we each become full persons when we reach out in service. We live our lives for others and thereby find ourselves. This is the meaning of Jesus' injunction, "For whoever would save her life will lose it, and whoever loses her life for my sake will find it" (Matt. 16:25).

In Annie Milhaven's sermon on depression (see p. 105) she describes the view that depression may be due to a lack of three characteristics or qualities of a healthy life: self-esteem, choice, and meaning. Depressed persons could well be encouraged to volunteer — to find important, worthwhile, satisfying work to do. When we are wrapped up in ourselves we die. Volunteering in the right assignment and organizational environment with good preparation and understanding support can draw us out of ourselves. Many volunteers have discovered themselves — who they are and what they can do — through volunteering.

In the same vein, medical researchers have documented that community service not only has a psychological benefit but also a physiological one. It seems that doing good is good for us, physically as well as mentally. Studies have shown that helping others is good for our hearts, our immune systems, and our overall vitality. Moreover, regular volunteer work, more than any other activity, dramatically increases life expectancy. The need for community, researchers have proposed, is a key part of our evolutionary heritage. As a species, we are communal; historically, to survive, we had to be, and the evolutionary process of natural selection has left its altruistic mark.

For many people, the primary vehicle for this humanizing process is volunteerism — though it may be initiated in individual as well as organized ways. Some people grow into volunteerism as naturally as they grow out of rompers and into school clothes. For others, the values need to be taught directly and intentionally. The family is one place where this can happen — but also in the schools, media, work place, church and synagogue, and retirement community. We need to teach people that the only way to care for themselves is to care for others, to lose their lives in order to find them. People need people, and this fact has profound theological implications.

But not only do we need to volunteer; we must recognize that everyone has a right to volunteer, and to volunteer to fullest potential. The stereotype of the Lady Bountiful with a basket over her arm is a reminder of the past. Today's volunteers come from all walks of life, all ages, all ethnic and socioeconomic groups. They are people with special physical and psychological needs, court-ordered community service workers, executives on the move, displaced homemakers, "yuppies," students who come and go with the semesters. Yet every one of them is a unique person who has been endowed with special gifts — gifts of love and laughter, gifts of artistic talent and sensitivity, gifts of management skills or a knack for children, gifts of appreciation for nature or understanding for those who are living with disabilities.

Elizabeth O'Connor in her book *The Eighth Day of Creation* tells a story about Michelangelo, who was rolling a large stone down the dusty road. A neighbor called from his porch, "Michelangelo, what do you want with that rock?" And Michelangelo shouted back, "There's an angel in here that wants to come out!" Michelangelo was a man who knew and used his gift of creativity to the glory of God. His story is for all of us. O'Connor writes, "We ask to know the will of God without guessing that God's will is written into our very own being. We perceive that will when we discern our gifts. Our obedience and surrender to God are a large part of our obedience and surrender to our gifts."

Each one of us is called to use that gift in service to others. Unless we do so, Thomas Merton notes, we will never be completely happy, will never uncover the divine within. The parable of the talents in the Gospel of Matthew (Matt. 25:14–30) is really an allegory about our own gifts. Jesus reminds us that all our gifts are important, that it doesn't matter whether we have one, two, or five, that they are of equal worth. Moreover, we are responsible for spending our gifts in the world, and God will hold us accountable. The one who is afraid and hides hers or his is symbolic of the experience of each of us when we hide our potential, of the suffering for what dies within us, unborn.

We need to help each other discover and use our gifts. There is an angel in each one of us that awaits the touch of a creative hand. This means being sensitive to the possibility in everyone, being committed to helping her or him grow as a person, encouraging participation in new opportunities for service. It means believing that *every* person has something to offer and believing it to the point where *every* one of us comes to believe so as well. We have a mandate to spend our gifts in the world and only when we spend them will we be fulfilled, or — to use more traditional language — will we be saved.

Finally, we have a responsibility to volunteer. We live lives of enormous blessings, most of us. Our land is one of freedom and opportunity. We have more than adequate material things and choices about how we shall live our lives. Granted, there are poverty and hunger, racism and fear of nuclear war, sickness and suffering. Yet as a people we know unprecedented abundance.

Three millennia ago a people enslaved in Egypt were delivered by a God who cared for the dispossessed, the vulnerable, the least of society — more than for the pharaoh. Yahweh's saving action turned the ancient world upside down. The Hebrew experience of Exodus is not simply a story of escape but also the story of the birth of social consciousness. The righteousness and compassion of God became a model for human community in the developing Hebrew nation. When one studies the laws governing relationships in the Book of Deuteronomy, it is clear how people are to treat each other: in a manner consistent with that of a loving God who hears and responds to the cries of those who are strangers, vulnerable, poor, outcast.

Jesus stands in this prophetic tradition. It is no coincidence that his "preaching the gospel of the Kingdom and healing every disease and every infirmity among the people" (Matt. 5:23) went hand in hand. The gospel of the Kingdom is embodied in the love and ministry of Jesus, and the message of the New Testament is that the gospel also is meant to be embodied in the love and ministry of each of us. How shall we enter the Kingdom? By feeding the hungry, by welcoming the stranger, by visiting the sick and the prisoner (Matt. 25:34–36) — just as Jesus did. By their fruits you shall know them, Jesus preaches (Matt. 7:15–20). Faith without works is a contradiction, James reminds us in his epistle (James 2:14–26). In truth, works create faith by radically changing the way we perceive ourselves and others — and ourselves in relation to God. The eternal triangle is underscored by Jesus in his teaching, "You shall love the Lord your God...[and] your neighbor as yourself" (Matt. 22:35–40).

In response to the goodness in our lives, then, there is joyful obligation to create a just and caring society. If we believe that the whole world is God's, that the whole world is sacred space and that there is no place where God is *not*, then what we do for each other and the larger world when we feed the hungry, clothe the naked, visit the sick, welcome the stranger, when we participate in loving service, that is, "unto the least of these" (Matt. 25:34ff.), to use Matthew's phrase, when we act as the "Christed Ones" in the world, then God is present. We realize — that is, you and I make real — the holy in the way we live and take responsibility.

How can we do this? How shall we take upon ourselves this overwhelming responsibility to make God's presence real in the world? Nobel Peace Prize winner Mother Teresa, a small, stooped woman in a faded blue sari and worn sandals, says we can do no great things — only small things with great love.

We live in a complex society that is in need of great love. We no longer know our neighbors. Intimacy is a commodity we purchase through computerized dating services. Violence and alienation are endemic. Nations rise up against nations, and carelessness and wastefulness threaten our very planet.

Such a society requires increased recognition of the significance of volunteerism. It is the vehicle through which the presence of God is actualized in community life, God's grace driving us from self-centeredness to other-centeredness, from emptiness to fulfillment, from death to resurrection.

To volunteer is to renew the community, to embody our deepest religious commitment to the way human life should be lived and cared for. And as we have seen, in the very act of giving the "gift of themselves," Terry, Christine, Mary, Susan, Becky, and Doris are becoming whole persons, fulfilled in the way they live and love. But not for themselves alone. For when we volunteer, when we reach out to others in service, we create divine space where God's presence is made real in our lives and in the lives around us.

So may God's grace lead us in the ways of volunteering, that by giving the gift of ourselves we may be blessed, and all the people of God's good earth will know love and justice in their lifetime.

AUTOBIOGRAPHICAL STATEMENT

Although a registered nurse by profession (with a degree in nursing from the University of Rhode Island), I loved my volunteer work best. Therefore, when I was divorced in 1975 and needed to work full-time to support myself and two small children, I responded to a job opening in volunteer administration. My years of volunteer experience in both policy-making and service capacities, particularly my years on Church Women United's national board, had prepared me well and provided me with the credentials I needed.

For fifteen years, then, I have been the executive director of Volunteers in Action (VIA), Rhode Island's central recruitment, referral, training, and informational center for volunteers and social service agencies. At VIA I have gained extensive experience in volunteer program development and an opportunity to design and lead numerous workshops for boards of directors and agency staff as well as to consult widely with agencies and service organizations in volunteer management and boardsmanship.

Although many women have used volunteerism as a launching pad for careers and have moved into paid work without looking back, I feel a responsibility to continue to contribute to the volunteer community by leveraging my skills and teaching others. Currently, for example, I am serving on my local United Methodist church's Parish Council and chairing the Stewardship Commission. I also am being called on by the ecumenical religious community for workshops on volunteerism with both clergy and lay persons.

Out of a concern for the development of the laity and the revitalization of volunteers in the church, I enrolled in Harvard Divinity School eight years ago and have completed a master of divinity degree. I believe that volunteering has religious significance and that much of the mission of the church is carried on by secular agencies. I also believe that the church — clergy and laity alike — needs to understand better how to mobilize its members. Perhaps if we could learn how to do that well, we could save not only the church but also an increasingly fractured world.

BACKGROUND INFORMATION

Periodically national studies are conducted to determine the extent of volunteering in the United States. The most recent and comprehensive survey was conducted in 1988 by the Gallup Organization for Independent Sector. It is available in summary form ($10.00) as well as with the complete findings ($25.00): *Giving and Volunteering in the United States: Findings from a National Survey*, 1988 Edition, Independent Sector, 1828 L Street, NW, Washington, DC 20036.

Some of the findings are pertinent background for the sermon, above. Consider these:

- *Giving and volunteering remain pervasive activities among Americans:* (1) The average contribution for all households in 1987, including non-contributors, was $562, or 1.5 percent of income. There were 91 million households in the United States. (2) The average hours volunteered per week in 1987 for all adults eighteen years of age or older, including non-volunteers, was 2.1. There were 176.7 million adults eighteen years of age or older.

- *The most frequently cited reasons respondents gave for starting to volunteer were that* they wanted to do something useful (56 percent), they thought they would enjoy the work (34 percent), a family member or friend would benefit (27 percent); or they volunteered for religious reasons (22 percent).

- *A strong commitment to certain personal goals and values has a marked impact on the level of household giving and on volunteering.*

- *Active involvement in religious organizations has a direct relationship to giving and volunteering.* Sixty-five percent of respondents reported that they held membership in religious organizations.

BIBLIOGRAPHY

Giving and Volunteering in the United States: Summary of Findings, 1988 Edition. Independent Sector, 1828 L Street, NW, Washington, DC 20036.
Scheier, Ivan H. *Exploring Volunteer Space: The Recruiting of a Nation*. Arlington, Va.: VOLUNTEER — The National Center, 1980.
Wilson, Marlene. *How to Mobilize Church Volunteers*. Minneapolis: Augsburg Publishing House, 1983.

For more information on the medical research showing a relationship between volunteering and health see the following:

Growald, Eileen Rockefeller, and Allan Luks. "Beyond Self: The Immunity of Samaritans." *American Health* (March 1988): 51ff.
Kohn, Alfie. "Beyond Selfishness." *Psychology Today*, October 1988.
Luks, Allan. "Helper's High." *Psychology Today*, October 1988.

An extensive booklist and catalogue are published biannually by VOLUN-TEER — The National Center and are available free. Contact your local Volunteer Center or write VOLUNTEER (see Resources).

RESOURCES

The *Journal of Volunteer Administration* is published quarterly by the Association for Volunteer Administration (see below) for professional administrators and other leaders of volunteers. It comes as a benefit of membership in AVA for $65 or to nonmembers for $24 per year.

Voluntary Action Leadership is a quarterly tool for administrators of volunteer programs, which is published by VOLUNTEER — The National Center (see below) for $16 per year.

Volunteer Centers (Voluntary Action Centers) can be found in hundreds of cities across the country. They serve as informational, recruitment, referral, consultation, and training centers for volunteers, leaders, and agencies. They will be listed in your telephone directory. If you need help in reaching the one closest to you, contact your local United Way organization or VOLUNTEER (listed below).

ACTION is the federal agency that oversees such government-sponsored volunteer programs as VISTA, RSVP, Foster Grandparents, Student Service Learning, and the Senior Companion Program. Contact your state office or ACTION, National Volunteer Agency, 806 Connecticut Avenue, NW, Washington, DC 20525.

The Association for Volunteer Administration (AVA) is the professional association for those working in the field of volunteer management. Membership is open to both salaried and nonsalaried professionals. AVA produces publications, including several newsletters and booklets and the *Journal of Volunteer Administration*. For further information, contact AVA, P.O. Box 4584, Boulder, CO 80306.

The National VOLUNTEER Center, a private, nonprofit organization, was created to strengthen the effective involvement of all citizens as volunteers in solving local problems. Among the wide range of technical assistance and support services VOLUNTEER offers are a national conference, publications, consulting and training services, national volunteer advocacy, and public awareness activities. Contact VOLUNTEER — The National Center, 1111 N. 19th Street, Suite 500, Arlington, VA 22209. Telephone: (703) 276-0542.

PART FOUR

Human Sexuality and Theological Discourse

12

Abortion: "Throw No Stones"

Karen Keating Ansara

SERMON

Who shall be the first to throw a stone?

In the eighth chapter of the Gospel of John, a group of lawyers and religious scholars circle around a woman accused of adultery. Their hands clutch stones. They are poised to throw. For committing adultery women *must* be stoned. The law says so. Ready... set....

Only Jesus lifts no stone. He scribbles in the sand. He lifts his head and says, "He who is without sin among you, let him be the first to throw a stone" (John 8:7b).

Thank God that in our society crowds no longer kill adulterers by stoning! But stoning still continues in other forms toward other persons. Some people throw words of stone — epithets and insults. Some beat with placards and megaphones. Some hurl lines from the Bible.

Stone-throwers are self-proclaimed lawyers, judges, and juries. Stone-throwers seek to purge the land of all impurity. They seek to obliterate all difference of opinion. They seek to force obedience to one infallible source of authority, whether it be the Bible, a certain preacher, the church, or the government.

Who are those stoned? Among others, they are free thinkers, gays and lesbians, racial and religious minorities, and women who choose to have abortions.

In the seventeenth century, Baptists were verbally stoned, ostracized, and even hung. Obadiah Holmes, the founder of one of the first Baptist churches in America, was hung by Boston Puritans for calling for religious beliefs to be free from the authority of any single church or state.

Like these early Baptists, the American Baptist Churches of the U.S.A. assert that no one person or institution has the right to dictate religious truth for another. All who are baptized with belief in

---

This is a sermon I plan to preach when called to ministry in an American Baptist congregation.

Jesus Christ are priests with the ability, authority, and responsibility to discern God's will for themselves. God alone is the sovereign of each conscience — no one else.

God alone is our judge. No person has the right to throw stones.

American Baptists ardently defended freedom of conscience. We call it "soul liberty." But we do not condone "soul anarchy." We do not encourage any person's beliefs and actions to be shaped only by their own desires.

Instead, Baptists defend a responsible freedom of conscience within certain limits. Through prayer and guidance from the Holy Spirit, we seek God's will as revealed in Scripture. We strive for consensus with fellow believers. We follow the model of members of the early Christian church.

We try to form our consciences prayerfully and responsibly. We use the minds God has given us. We reason and we reflect on our experience. But we are careful not to rely on our reason and experience alone, for our perceptions may be flawed. We admit that we do not fully share the mind of God. We confess that we do not always exemplify the grace of God.

Because we are fallible, because we sin, we are in no position to throw stones. "No one is righteous, no, not one" (Rom. 3:10).

Sad to say, some fundamentalists masquerading as Baptists have strayed from these roots of the Baptist faith. They have forgotten their human limitations. They posture as infallible religious authorities, the very megaphones of God. They parade as the guardians of morality and soldiers for Christ. They appoint themselves as the teachers of intolerance. They preach as the philosophers of easy answers.

They all too readily throw stones.

Stone-throwers rarely ask to hear their targets' stories. They seldom try to see the world through their victims' eyes. They are too busy to listen — too obsessed with collecting stones.

Was the adulterous woman ever asked to tell her story? Probably not. Women were rarely spoken to — less heard from — in Israel in those days. Jesus is the only one who speaks to her. "Woman, has no one condemned you?" he asks.

Stone-throwers do not solicit the stories of women who choose to have abortions unless those women say they have regrets. Women who have faced the decision rarely volunteer to speak because there is so much stigma attached and so much danger of being attacked. And so most Americans contemplate abortion in the abstract.

If we are like most Americans, many of us would say we could never have an abortion ourselves, but others have the right to make that choice. I would wager that many of the women who have chosen to have abortions once thought they could never make such a choice.

One's view often changes when abortion becomes no longer abstract, but very real — a dilemma of a real woman's life within a real-life situation.

I would like to share with you the stories of two women I know. Let us try to see their lives through their eyes. If you were faced with their pregnancies, what do you think you would do? How would you choose? What beliefs, what values, what circumstances would influence you? Where would you go for guidance and advice?

A young girl lived on welfare with her mother and her mother's boyfriend, an ex-convict. The mother and daughter, while they loved each other, had a stormy relationship. The mother had a history of emotional instability and depended on the daughter for emotional support. The daughter was always rebelling and trying to stay away from home. Nevertheless, the protective mother kept tight reins on her little girl.

One day, not long after her fourteenth birthday, the daughter was hit by a car and rushed to a hospital. While examining her injuries, the doctors discovered that she was five months pregnant. The mother greeted the news with horror and disbelief. How could it have happened? Then she was angry. Why had her daughter not told her before, when there was still time to have an abortion?

Unbeknownst to the mother, the mother's boyfriend had been forcing her daughter to have sex with him for over a year. He had silenced the girl by threatening to have her mother committed to a mental institution. Like most young and bewildered teens, the girl had denied to herself the fact that she was pregnant.

She did not have an abortion because of the late stage of her pregnancy. But as I accompanied this humiliated girl and her mother to childbirth classes, as I coached her through thirty-six hours of agonizing and terrifying childbirth, as I counseled her about keeping the baby-to-come or surrendering it for adoption, as I watched her and her mother look at the child through the nursery glass for the first and last time, there was no question in my mind which option I would have preferred for her if there had been time for a choice. *Nothing* could justify the emotional and psychological scars that this entire experience had left on them...not even that new human life.

Another story, less dramatic, is perhaps less clear-cut. It is one woman's story and also many women's story. It is the unsensational, typical dilemma that many single pregnant women face.

A nineteen-year-old college student found herself six weeks pregnant by a young man with whom she had been going for a year. She was stunned because she had always been responsible about using birth control. But she had not been knowledgeable enough or mature enough to obtain the most effective method from a doctor. She joined the dreaded statistics of women victimized by contraceptive failure.

She and the young man expected that they would one day get married. Perhaps this pregnancy meant that the time was right? But she had doubts. She had not known this man long enough. She did know that she was too young. Her parents' divorce taught her never to run into marriage.

She knew that her rigid Irish Catholic family would be mortified by either a "shot-gun wedding" or an illegitimate child. She would irreparably tarnish the family name. She and her child would be disowned. They would be verbally stoned. She could bear the chastisement and ostracism, but was it right for her to cause her family and a future child so much pain? She loved them too much to make them pay for her mistake.

She and her boyfriend met with the Protestant college chaplain. He was compassionate and understanding of their complex situation. Adoption was not an option, as the couple could get married and keep the baby. But was a teenage marriage and premature motherhood the most responsible course?

The young woman felt abortion was a sin because it did not conform to God's original plan. In the perfect world God had planned, every child would be wanted and every child would be a blessing. But the world had not been perfect since humanity's fall. Things do not always go according to God's plan — and this pregnancy was *not* a part of God's plan.

This pregnancy was a result of irresponsible actions: not taking the God-given power of reproduction in a serious and answerable manner. The couple never talked about nor did they assume responsibility for the possibility of pregnancy. They sinned by not seeking the best contraception or by not postponing intercourse until they were prepared to be parents. Further, the young woman did not want to sin again by inflicting pain and shame on her family or on a future child.

Freely she searched her conscience and the word of God. Repenting of her sins, she felt God listened with compassion. She drew closer to God as she weighed her options. The Most Holy knew her heart, and she let God alone be her judge. In the end, she knew that abortion was a moral choice she had to make. She made her decision responsibly and boldly; she had an abortion at seven and a half weeks. The embryo within her was less than one inch in length.

Today, her circumstances are very different. She and her husband (a different man) face infertility. She has achieved maturity and enjoys stability and solid support in her life. In these circumstances she would make a different choice: she would not have an abortion.

Nor would she, on the other hand, change the decision she made at age nineteen. She has never regretted that decision. Nor has she ever longed for that embryo to have become a child.

In each of these stories, I wonder, where did you stand? What would you have done? What would you choose to do? What would you have advised? How would you attempt to enter into the lives and experiences of these women?

Making ethical choices — to have or to forego an abortion — is very difficult and complicated. Having the power to face God directly, having the freedom to form our own conscience, having the legal liberty to act on whatever choice we make sometimes feels more like a burden than a blessing. Faced with such dilemmas, how much we long for the philosophers of easy answers! But the easy answer is not always the wise answer or the responsible route to take.

In search of wisdom, Christians are called first to search the Scriptures for guidance in ethical matters. But we must do so carefully and honestly. We can be tempted to search for easy answers, for simple texts to support our preconceived opinions. We may forget that some passages meant something different in the time and place for which they were written than they seem to mean today. We may forget that the writers drew not only upon divine wisdom, but also upon the more limited wisdom of their own experience.

We may forget that women in ancient times were not allowed to write Scripture. Their stories were rarely heard, so their experiences were often obliterated. So it is not surprising that abortion was of little concern to the Bible's writers. After all, they weren't women facing unwanted pregnancies. And abortion, while it occurred, was not prevalent among ancient Jewish and Christian women, even though it was widely practiced by pagans.

The most significant biblical reference to abortion is to abortion by accident. Exodus 21:22–25 specifies that a man who accidentally hits a pregnant woman and kills her must pay with his life. In contrast, he is required to pay a mere fine to her husband if she lives, even though the fetus dies. Clearly, the life of the fetus was not of the same value as the life of the woman. This position is maintained in Jewish law until this day.

The New Testament contains no clear mention of abortion. One biblical scholar has interpreted certain words in Galatians and in Revelation as possibly referring to abortifacients — abortion-inducing poisons or drugs. The use of such drugs, which were supplied by sorcerers or magicians, was prohibited for early Christians.

The Bible contains many poetic references and instructions regarding the value of life and the blessings of children. In ancient Jewish and Christian societies offspring were needed to increase the community's strength. So God said, "Be fruitful and multiply." Scripture called children a blessing.

Anti-abortionists claim these passages are equally applicable today and they condemn abortion by inference. Because anti-abortionists consider only the value of fetal life and not the value of the woman's life, or of her existing family's life, they charge that abortion always devalues life.

But times have changed. With today's world crises of overpopulation and fractured family structures, of sexual abuse and rape, could a loving God really will that every fertilized egg should be born?

In examining the morality of abortion, an appeal to Scripture alone is insufficient. We may look also for insight from the early Christians. We find that an early second-century "manual of church life and order," called the *Didache*, prohibited abortion. The *Didache* said, "Thou shalt not murder a child by abortion/destruction."

By the fourth century, however, more church writings were making a distinction between the abortion of an unformed fetus and a formed fetus. Greek philosophy had gained sway. The Greeks believed that a fully physically formed fetus was a person before birth. Christians then came to believe that when a fetus became fully formed, God gave it a soul — a mark of personhood. So, the Church Fathers ruled that abortion after formation, *after ensoulment*, was the killing of a person, and a more severe sin than abortion before formation and ensoulment.

To regulate abortion, the Church Fathers pinpointed the moment of ensoulment. They said that male fetuses were fully formed and given souls at forty days from conception; females at eighty days from conception. As a result of this curious distinction, aborting a female fetus was not as bad as aborting a male!

While the timing of abortion and the sex of the fetus changed the severity of the sin, abortion was never condoned by the early church. Abortion at any time was condemned, not because it was an act of murder, but because it was always assumed to be a cover-up for a woman's act of sexual immorality — for which she should be willing to bear the shame and punishment! She must be willing to bear her child and wear her "scarlet letter"!

Did the Church Fathers ever ask the early Christian women their opinions? Did anyone ever listen to their stories? Undoubtedly not. Women were told to keep silent.

Debate continues over the moment of ensoulment and the motivations for abortion. The curious historical church rulings on the issue illustrate why Baptists are wary of church leaders who claim infallibility, why Baptists are skeptical of centuries of man-made religious tradition, and why Baptists place more credence in the Bible.

Today the Roman Catholic hierarchy asserts that abortion is murder at any time in pregnancy, for any reason, for they now teach that God infuses a new soul at the moment of union between sperm and egg. In contrast some Baptist theologians and others have argued that the moment of ensoulment cannot be proven, but that the Bible implies ensoulment at the moment of birth. They cite Genesis 2:7: "And the Lord God formed man out of the dust of the ground and breathed into him a living soul." This ongoing disagreement shows why Baptists should oppose any one particular religious position on abortion being imposed as civil law.

We have examined Scripture and church tradition and find no easy answers to the morality of abortion. We hear few or no women's voices.

But we have additional resources to consult that can shed light — albeit tinted light — on what little we have gleaned on this subject from Scripture and church pronouncements. We can consult the voice of reason and heed the voice of experience.

Our ability to reason allows us to look beyond the minutia of religious laws to seek the central values with which to form our consciences — values like love and forgiveness, mercy and responsibility. Through reason, we may recognize that following an ancient law to the letter in a particular modern circumstance may contradict Jesus' message of freedom and toleration. Through reason, we may discern that God has not granted us crystal-clear insight — that we do not have all the answers — and that we are in no position to throw stones.

We can look to the lessons that life experience teaches us. The Hebrew Scriptures teach that divine wisdom is imparted through human experience as well as through Scripture. So we can look at reality, at the circumstances of our own lives and of persons with lives very different from our own. When we hear their stories we will be less likely to throw stones.

When we look to reason and experience, we can recognize that each person's reality and perception of reality are not exactly the same as our own. Our different realities and worldviews, as much as our religious beliefs, shape our positions on abortion. And so we cannot impose our position on another woman — no matter how strong our convictions. Nor should we insist that we would impose our present positions on ourselves if our circumstances become different.

Still, the ambiguities and complexity of the abortion dilemma do not allow us to be silent or inactive on the issue. We must speak with the voice of faith and reason, love and mercy. We must find the courage to tell our stories.

Out of compassion we should support women financially and lovingly as they face unwanted pregnancies — whether they choose to bring their pregnancies to term *or* to obtain abortions. We must enable them to be sensitively counseled by church, family, and clinic. We must free them to make their own moral decisions before their own God, without interference from civil laws. We must protect them from persecution for their actions and beliefs.

The fourteen-year-old girl who bore her abuser's child in terror and pain, as well as the nineteen-year-old woman who prayerfully chose to spare her family shame, must be treated with the same respect and dignity.

No one — no, not one — has the right to throw stones!

AUTOBIOGRAPHICAL STATEMENT

I worked for Planned Parenthood for four years. As a political organizer and liaison to forty other pro-choice organizations, I came to know hundreds of women who had had abortions — women with no regrets who fought with determination to preserve abortion as a legal moral choice for others. I heard many stories about abortions chosen for countless reasons by women of diverse faiths. At Planned Parenthood and as a board member of a coalition to lobby for women's legislation, I became convinced that preserving women's right to choose abortion or childbearing was inextricable from other efforts to guarantee their empowerment and well-being.

In my work to promote access to family planning and abortion services, I was confronted with the real-life casualties of insensitive church decrees on birth control and abortion. At the same time, I began to examine my faith systematically. Raised a Roman Catholic, I converted and joined an American Baptist church. For Baptists, the Bible, and not church traditions or hierarchies, is the ultimate authority for matters of faith and ethics. Besides Baptist theology, I was attracted to the American Baptist churches because of their non-hierarchical and decentralized structure, their affirmation of women, their defense of freedom of conscience, and their pro-choice policy statement.

To explore the intersection of feminist theory and faith, I attended the Women's Theological Center in Boston for one year. I worked with and heard the stories of women who had been battered and sexually abused. I now attend Andover Newton Theological School in Massachusetts and am working for a master of divinity degree.

BACKGROUND INFORMATION

Since women began to gain access to legal abortions in the United States (as early as 1967 in some states), abortion has been the subject of incendiary debate. Certain religious groups have fanned the flames, condemning abortion for any reason as an intolerable sin against God. The fire of protest intensified in the 1980s as the anti-choice National Conference of Catholic Bishops gained political sophistication, as fundamentalist and conservative evangelical churches amassed more members, and as right-wing Christian lobbying groups entered into a courtship with the White House.

All the while, the vast majority of religious bodies in the United States have continued to support the legality of abortion or to remain officially silent on the issue. The Religious Coalition for Abortion Rights counts thirty religious and ethical organizations in its membership.

Despite vehement anti-choice crusades, most religiously identified Americans support the *legality* of abortion in at least some circumstances, with little difference between Catholics and Protestants. In 1982 during the height of anti-abortion activity in Congress, 74 percent of Catholics agreed that the abortion decision should be left entirely to a woman and her doctor;[1] in 1977, 76 percent of all Protestants agreed.[2] Two 1985 polls disclosed that 55–60 percent of Catholics believe "that the legality of abortion should depend on the circumstances."[3] When it comes to federal *funding* of abortions for poor women, an equal percentage of Catholics and of Protestants, 54 percent, said they were opposed to a funding ban in 1982.[4]

Greater variation in opinion occurs regarding the *morality* of abortion in specific circumstances. In 1982 between 83 percent and 86 percent of Catholics endorsed abortion in cases of rape and health endangerment to the woman, compared to 89 percent and 93 percent of Protestants; in contrast, only 48 percent of Catholics as well as Protestants viewed poverty as a justifiable case, and only 39 percent of Catholics and 37 percent of Protestants sanctioned abortion for any reason.[5]

These ranges of religious opinion reflect the moral complexity of the abortion decision and the necessity of discussing it not in abstract, absolutist terms, but in concrete, situational language.

The Roman Catholic Church and fundamentalist and conservative evangelical Protestant churches speak in the abstract. They condemn abortion based on absolute moral laws. The Roman Catholic hierarchy claims to derive these unchanging laws from God's revelation in nature, discerned through reason, and recorded in the church's two-thousand-year tradition. Rejecting the authority of much of church tradition, conservative Protestants cite Scripture as the source of divine laws.

Mainstream, liberal Protestants tend to be less bound by absolute ethical laws. They examine the historical context in which Scripture and tradition were formed to see if ancient teachings are appropriate to address complex, present-day circumstances. They are apt to be more concerned with following the spirit rather than the letter of the law. They may consider the *consequences* of imposing a moral law to establish its merit in a particular case.

As feminist historian and Roman Catholic theologian Elisabeth Schüssler Fiorenza has argued, Scripture and church tradition must be examined with a "hermeneutics of suspicion."[6] The pronouncements of the church Fathers throughout the history of the church become less credible when one discovers that these leaders viewed women as more physical, more carnal, and more sinful than men. Women were described in ancient church writings as inherently immoral and the downfall of the other sex. These perspectives were not challenged because women were increasingly banned from the emerging church power structure; their perspectives and life stories were rarely heard.

A theology of abortion must consciously reject as sinful the words of Scripture and the tradition that make women invisible, or that brand them as weaker and more sinful beings than men. It must reject as paternalistic and oppressive two thousand years of church decrees on sexuality and abortion that never consulted women, yet sought to define and control them.

Because the mention of abortion in Scripture is scant and the message of tradition is suspect, the morality of abortion cannot be honestly evaluated apart from reason and contemporary human experience.[7] One must consider the reality of women's lives.

The lives of real women in the church show a degree of acceptance of the abortion choice. Only nine years after the nationwide legalization of abortion, a 1982 study revealed that 8 percent of Catholic women and 7 percent of Protestant women had had abortions.[8] Today those percentages will be much higher, since over 1.5 million abortions continue to be performed in the U.S. each year. We know that Catholic women continue to be more likely to obtain abortions than Protestant women as a whole, although fundamentalist Protestants are the least likely of any religious group to have abortions.

NOTES

1. From a 1982 Associated Press/NBC poll cited in "Who Should Be Involved in the Abortion Decision?" *Public Affairs Speakers Manual* (Cambridge, Mass.: Planned Parenthood League of Massachusetts, 1985).

2. From a 1977 New York Times/CBS poll cited in *Public Affairs Speakers Manual*.

3. From a January 1985 Gallup poll and a September 1985 Harris poll as cited in *A Church Divided: Catholics' Attitudes about Family Planning, Abor-*

tion and Teenage Sexuality (Washington, D.C.: Catholics for a Free Choice, 1986), p. 13.

4. From a September 1982 Gallup poll cited in *A Church Divided*, p. 13.

5. From a 1982 poll conducted by the National Opinion Research Center, University of Chicago, cited in *Public Affairs Speakers Manual*.

6. Elisabeth Schüssler Fiorenza, *In Memory of Her: A Feminist Theological Reconstruction of Christian Origins* (New York: Crossroad, 1985).

7. I am indebted to two unpublished papers for asserting that a theology of abortion is shaped by the degree of authority one invests in either Scripture, tradition, reason, or experience: Johanne Dame-Brusie, "Some Considerations About the Abortion Issue," Andover Newton Theological School (A.N.T.S.), May 1988, and Cindy Maybeck, "The Political Ethics of Abortion in the American Baptist Churches," A.N.T.S., November 1986.

8. From a study published in *Family Planning Perspectives*, March/April 1982, p. 61, and cited in "Percentage of Women Who Report Ever Having Had an Induced Abortion, by Various Characteristics," *Public Affairs Speakers Manual*.

BIBLIOGRAPHY

A Church Divided: Catholics' Attitudes about Family Planning, Abortion and Teenage Sexuality. Washington, D.C.: Catholics for a Free Choice, 1986. Contains extensive public opinion data showing lay Catholics' dissent from the official positions of the Roman Catholic Church on sexuality-related issues.

Gilligan, Carol. *In a Different Voice: Psychological Theory and Women's Development*. Cambridge, Mass.: Harvard University Press, 1982. Landmark psychological studies revealing differences in male and female moral decision-making processes. Females consider personal relationships, responsibilities, and circumstances more than absolute norms. Includes many interviews of women who chose abortion.

Gorman, Michael J. *Abortion and the Early Church: Christian, Jewish and Pagan Attitudes in the Greco-Roman World*. New York: Paulist Press, 1982. A short, well-researched anti-choice account of early church tradition on abortion.

Harrison, Beverly Wildung. *Our Right to Choose: Toward a New Ethic of Abortion*. Boston: Beacon Press, 1983. Groundbreaking scholarly analysis of Christian abortion theology and proposal of a pro-choice, feminist theology of abortion.

Hurst, Jane. *The History of Abortion in the Catholic Church: The Untold Story*. Washington, D.C.: Catholics for a Free Choice, 1983. From a pro-choice perspective, a concise interpretation of the inconsistencies and loopholes in the Roman Catholic tradition on abortion.

Simmons, Dr. Paul D. *A Theological Response to Fundamentalism on the Abortion Issue*. Washington, D.C.: Religious Coalition for Abortion Rights, 1985. A concise analysis of fundamentalism and civil religion and a biblical, pro-choice discussion of providence and personhood by a Southern Baptist.

RESOURCES

Catholics for a Free Choice
2008 Seventeenth Street, N.W.
Washington, DC 20009
(202) 638-1706

National voice of pro-choice Catholics. Publishes tracts and research written by scholars for the general public on Roman Catholic theology and issues of abortion, sexuality and the relationship of church and state. Publishes a bi-monthly journal *Conscience* with opinions and research by dissenting pro-choice and feminist Roman Catholics.

Planned Parenthood Federation of America, Inc.
810 Seventh Avenue
New York, NY 10019
(212) 541-7800

This national office, as well as many local affiliate offices, monitors political developments and provides extensive data regarding national and international abortions, family planning, and sexuality. Various journals sometimes contain articles on religion and abortion. Affiliate clinics provide sensitive, nondirective counseling and services.

Religious Coalition for Abortion Rights (RCAR) and RCAR Educational Fund, Inc.
100 Maryland Avenue, NE Washington, DC 20002
(202) 543-7032

Organization of thirty religious and ethical groups supporting legal abortion. Publishes quarterly newsletter. Produces issue pamphlets and tracts on abortion from Protestant and Jewish pro-choice perspectives. Organizes membership around abortion-related legislation. Has state chapters of clergy and laity.

13

Overcoming the Fear of Love

Mary E. Hunt

SERMON

Everybody loves a party. Holidays provide a convenient excuse for getting together with loved ones. Birthday parties, even as we grow in years, are a great way to celebrate the lives of people we love. Election watching, the Super Bowl, Halloween, New Year's Eve, Sisterfire, Mardi Gras all offer opportunities to gather the clan and enjoy food and drink in a festive spirit.

Everybody wants a clan with whom to gather on these occasions. Even the most introverted among us want to know that we bumble along in this life with others. That is where love comes in, to give us a way to stretch beyond our own finite bodies and spirits to others who are stretching back. Love is more than emotional aerobics. It is the fundamental human emotion that persists and prevails when and where we least expect it.

Nobody likes to go to a party not knowing anyone. There is that awkward moment at the door when greeting the hostess or host with a mumbled introduction, when the guest wishes that she or he had stayed home. There is that beeline for the coatroom and quick glance around to find someone, anyone at all, who looks the least bit familiar. Sometimes there is a fast retreat to the libations in order to cushion the uneasiness a bit. Or, there may even be an early exit because everyone else seems to be having such a good time with people they know.

In most hospitable groups one does not stay a stranger very long. Common humanity, if only conversation about the weather, dictates

---

This sermon has not been preached, in part because Roman Catholic women are not officially permitted to preach at masses. It would be well received by a Dignity, Conference for Catholic Lesbians, or Metropolitan Community Church group. However, it needs to be preached at mainline denominational gatherings so that the content can make a difference in future church policies.

Note that it is a homily in format — short, addressed to the group gathered, and tied to the Eucharist about to be celebrated. It could be adapted to a Protestant setting with the addition of relevant biblical texts. Here I use women's lives as text.

that we find things to talk about, interests and experiences to share. Before we know it there is a common friend, or perhaps we work in the same place, or we admire the same sports heroine. Few people leave parties feeling lonely. Many people leave with new-found friends and an invitation to another social event. Such is human community because love is at work.

Churches, at their best, put on a good party every week. Yet lesbian/gay people are made to feel unwelcome all the time. No one greets us at the door affirming who we are. We are told in sermons and church teachings that our way of loving, of stretching to build human community, is sinful, unhealthy, unnatural, anything but holy. We are all but disinvited from the party. Surely we ought not approach the table expecting that we too shall partake of the hostess or host's freshest bread and best wine because, we are told in a thousand ways, we are uninvited guests who have crashed the party to the discomfort and embarrassment of the invited guests.

What causes such shameful lack of hospitality? My sense is that people who reject lesbian/gay people do so because they fear love. This may seem a reductionistic argument, one that leaves aside the academic nuances of scriptural exegesis and dogmatic deciphering. But having done all of that for some years I have come up intellectually empty-handed on the question. I can only conclude that it is an irrational fear.

There is to my mind no persuasive theological or scriptural prohibition on same-sex love that squares with contemporary scientific findings that some of us are oriented homosexually and others heterosexually. Rather than rehearse the old arguments that seem to get us nowhere, I want to explore why some people fear love and what faith communities can do about it.

Love comes in many packages. Love is one of the few things that never needs a defense. In fact, it is demeaning and degrading, fundamentally disrespectful, to expect that people will defend their love. I never do it even when I realize that people expect me as a lesbian woman to make excuses or find a way to make them feel comfortable with the fact that I love women, especially one wonderful woman with whom I share a welcoming home and a fulfilling life. Such love needs no explanation. "For those who have eyes to see" it is plain as oatmeal. For those who prefer not to see, it is still as plain as oatmeal. Their fear, and not my love, needs attention.

Complex personal factors are at play. Some people do not feel worthy of love; others consider love so limited a commodity that it must only come in one wrapper. But those are issues for my therapist friends to deal with. I do not think that fear of love can be psychologized away. Neither do I think that it is *only* a psychological phenomenon. It has important theological factors as well. Let me name three.

First, people fear love because *their God is a tyrant.* The wrath of a jealous, vengeful God stays with them from childhood. As children they were taught that things ought to be a certain way in love and family, and that this omnipotent, omniscient, omnipresent God makes it so. Any deviation is sin and will result in punishment.

The love of a merciful, tender, maternal God/ess pales by comparison in a culture in which power is prized. The image of a macho God-father, with his amazing Son and their sidekick Holy Spirit has so dominated the Christian consciousness since the Middle Ages that we have had few other images. Without a change in the concept of God I am convinced that there is little hope for overcoming heterosexism/homophobia.

Luckily in our time the "feminization" of theology has given us some new options. It will take several generations to wear down that old image of the Ruler, Lord, King who dictates how love will be and family will form. Many fear that any tinkering with God will, à la the Wizard of Oz, make the whole Christian myth fall apart. Of course people fear "inappropriate" love in this setting. The stakes are simply too high. Not only will they lose what they thought was "the way things are," but they will also lose their God.

I suggest that we start by holding our God lightly, letting her go and evolve rather than guarding a tight-fisted faith. This way we can be more flexible in our worldview, shifting as we must with new knowledge and insight. Lesbian/gay love understood as completely normal and natural for many of us is new data that requires revising some deeply held beliefs. If our God/ess is not big, elastic, and embracing enough to make the change then I wonder what we mean by the divine.

Second, people fear love because *they hate themselves.* Self-love, especially for women, is a rare and fleeting phenomenon. Sin, guilt, and death have so overshadowed love, celebration, and solidarity that there seem to be two distinct strands of the Christian tradition. The predominant one has led to female self-hatred since women are identified with the body and the body with base, sinful instincts; men are seen as rational, logical, and goal directed. They are above the flesh. The subordinate strand teaches the equality of women and men, loving our neighbors, ourselves, the earth, and our God/ess as one. Unfortunately the predominant one obscures it and we all lose.

Instead of understanding human frailty as the impetus for human community, i.e., what I am individually is enhanced by what all of us are collectively, we are taught to be "all things to all people" as mothers and wives. This impossible job description leads us to hate our "inadequate" selves. Something is wrong with this picture. We have been set up to fail. It is logical to fear loving ourselves when we are not able to measure up to the demands of society. But this perverse logic is what needs to be eradicated. Then we can see ourselves as whole persons who enter into relationships and webs of connection out of strength, not out of weakness. We are bodies and spirits, feelings and thoughts.

I suggest that we begin to revise our anthropology, our way of naming and claiming what we consider to be the essence of humanity. We will find no pure type but instead diversity, particularity, complexity as we appreciate humanity anew. Only then will lesbian/gay love be seen for what it is: a way, among many ways, in which all people seek the most basic companionship that life offers. Then we can delight in ourselves, all of us.

Third, people fear love because *it is awesome to imagine how much there really is*. The power of love when it is unleashed in all of its frenzy is something to behold. Who does not think twice when parents gaze upon their child for the first time, when couples profess their love publicly, when we see long, well-tended love in friends who are celebrating a holiday in a happy home. This is love in its most ordinary dress.

Our joyful tears are tinged with the awesome power of what love means. We cannot live at that level of attention or consciousness about love all the time. But just as surely we cannot live without it either. The paradox induces fear. What would it be like if the power were set free?

I suggest that we revise not only our concept of God/ess and our anthropology, but also our doctrine of salvation. It is time to admit that the Christian promise of eternal life is meant for everyone, not just for a chosen few. Jesus died once for the sins of the world; it is not necessary to repeat his performance. It is time to flesh out the notion of Eucharist so that it really means bringing together a community to give thanks and praise for the fact of new life after death.

Without some deep affirmation of this basic Christian notion of the sacramentality of the whole of creation there is no way to admit newness, diversity, fresh revelation. And without admitting new revelation there is no chance of Christian communities ever coming to an affirmation of same-sex love since it has only come in my generation as a result of the women's movements and the gay/lesbian pride movements. With such an affirmation there is every hope that we might move together toward a real communion.

These three factors, a new concept of the divine, a new anthropology, and a new grasp on salvation are at play when same-sex love is at hand. These concepts may seem lofty or extraneous, but the irrational fear of the "gentle, angry people" who will no longer tolerate discrimination because of whom we love cannot be explained otherwise. When I think of my friends — a young woman with a deep commitment to empowering women, a couple made up of a dedicated pediatrician and a tireless fundraiser for justice work, an elegant elder churchwoman, a store owner, a dozen teachers — it is inconceivable that their passionate love should be the cause of fear. The God/ess of right relation smiles on lesbian women as on all. We feel her warmth and approval when we cuddle and caress, when we enjoy sexual pleasure and relax in the arms of someone who cares. What is to fear?

The temptation is to say there is nothing to fear from women, but gay men give lesbian women a bad name. This is strategically unacceptable. In a sexist society no distinction is made between gay men and lesbian women when homosexuality is condemned. In a way it is easier to get society to accept lesbian women. There is none of the cruising in the parks, transmission of AIDS, or flamboyant behavior that the media has taught us characterize gay men. A well kept secret is that most gay men do not engage in these activities, but that is a topic for another sermon. The point is that I will not buy respectability on the backs of my brothers who are particularly hard hit by AIDS. I prefer to deflect the fallout of hatred with a shield of solidarity.

Fear is overcome most effectively by facing what produces it. In our communities it is the fear of a loving God/ess, a fear of expanding the definition of what it means to be human, and a fear of allowing for the salvation of all that is hamstringing human community. If I had a magic cure, I would offer it around like a taste of fine wine. It would be a way of saying drink from the same cup and be whole.

Instead, I suggest that we gather around the table as a first step. Let us imagine ourselves at a party. Let us eat and drink to enjoy and fortify ourselves. Then we can go home confident that we have taken a step toward overcoming the fear of love.

AUTOBIOGRAPHICAL STATEMENT

I am a Catholic feminist theologian, co-founder and co-director of the Women's Alliance for Theology, Ethics and Ritual (WATER, Silver Spring, Maryland). WATER is a grassroots education center that develops programs, projects, and publications on women's issues in religion. Our work necessarily involves us in pastoral ministry since feminist resources are few and far between, and feminists experience loss, doubt, illness, and death just like everyone else.

I preach occasionally at a local Presbyterian church and sometimes at masses sponsored by Dignity chapters throughout the country. My own local church, SAS, or Sisters Against Sexism, a women-church base community, does not favor sermons. Instead, we rely on discussion by the whole group, or sometimes one-to-one or small group discussions, formats that encourage participation and shared leadership. Sermons like this one, however, need to be preached occasionally if ministerial leadership is to be used to best advantage for social change.

I grew up in the Catholic tradition, what sociologists call a "cradle Catholic." I did not use the word "lesbian" to describe myself until I was twenty-three and had had some sexual experiences with women. But looking back at my earlier relational patterns and taking account of the fifteen years since, I can say that mine is a consistent pattern of good male friends and outstanding, erotic, and fulfilling friendships with women. I embrace the word "lesbian" as a deliberate way to affirm my love for women in a culture that rejects it.

Other lesbian women have different histories, of course. Many entered religious orders; some married and had children. Others lived alone or with few friends. But my particular history stands me in good stead as I comment on the ordinary, delightful, relatively uncomplicated love I know. After all, if I did not love women in the fullness of commitment, romance, and sex, I might not love at all. Is any love so fearsome that it makes this a desirable alternative for anyone?

Why anyone would fear women's love for one another is beyond me except that the power of love is awesome. The extent to which we change our lives because of one another, the degree to which we are modified in our dress, behavior, jobs, and politics because of close friends never ceases to amaze. But only a culture that is protecting male privilege and the hegemony of heterosexuality will decry these very human events when they take place between women. Only a society and a church that is invested in a very limited way of loving would scorn love in any form.

By contrast, those who notice the lack of love in our militaristic society herald love wherever they find it. Sister Theresa Kane, R.S.M., made this clear when she spoke of her own uncertainty about same-sex love and how she came to look at it more closely and kindly. She spoke of attending a conference sponsored by New Ways Ministry, a Catholic group that works with lesbian/gay people, their families and friends. She said that she did not know much about homosexuality going into the conference, but, she "saw love there" between women and between men. "As a Christian I had to take notice," she witnessed. No wonder Catholic women are not ordained and in leadership in the church. Imagine what the Theresa Kanes of this world would do!

I have the privilege of belonging to the Conference for Catholic

Lesbians, a network of women who seek the healthy integration of our Catholic and lesbian identities. Members meet in local groups and periodic national gatherings where the talent and generosity of the members continue to astonish me.

My professional theological interests include feminist ethics and public policy, especially reproductive choice. I am deeply involved in the encouragement of global feminist theology, especially focused in Argentina and Uruguay through WATER's "Women Crossing Worlds" project. I know dozens of Catholic lesbian women in Latin America. I am moved by their courageous attempts to hold together lesbian pride and spiritual search under the duress of dictatorship, economic hardship, and a repressive church. This sermon honors them.

BACKGROUND INFORMATION

Sermons on love are everyday fare in most churches and synagogues. Examples are chosen from Scripture and life experiences to illustrate the great commandments to love God/ess and our neighbors as ourselves. Preachers tell how mothers love their children, how fathers sacrifice their only sons to save the world, how siblings give kidneys to keep each other alive, how perfect strangers act heroically. These are all aimed at making love visible so that we may be edified into doing the same.

Never have I heard a preacher cite the altogether ordinary love of one woman for another. Yet this is day-to-day life for millions of lesbian women, just as a man loving a man is standard fare for gay men. After years of dealing with homophobia and heterosexism as a theological professional and as a lesbian woman, I am left to conclude that some irrational reason is all that can account for this obvious lacuna. Fear is my best guess for why such simple yet apparently threatening examples are systematically passed over.

Love is the legacy of religious traditions. It is the reason for adhering to the otherwise foolish notions of self-giving, concern for others, and a sense that life everlasting will be enjoyable for all. Love is alleged to make all things new, at least until same-sex ways of loving are broached. Then, as if by magic, the curtain falls and love that is love is denied, demeaned, destroyed by religiously sanctioned ideology.

The miracle is that any lesbian/gay people continue to count ourselves among traditions like Christianity. My own brand of it, Catholicism, has been outstandingly virulent in its condemnation of homosexuality. Theological power structures fall into self-contradiction in the face of same-sex love. Yet we stubbornly refuse to let them off the hook so easily by leaving their folds. We know their fear of love, and we graciously offer them a way beyond it. Perhaps because we too have feared loving due to the high price it exacts in a patriarchal, heterosexist culture, we can spot the symptoms. Our love for our enemies is an act of solidarity.

No one knows how many lesbian women there are in the United States. I have often joked that there really are only two kinds of women, lesbian women and pre-lesbian women. I want to make the point that all women have a bit of women-loving in us. Or if we do not, we need to develop it. As Sweet Honey in the Rock sings, "Let every woman who ever loved a woman stand up and shout out her name. Mother, daughter, sister, lover."[1]

This is the point of Adrienne Rich's now classic essay, "Compulsory Heterosexuality and Lesbian Existence."[2] Rich argues that there is a continuum on which all women find ourselves. Critics have questioned the usefulness of Rich's analysis, i.e., if all women are lesbian then why all this fuss? But for present purposes I assume that lesbian women are those who find ourselves clustered toward one end of that continuum. We are women whose primary affective, sexual, and political partners are women. Our sisters are those whose primary focus, while it includes women, is more directed toward men. In fact, most women find very little difference between and among lesbian, bisexual, and heterosexual women. Lesbian women find more affinity with bisexual and heterosexual women than with most gay men. Women, after all, are women.

A conservative guess is that there are fifteen million lesbian women in the United States. But the fact is that no one has hard data. This is based on the long accepted, but just as long debated, statistic that 10 percent of the population is lesbian/gay. Numbers are not the important issue here. The point is that "normal" life has many manifestations. Same-sex love is not just different from or beyond the "normal." It is part of the diversity of creation, something to be taken seriously but not dissected, something to be celebrated but not put on display.

Same-sex love, for those of us who are oriented in this way, is as ordinary as a well-worn bathrobe and a cup of herb tea. What is extraordinary is the shock, scorn, and discrimination that is visited upon us by people who have not yet internalized the fact that same-sex love is just as healthy, good, natural, and holy as other-sex love. What is remarkable is the dissonance that is created, especially for young people, who find themselves punished for doing what they were taught was good, namely, for loving, when they love people most similar to themselves.

No one knows why some people are homosexually and other people heterosexually oriented. Nor does anyone have any idea what causes anyone to be straight or lesbian/gay. The best evidence that we have, and I underscore that it is good scientific data, is that sexual orientation is fixed either *in utero* or shortly after birth. No parent can take credit or blame for what is seemingly in the stars.

What we do know is that homophobia/heterosexism are pre-existing social, economic, religious, and political conditions into which all of us are born. While no one causes sexual orientation, there are powerful forces led by powerful people in powerful places like churches, schools, the media, and families that assure that the message of compulsory heterosexuality is learned early and well. They make sure that same-sex love is condemned out of hand regardless of its quality. Still, nature rules and millions of lesbian/gay people make our way into the mainstream of U.S. life. In fact, some of us are leaders in intellectual, religious, governmental, artistic, scientific, and athletic arenas. Many of us are very public about our sexual orientation. Others are quite content to live and love without any public reference to it.

There is some reliable social scientific data on lesbian couples, but samples are small and research is only beginning to be a priority. What we know is that there are "many ways a woman can be" (as Theresa Trull sings). Heterogeneity is the norm. Lesbian women live alone, in couples, and in groups. We come from every race, class, ethnic background, and religious tradition.

The only thing we have in common, and even that varies from person to person, from group to group, is that we suffer external and internal repression at the hands of a patriarchal, heterosexist society. Paradoxically, we are censured for loving even in those places such as churches where love is valued above everything. Is it any wonder that we ask questions about most things that others take for granted? No wonder some fear our love. Loving as we do is a challenge to how we were told things are to be. If society is mistaken about the strictures placed on sexual orientation, maybe other errors abound, like consumerism, class privilege, racism, and abuse of the environment. Just maybe....

NOTES

1. Bernice Johnson Reagon, "Every Woman," sung by Sweet Honey in the Rock.

2. Adrienne Rich, "Compulsory Heterosexuality and Lesbian Existence," *Signs: A Journal of Women in Culture and Society* 5, no. 4 (Summer 1980): 631–60.

BIBLIOGRAPHY

I suggest a visit to the local women's bookstore. March boldly to the section marked "lesbian" and peruse the literature. You will find books on health care, legal rights, having children, even self-help sex manuals like heterosexuals have. Be sure to note your feelings, especially if you are a straight woman. Your boss, your mother, your superior, your district superintendent may find out. Then again, she may be on the other side of the bookcase.

Among the best resources on the topic of lesbian women and religion are:

Beck, Evelyn Torton, ed. *Nice Jewish Girls: A Lesbian Anthology.* Trumansburg, N.Y.: Crossing Press, 1982.

Heyward, Carter. *Our Passion for Justice: Images of Power, Sexuality and Liberation.* New York: Pilgrim Press, 1984.

Hunt, Mary. *Fierce Tenderness: A Feminist Theology of Friendship.* New York: Crossroad, 1990.

Hunt, Mary, and Carter Heyward. "Roundtable: Lesbianism and Feminist Theology," *Journal of Feminist Studies in Religion* 2, no. 2 (Fall 1986).

Nugent, Robert. *A Challenge to Love: Gay and Lesbian Catholics in the Church.* New York: Crossroad, 1987 (see especially Mary E. Hunt, "Lovingly Lesbian," pp. 135–55).

Open Hands: Journal of Reconciling Congregation Program, published by Affirmation: United Methodists for Lesbian/Gay Concerns, Inc., P.O. Box 23636, Washington, DC 20026.

Zanotti, Barbara. *A Faith of One's Own.* Trumansburg, N.Y.: Crossing Press, 1986.

RESOURCES

The best resource materials for dealing with this issue come from talking with lesbian women friends, parishioners, co-workers who are the experts. Our life experiences as lesbians, our insights into loving against the odds, and the day-to-day ordinariness of our lives is a revealing source.

Most mainline Christian denominations have lesbian/gay groups. Check your local lesbian/gay newspaper or the denominational headquarters for the address of a chapter near you. Among the many national groups are:

Conference for Catholic Lesbians
CCL Membership
PO Box 436, Planetarium Station
New York, NY 10024

Consultation on Homosexuality, Social Justice and Roman Catholic Theology
527 Riverside Drive, #3J
New York, NY 10027

Dignity (Catholic)
1500 Massachusetts Avenue, NW, Suite 11
Washington, DC 20005

Integrity (Episcopal)
4550 Connecticut Avenue, NW, #605
Washington, DC 20008

New Ways Ministry
4012 29th Street
Mt. Rainier, MD 20712

United Church Coalition for Lesbian/Gay Concerns
18 North College Street
Athens, OH 45701

14

"Blessed Singleness":
A Journey in Uncharted Waters

Frances Kissling

SERMON

As a young girl growing up in the pre–Vatican II Roman Catholic Church, I was taught that I would be called to one of three states of life. The first — and the highest — was a religious vocation. In it one made a lifetime commitment to devote one's self to the service of God (now we would say God's people) through membership in a religious community. In this state of life, we were informed, through prayer, surrender, and service we would be closest to God.

If we were not blessed with a religious vocation, the next state of life, marriage, also offered opportunities for holiness. For in establishing a Christian marriage and bringing children into the world we would be living examples of the love God had for the church and give witness in the world to Christian hope in the future.

The third state of life, singleness, was simply never discussed. No deep spiritual meaning was ascribed to it. Indeed, in the 1950s singleness was the exception rather than the rule and rarely thought of as a conscious choice. You were single because you could not find someone willing to marry you, or, because of a great tragedy — the sick parent, a terminal illness, dementia, or the great love who died in the war.

By inference, we all assumed that if a religious vocation constituted the highest calling, then singleness was surely the lowest. Being a classic overachiever, I tried first, at the tender age of nineteen, the highest, and "fell" rapidly (after less than a year) and by choice to the lowest state, where I have determinedly remained and expect to remain all the days of my life.

Parts of this sermon, particularly those related to the Roman Catholic Church's view of women and sexuality, were given at the Women-Church Speaks Conference in October 1987. While this was an almost all-female event, I envision this sermon as preached to any congregation. It might be an interesting challenge to preach it on Mother's or Father's Day.

As the years have passed, my interest in a faith community has increased. Many occasions have provided the opportunity to think about single life, its values and problems as well as the institutional church's response to singleness. Today, I want to share with you not only the facts about single life in the United States, but also my reflections on some key value questions singleness raises in a faith community — questions of justice, of autonomy and community, of hope, and of sexual ethics.

These questions when answered in the context of the phenomenal growth of singleness in our society challenge traditional Judeo-Christian concepts of the purpose of life, of relationships, and of family.

Look around you in this church today. Do you see only traditional nuclear families — mom, pop, and the kids? Or do you see single mothers with their children, men and women in their thirties and forties who have never been married, or are living together without being married, the divorced, the widowed, and the separated. Hopefully, they are with us today for they make up one-third of the adult (eighteen-plus) population.

According to March 1987 census data, thirty million adult women and men are ever single (have *never* married), thirteen million are widowed — eleven million of them women, thirteen million divorced, six million live in homes where the spouse is absent, and four million are separated from their spouse. A full 24 percent of children live in a single-parent household, most frequently headed by women at low income levels.

To some extent, we have come to understand the widowed, the divorced, and even the single parents in our community. They have participated in the rituals and practices the community considers normative — often marriage and certainly children. While they may have "failed" in partnership or lost their spouse through death, they share with the community the values and practices historically central to our faith traditions. We also, in many cases, respond to their special needs — food, clothing, and shelter for mothers and children; comfort and companionship for the widowed and divorced.

Yet so little is known of the ever single in our midst. There are no rituals or sacraments to mark passages in our lives. Marriage, baptism, confirmation are "family affairs." From the onset of adulthood (confirmation) till death there is no time we enter the church community to celebrate the meaningful moments of our lives.

Most often we are invisible; we become "real" only in the church's frequent forays into the pelvic zone to repeat the single word known to all single people — "no."

As the number of ever-single people and those who delay marriage increases so do our questions about this "no." We experience the deep burden of the historic revulsion and hatred of the body, of sexuality, and of women inbred in the Christian tradition.

Early Christians saw sexuality as a distraction from man's purpose, which was devotion to the spiritual life. Women and women's bodies were seen as a primary source of temptation. Women were directed not only to cover their bodies, but to make themselves as unattractive as possible: "Good looks are to be feared because of the injury and violence they inflict upon men who look upon you." The body was seen as an encumbrance to the ability to worship God. Note St. Jerome pleading, "Take from me this body that I will then be able to bless the Lord again."

Sexual activity of any sort — even married sex — was seen as debased and animalistic. It could be redeemed only by procreation. Even then pleasure was to be avoided. Early Church Fathers frequently dealt with sexual matters. St. Ambrose writes, "Virginity is the one thing that separates us and keeps us from the beast." St. Jerome exhorts a wealthy widow contemplating remarriage, "You have tasted the bitterest of gall. How can you return to it like a dog who has returned to his own vomit?"

In the seventeenth century, priest theologians developed "guidelines" for married couples on when they could engage in intercourse: not during pregnancy, menstruation, or lactation, not during Lent or Advent or on ember days, not before communion and never on Sunday, Wednesday, or Friday!

As late as the nineteenth century, the Vatican was preoccupied with the question of whether married sex could ever be engaged in without committing at least a venial sin.

In all instances, this fear of sex was accompanied by distrust and blame of women. The sin of Eve branded woman forever as temptress. The price of Eve's sin, which came to be seen as pleasure in sex, is pain in childbirth. The locus of original sin is the birth canal.

This distrust of women is not just part of our history, but a reality for women in the church today. It survives in the prohibition on contraception and abortion, in the refusal to ordain women to the priesthood.

Perhaps the most recent manifestation can be seen in the papal document *Mulieris Dignitatem* by John Paul II. This document claims to lay the theological and anthropological foundation for the church's position on women. While it repeats the prohibition on women priests, what is most disturbing is this pope's "vision" of women. It is a romanticized Victorian concept. Again, we are defined by our biology. Only two routes are open to us: virgin or mother. Our value is not inherent in our personhood but is rooted in our capacity to bear children. Our sexuality is limited again to either procreation or denial. Only men without true experiences of equality with women could see us in this way.

Single people who understand this history seek to develop a new paradigm for sexual ethics. We start by affirming sexuality as good, healthy, and holy. We move quickly to justice as the model for evaluating sexual relationships. While much work needs to be done by the churches and by single people in articulating the justice paradigm for sexual ethics, some points are immediately apparent: Expressions of sexuality must be responsible to our obligation to create new life only when we are able to sustain and support it; promises and partnership commitments must be scrupulously kept; mutual respect and equality are critical; the weakness or need of a partner should not be taken advantage of; above all we must want and work for the good of our partner.

Applying these principles to singles is challenging to our religious denominations — at best most want to pretend sexuality does not exist.

They are not, by far, the most serious challenges presented by the rapidly growing category so melodically and absolutely named "ever single" by the Census Bureau. A full one-third of the population remains single through age twenty-nine. Thirty million adults — 22 percent of the adult population — have never married. Marriage rates have dropped to historic lows. For example, in 1987, among unmarried women fifteen to forty-four there were fewer than 100 marriages per 1000. Compare this to 1946 when there were 199 marriages per 1000. In case you are tempted to view this as a momentary blip on the screen related to the end of World War II, let's look at marriages in 1970 as compared to those in 1986. In 1986 41 percent of men twenty-five to twenty-nine had never been married; in 1970 only 19 percent were in this category. Among women in the same age group 28 percent had never been married in 1986, only 11 percent in 1970.

The ever-single person appears to defy our understanding of the Genesis story and the Creator's wisdom: "It is not good that the man should be alone; I will make him a helper fit for him." (Gen. 2:18, RSV) "A man . . . cleaves to his wife and they become one flesh." (v. 24) How, you may wonder, do those who do not come together in a lifelong commitment to share themselves fully with one other person ever feel complete?

The ever-single person often appears to defy our understanding of family, of children. (It should be noted that increasing numbers of single persons, both men and women, are parenting both biological and adopted children, although most still remain childless.) How, you may wonder, do single persons express hope in humankind, in the future? How do they fulfill the directive "Be fruitful and multiply."

The ever singles who do not join a religious congregation appear to defy our sense of community, the common good. We believe that a sense of duty to each other is developed in family. Can those who appear to value individuality more than family develop moral relationships with persons in the community? Will they support the same values, attitudes, and virtues that the community holds dear. In short are they, can they, be part of a community, or are they by their experiences and values alienated from the religious community, which has — let us make no mistake — defined family as the basic unit.

Conservative theologians and political scientists have answered these questions by reaffirming traditional concepts of family and community and by blaming liberalism. Singleness, particularly in women, is seen as the height of selfishness; moral individuality and the drive for autonomy are derided as symbolic of a liberal culture that equals the death of community.

But singleness is not synonymous with alienation, isolation, or loneliness. This is known by all married people. Wholeness and fulfillment come from inside each person, not from the outside or the other. Meaningful, committed relationships can be developed among friends, co-workers, and in the community at large.

Surely life can be fruitful in ways other than through children. Our lives are immeasurably enriched by the teachers, doctors, writers, artists, and friends who have unselfishly moved beyond blood to offer their gifts to anyone in need. Surely those without children who remain engaged in life and in the struggle for justice show great hope in the future.

In my own life I have been struck by the increased opportunities for risk taking that the absence of husband or children has granted me. I need not fear losing a job and being unable to support a family if I take an unpopular stand. Nor do I hesitate to speak the truth or dissent from church teachings because my family — or religious community — will suffer.

Each single person faces the awesome task of knowing moral decisions must be made solely on the merits of and in accordance with how they serve the whole community, that family Jesus embraced when he said, "Who are my mother and my brothers? And looking around on those who sat about him, he said, 'Here are my mother and my brothers! Whosoever does the will of God is my brother and sister and mother'" (Mark 3:33–35).

I am reminded of Elaine Pagels's description of first-century Christians who:

saw themselves participating at the birth of a revolutionary movement that they expected would culminate in the total social transformation that Jesus promised in the "age to come."

To prepare themselves for these events, Jesus commanded his
followers to forget ordinary concerns about food and clothing,...
divest themselves of all property, and abandon family obligations,
whether to parents, spouses, or children, for such obligations would
interfere with their dedication to the apocalyptic hopes Jesus announced; the disciple must become wholly free to serve God....The
coming new age demand[ed] new — and total — allegiance, no
longer to family and nation but to the kingdom itself. Thus Jesus
urge[d] his followers to break their merely natural relationships in
favor of spiritual ones.

We might ask as we face a planet on the brink of both nuclear
and environmental destruction, do our times demand the same? Is
singleness actually more expressive of good stewardship than either
married or religious life? Is this the age of the Lone Ranger? Hopefully, we have learned that the planet needs *diversity* in human nature
as well as in plant and animal nature. It is the inherent dignity of
each person that has value, not any of the three "states of life" to
which we are called.

We need the trinitarian oneness of those who stand alone, those
who join in family, and those who create discreet communities with
purpose. Let us never forget, however, that we are not separate —
we are one!

AUTOBIOGRAPHICAL STATEMENT

For the past twenty years my professional life has been focused on
supporting the legal right of each woman to decide when, whether,
and — most recently — how she will bear children. The most contro-
versial aspect of this work has been my support for legal abortion as
a legitimate option for pregnant women.

Twelve years into my work on abortion rights, my focus shifted
from the secular world to the world of religion — particularly to the
Roman Catholic tradition — when I became executive director of
Catholics for a Free Choice. Increasingly I have become convinced
that religious objections to abortion are based not on a serious concern for fetal life, but rather are rooted in institutionally entrenched
negative attitudes toward women and sexuality.

However, I was shocked by what I found, not just in the traditional church circles, but even in the most progressive feminist groups
and gatherings. I had entered another world. My singleness outside a
vowed religious community was both an oddity and suspect.

I remember attending a weekend workshop to explore founding the Women-Church Convergence. Not once was singleness mentioned. A stunned silence greeted my comment on this, which was coupled by the announcement that I was forty-plus, never married (although not without past long-term committed relationships), and heterosexually active — a set of circumstances not unknown in the world at large. I later learned one woman leader left the meeting saying she had lost considerable respect for me as a result of that admission.

This experience and others like it have compelled me to take on the task of publicly dealing with the challenge of being single in a church — even Woman-Church — where single people are invisible.

BACKGROUND INFORMATION

Seeking resources in a major university library on Single Women/ Women Who Never Married was like Virginia Woolf's search earlier in the century. In *A Room of One's Own* she describes her search in the British Museum for books on women written by women. She found slim pickings. But, she asked: "Have you any notion of the volumes upon volumes written by men about women?"[1]

Similarly in this search for information on single women, books abounded on the single parent, all save one related to women. Single cell division claimed an avalanche of titles. But the volumes on single women were few. Barbara Levy Simon's is the best of the few available titles on single women. *Never Married Women* is a recent work. Yet, it has severe limitations, exploring the lives of fifty retired women.[2] Interestingly, Simon describes these women as "rebels" who disobeyed patriarchal rule and flouted society's expectations of marriage and child bearing/caring. They chose to swim upstream.

Magazines and journals deal with many issues of single women: education, career, promotion, travel, and money-management. Few if any articles, even in magazines like *Christian Century, America,* or *Commonweal,* deal with the spiritual lives and welfare of the millions of single women in our society.

All women in our society are to begin with still marginal, enduring handicaps that feminists are increasingly calling to our attention. But single women are often more marginalized, forming, as Simon notes, a subculture of their own.

The classic, still pervasive "Old Maid" image projects characteristics that the successfully married flee. Such characteristics as oddity or barrenness have enjoyed a long history in literature and popular culture, although this was not always true in the United States.

White single women of the middle and upper classes who expanded their social roles drew great respect between 1810 and 1860. As Simon notes: "The 'Cult of Single Blessedness,' as it was called, upheld the single life as both a socially and personally valuable state [and] offered a positive vision of singlehood rooted in Protestant religion."[3]

Between 1860 and 1960, a deviant picture of the single woman reemerged, fitting as it does into the social canonization of home, family, and child care as women's "proper" domain. Then the women's movement, Betty Friedan's *Feminine Mystique*, and the general cultural upheavals of the 1960s influenced many women. As a result, a higher percentage of American women now remain single.

Those who choose to remain single can do so due to the increased female participation in work that leads them to financial independence; increased availability and use of contraception and abortion make heterosexual relationship without marriage more likely. The influence of the gay rights movement also opens doors of dignity, choice, and meaning to lesbian single women.

According to the Census Bureau, in 1987 14.6 percent of women between ages of 30 and 35 have not been married, as compared to 8.4 percent of women ages 35–39. The percentages decrease with age: 6.4 percent of women aged 40–44, and 4.5 percent of the 45–54-year-olds never married. In fact, 6.4 percent of women over 75 had never married.[4]

According to the Simon study cited above, women in that group may have sought marriage, but they refused to answer questions about sexual matters. Similarly, we have no information on the desires or hopes for marriage of the millions of never married women. Single women in poll after poll proclaim that they are more content and happy in their life situations than are their peers who married and had children. They cite freedom, friendships, close family contacts, and extensive volunteer work.

Further, the American Association of Retired Persons (AARP) states that single women make the best adjustments in retirement.[5] This at a time when the suicide rate for retired men is catching up with the group most at risk for suicide — eighteen to twenty-four years old. A lifetime of self-reliance seems to bring its own advantages.

NOTES

1. Virginia Woolf, *A Room of One's Own* (New York: Harcourt Brace & Jovanovich, 1929), pp. 26–27.

2. Barbara Levy Simon, *Never Married Women* (Philadelphia: Temple University Press, 1987), p. ix.

3. Ibid., p. 9.

4. *Statistical Abstract of the U.S* (Washington, D.C.: U.S. Department of Commerce, Census Bureau, 1989).

5. American Association of Retired Persons, Pamphlets on Being Single in Retirement.

BIBLIOGRAPHY

Armstrong, Karen. *The Gospel according to Woman: Christianity's Creation of the Sex War in the West.* Garden City, N.Y.: Anchor Press/Doubleday, 1987.

Badinter, Elisabeth. *The Myth of Motherhood.* Trans. Francine du Plessix Gray. Souvenir Press, 1981.

Badinter, Elisabeth. *The Unopposite Sex: The End of the Gender Battle.* Trans. Barbara Wright. New York: Harper & Row, 1989.

Belenky, Mary Field, et al. *Women's Ways of Knowing: The Development of Self, Voice, and Mind.* New York: Basic Books, 1986.

Boulding, Elise. *The Underside of History.* Boulder, Colo.: Westview Press, 1977.

Calvocoressi, Peter. *Who's Who in the Bible.* New York: Penguin Press, 1988.

Chesler, Phyllis. *Women and Madness.* Allen Lane, 1974.

Fisher, Helen. *The Sex Contract.* Granada, 1982.

Guttentag, M., and P. F. Secord. *Too Many Women: Demography, Sex, and Family.* New York: Basic Books, 1983.

Hardy, Sarah. *The Woman That Never Evolved.* Cambridge: Harvard University Press, 1981.

Jacobsen, L., and F. Pampel. *Living Alone in the U.S. 1940–1980: A Test of Competing Explanations.* Iowa City: University of Iowa Sociology Work Paper Series, 1987.

Mead, Margaret. *Male and Female.* Pelican Books, 1962.

Novak, W. *The Great American Man Shortage.* New York: Rawson Associates, 1983.

Pagels, Elaine. *Adam, Eve, and the Serpent.* New York: Random House, 1988.

Parke, R., and P. C. Glick. "Prospective Changes in Marriage and the Family." *Journal of Marriage and the Family* (Minneapolis) 29, no. 2 (1967): 249–56.

Preston, S. H., and A. T. Richards "The Influence of Women's Work Opportunities on Marriage Rates." *Demography* (Washington, D.C.) 12, no. 2 (1975): 209–22.

Shostak, Arthur. "Singlehood." In *Handbook of Marriage and the Family.* Ed. Marvin B. Sussman and Suzanne K. Steinmetz. New York: Plenum, 1987.

Tanner, Nancy, and Adrienne Zilhman. "Women in Evolution: Innovation and Selection in Human Origins." *Signs* 1, no. 3.

U.S. Census Bureau. March 1987, March 1986, March 1985; 1989. *Marital Status and Living Arrangements,* Current Population Reports, Population Characteristics; Washington, D.C.

PART FIVE

Neglected Issues Women Want Proclaimed

15

Divorce as Grace, Empowerment, and Sacrament

Janice P. Leary

SERMON

Before I formed you in the womb, I knew you: You existed in my mind long before you came to be; precious, loved, unique in time, destined for eternity. I am with you: Be not afraid!
—Psalm 139:13–15, paraphrased

Divorce is a major turning point for women and men, and too often this experience has been fraught with fear. A divorced woman's standard of living falls by an average of 73 percent in the year after the divorce, while the divorced man's standard increases an average of 42 percent. Millions of women are a divorce away from destitution. The suicide rate for divorced men is three times higher than for married men. Divorce has become a reality of modern-day life, but is there a better way we can go about living out this reality? I have been asked to offer this sermon on my experience of the "practicalities and the spirituality of divorce" today, and in this light I will not be presenting the stereotypical image of divorcing spouses who feud bitterly as a result of their fear. Instead I wish to share with you a different perspective, which I worked through in my own experience with divorce, a perspective that has allowed my children, myself, and my ex-husband to remain friends.

My words today are offered to those of you who have experienced loss or rejection in the reality of separation. Your feelings may take the form of frustration, anger, helplessness, and grief, each of which is inherent in the emotional dimension of most individuals' divorce process. And my words are offered with the hope of empowering individuals in a separation/divorce situation where there is a "significant other" involved. I also wish to offer an affirming perspective to individuals who are facing the divorce court system of American legal

---

I cannot, at present, as a Catholic woman preach this sermon in my church. Were I enabled to do so, it would be appropriate at any time of the year.

179

justice, particularly women, who *can* gain some economic security in an equitable settlement but who *think* they will be "powerless" during the legal process of a divorce court experience. My words are for those of you who are willing to create a new path, a positive turning point for yourselves as your divorce progresses from condolences to congratulations, from sadness to sacrament! For I propose here a more creative and more positive approach toward what women and men are beginning to experience as the sacrament of divorce.

Divorce as a process moves along a developmental pathway. Usually the initial period of denial is followed by a dawning awareness that the marriage will not endure. Often this entails a time of mourning, a sense of loss, and a withdrawal from social contacts. Feelings of anger at the spouse are intermingled with feelings of failure. These feelings, which I term "separation distress," result from a nostalgic yet fierce attachment toward one's "departed" partner. Eventually a period of readjustment begins as hostility toward the spouse, and oneself, lessens. In today's sermon I would like to share with you some results of my own research concerning four "phases" of coping with the chronic stress of a dysfunctional marriage and divorce. These four phases are: (1) the crisis phase; (2) the initial coping phase: working toward accepting the *emotional* realities of separation; (3) the ongoing coping phase: working out the *practical* realities of divorce; and (4) post-divorce altruistic coping: a time of deepening psychological and spiritual growth. Each divorcing couple is unique, and while it often takes nearly three years to resolve the psychological issues from the dysfunctional marriage and the divorce process, these "phases" will be experienced at varying times for each person as they move toward a new post-divorce life. The underlying message of this sermon is to recall the words of the Psalmist: "Be not afraid!"

The Crisis Phase. In my own experience with divorce and from what I have observed as a pastoral counselor with clients going through separation and divorce, the crisis phase often begins silently with unspoken expectations. Before today's generation, women were expected to remain at home and "carry" the emotional life of the family, and men were expected to shoulder the problems at work without the benefit of support systems such as "employee assistance programs." Judith Viorst has noted that "enmities arise because our unmet expectations become metaphors for all that our marriage lacks." Before the late 1960s few books of substance offered guidance and affirmation to those in troubled marriages, and groups that focused on separation, divorce, and post-divorce were relatively unknown. As a result very few women and men had access to psychological guidance with which to take positive steps to enhance their own marriages. I believe that the women's movement in the late 1960s and early 1970s was an important step toward an evolving awareness of constructive mutuality and empathic connections between women and men. But we are only beginning to learn how to put this deeper awareness into common practice.

The Catholic Church's stand on birth control was devastating to many married couples who took the dictates of Rome seriously in the 1950s and early 1960s. Within the first four years of our marriage, we became parents to three infants within thirty-three months. The birthing, care, and provision for three children required a primary focus of time on nurturant parenting rather than a concentration on our development as a couple during the formative years of our marriage. At the time it was almost unheard of for men to choose to be an *equal* partner in co-parenting, and so I took on the primary responsibility of full-time parenting until our daughters reached adolescence. Did the crisis phase occur as the result of his career pressures, with few other outlets to vent his frustrations except at home? Did the crisis result from a resistance to counseling that could have healed the emotional distance in our marriage? Did it occur because I went back to school and caused a jolt to the expected family routine? The answer is never clear after three decades, but certainly there was not just one reason; more likely it was a combination of each of these pressures, including aspects that will never be quite clear. One thing is clear, though: unless some form of therapy is accepted by both partners, the crisis phase cannot heal of itself; the dysfunction may wane but it re-emerges in another form, on another level of frustration.

The Initial Coping Phase. Once the crisis phase of divorce has been "negotiated" or journeyed through, the next phase begins — that of dealing with and ultimately accepting the reality of separation and the emotional loss of the significant relationship. In my work and research with mothers of multi-handicapped children, I was taught valuable lessons in coping with chronic stress. Although I learned how to deal more positively with my own dysfunctional marriage, that was not enough to stabilize our marriage. And so I learned to cope constructively with the challenge of separation and divorce. The second phase, the "initial coping phase," centers on getting through the emotional realities of the separation and divorce crisis. An important challenge inherent in this phase is to tolerate the ambiguity of the see-saw feelings in divorce: one moment perceiving the opposing partner with compassion, love, and kindness, and the next moment with disdain, anger, and diffidence. At the time my husband told me he wanted a divorce, I was just beginning to prepare for my final comprehensive exams to complete a doctoral degree. More than a few of my feelings and experiences during this time of crisis were reflected in Abigail Trafford's *Crazytime*.

The feeling that one does not have control of the situation during divorce, and that everyone knows it, is a self-diminishing attitude. It is good for your morale to look your best ("looking good is the best revenge!"), that is, it is important to maintain your best outward appearance even if this is felt to be a "front." There are times when what you feel on the "inside" need not be demonstrated to the world in general, or to your "opposing partner" in particular. Carol Gilligan's research indicates that the most advanced moral level occurs when a woman feels care for herself as much as she experiences care for others. To work through to the goal of positive resolution, the decision to "do the best for yourself" is of *prime* importance. Once you decide to take good care of yourself your outer presence will become more natural and you will achieve an important level of inner confidence. Be not afraid!

When interacting directly with the opposing partner, actions that take a person's attention away from what is best for an amicable and satisfactory divorce resolution must be set aside. It is important though to vent negative feelings in a therapeutic setting, *without* the "opposing partner" present. A trusted therapist can help a woman or man direct intense feelings into a constructive direction. Keep in mind that not only is your "almost-ex" a significant person in your children's development; he or she is the one with whom you must negotiate a fair settlement. Confronting the rejecting spouse with anger is a "no win" drain of energy. If there is any chance that the marriage might survive, couple counseling is also beneficial.

It is essential to "call a truce" on whatever bitterness may have existed between you and your "almost-ex" in order to obtain a stable economic future for your children and yourself. Make a pact early on *not* to use the children or money as objects of retaliation or to wield power for advantage. This mutual decision was key to the ease with which fairness has characterized my own post-divorce relationship. Research by Darlene and Roger Duncan found that the single most important aspect that helps children, of any age, adapt to the splitting of their sense of family security *depends on the quality of the relationship between their parents during and after the divorce.* Bear in mind that your opposing partner, whether father or mother, will continue in that role for the rest of the children's lives. Be not afraid!

One of the thorniest issues during a separation and divorce is the presence of a "significant other" on the scene of a marriage dissolution. If you allow yourself to become involved emotionally with your opposing partner's romantic affairs, you will experience a self-defeating diversion from your primary task of achieving what is in your own best interest. Anger and jealousy only weaken an individual's clarity and dignity, and ultimately the bargaining position for the divorce settlement is also weakened. It is to an individual's advantage that her or his feelings, fantasies, and actions about dating others be reserved until after the divorce is settled amicably and after the time when a peaceful closure to the divorce process is secured — when one is celebrating and not acting out of misguided retaliation.

If a person is to embark upon a constructive and meaningful journey of divorce, she or he must be willing to put in the necessary time. One of the most important points regarding the initial coping phase is that a single-minded concentration of focused time is essential to one's eventual inner confidence during the challenge of divorce. I did not focus energy on my separation problems until many months after the initial announcement. At times I silently berated myself for not accomplishing the doctoral work with more efficiency. Finally I realized that if I were to help myself and accomplish the divorce positively and creatively, it was incumbent on me to be particularly single-minded. I set aside the doctoral research work even though to my immediate world that "inaction" seemed to indicate a lack of coping. There were times when I, too, was not certain the single-minded focus was the right thing, but in retrospect it was the only thing to do. This need to re-center oneself to reclaim a concern for one's own life is a primary message of this sermon. No one else can achieve this for you; a single-mindedness about the divorce process must come from your own inner direction and confidence, or what Judith Jordan terms "self-empathy." I believe this inner confidence is the most important aspect of coping with the disequilibrium caused by the jolt of separation. An alternative choice is the victim role, which is totally self-destructive. *Be not afraid!*

Positive growth during each of the coping phases cannot happen in isolation; good friends and community support are essential. Carolyn Osiek's book *Beyond Anger* provided me with insights and comfort as I was trying to cope with divorce. The last pages of her book offer thirteen strategies for "surviving... even thriving within a structure (whether church or society) otherwise guaranteed to cause premature gray hair." To paraphrase her words, it is time we move "beyond anger" and allow ourselves a conversion process in divorce. Osiek observes that "when the darkness and pain of the impasse experience is fully lived through, not bypassed or shortened, genuine change can take place." The words of the Psalmist speak directly to each one of us in our experience of frustration and helplessness: "Be not afraid," for in your work of achieving a positive, empowering divorce you will *not* be alone.

The Ongoing Coping Phase. Once there is an inner sense of adjustment to the immediate emotional issues inherent in the divorce process, we can move on to the next coping phase, which includes choosing a lawyer and concludes with the actual court legalization of the divorce process. "Ongoing coping," which is my term for this third phase, is a time of working out the practical realities of divorce. This phase began for me when I drew up a list of lawyers who had been recommended to me — all men. Research has indicated that the majority of people who divorce hire the first and only lawyer they consult. Here again is a time to maintain an inner confidence in yourself and not give over complete control to a lawyer! Initially, I had reservations about lawyers in general and about where to start in particular, but once I took a first step in what may be considered informative "lawyer shopping," I found this to be a meaningful and rewarding experience. During my direct phone call with each lawyer (I did not leave long messages with secretaries), I explained that I wished to meet at his office to see if we might work together. I said that I was not making an appointment for any legal advice and as long as there was no charge for the approximately twenty minutes, I would be there at his convenience. I never decided on the spot to employ the lawyer. After a few hours' reflection I often had a sense that a particular lawyer could become adversarial with the "other side" during the legal process, and I wanted a lawyer who would work from a negotiated, nonaggressive perspective. My first list ended *without* a choice. And so I made a second list — of women lawyers. The time I put into determining which lawyer was likely to establish a working relationship with me was well worth the effort. My choice was an affirming woman lawyer who took seriously each of my suggestions. She helped me through the maze of potential legal tangles and supplied the necessary legal language. To this day I value the deep satisfaction of an excellent working relationship with this woman.

With regard to the formal divorce agreement, it was to my advantage to do as much of the work as possible. Reading pertinent material regarding the practical and legal dimensions of divorce is an important step toward coping with this experience. It has been my own experience with the divorce process, both personally and as a therapist, that many separation or pre-divorce rules are arbitrary and not inflexible, although this won't be expressed often or freely. The sky just does not fall in when a rule is transgressed for a valid reason; there is no rule made that cannot be broken for a greater good. Once my thoughts were clear and the most recent financial concepts were on paper (with the help of a Macintosh word processor), before my lawyer made any further legal step I contacted my opposing partner and made plans to meet and discuss the most recent developments of the divorce agreement with him. During this coping phase, negotiation was the mode of our communication. I would highly recommend Fisher and Ury's book on negotiation, entitled *Getting to Yes*. Research by Sanford Katz has suggested that individuals in a divorce are much more likely to accept a settlement if they have been involved in *negotiation*, rather than having a settlement imposed upon them. The two of us met five times without any lawyers present; each discussion-negotiation lasted about four hours. Wherever it was possible I considered the advantages and disadvantages of each proposal, financial or otherwise, for the man with whom I had spent twenty-five years. This led to knowledge that was to our mutual benefit, as well as allowing each of us the courtesy and dignity not typically associated with divorce. There were numerous times when I made or agreed to a decision that benefited him, and that decision usually came around to benefit me in return. The negotiations entailed a conscientious effort, yet I recall those discussions as the most mutual and productive conversations of our entire twenty-five years together!

This third phase culminates with the court experience. My lawyer and I discussed the time for the divorce, and I had a voice in the decision regarding the choice of judges who would hear our case. Because I had never been in the courthouse where my divorce would take place, a week before our court appointment I chose to familiarize myself with that environment. I phoned to find when the judge who would hear our case was sitting, and then I went to his courtroom during a few of the divorce cases he heard that day. This increased my confidence. I asked a trusted friend to accompany me to my court proceedings and after the divorce was completed, my friend and I enjoyed lunch together: recalling with fondness the judge's expression of sadness about the necessity of divorce, sharing a feeling of amazement regarding the confidence I felt while talking with the judge on the stand, and laughing about my momentary memory lapse in response to one of his routine questions. The time of condolences was over, I appreciated celebrating a time of congratulations for an empowering divorce experience.

On the day of the divorce we signed a personal agreement in the presence of our lawyers; this agreement dealt with five issues not associated with the court proceedings. The third item involved participation in joint counseling. The post-divorce period is potentially a time for entering into counseling for emotional, and possibly confrontative, issues that it may not have been advisable to deal with while negotiating the divorce settlement. Diane Vaughan's research reveals that even after the proceedings are long over, it is not uncommon for divorced individuals to yearn to know what went wrong, often to the point of obsession. Shortly after our divorce we met four times in counseling sessions with two trusted therapists, once a month for two-hour sessions. We discussed issues still present from the dysfunctional marriage and issues for the future, especially concerning our relationship with our daughters. The fifth and final counseling session included our three daughters, who were invited to share whatever feelings they wished. Today I still recall those five meetings as very sincere, emotional experiences in an empowering atmosphere that culminated in a basic sense of contented "re-equilibrium." The result has been the ability to see the marriage more objectively, and we both have been enabled to value the other as a friend. Elizabeth Stark aptly describes a relationship such as ours as "kinship."

Post-Divorce Altruistic Coping. A fourth coping phase, which I term "altruistic coping," is quite possible in the post-divorce period. An opportunity is usually present in separation and divorce to find new grace, empowerment, and meaning. As one progresses through the phases of coping and readjustment, she or he may experience the paradox that successfully negotiating a crisis results in a deeper sense of faith and inner strength. The importance of community now becomes a more reciprocal dynamic for the divorced individual. In her most recent book, on community in American life, Madonna Kohlbenschlag refers to our generation as the archetype of "spiritual orphan." Most individuals facing the challenge of the separation and divorce process will recognize their own reflection in her words. It is likely that the orphan archetype also motivates many of us who have emerged from the difficulties of separation and divorce to reach out to those others who are beginning to face an emotional and economic path similar to the one we have traveled. As a pastoral counselor I have been particularly motivated to support individuals facing the challenges of divorce — by offering listening attention, emotional encouragement, instruction with the Macintosh, and accompaniment through the court experience.

Divorce as a "Sacrament"? This sermon is shared with you in the hope that you begin to experience and to recognize the grace and *sacrament* of divorce within yourselves, that you and I may reach out to each other as community and minister as Jesus did by "binding up the broken-hearted, proclaiming release to the captives, setting at liberty those who are oppressed, and comforting those who mourn" (Isa. 61:1–2 and Luke 4:18). While I am grateful for the degrees that I have earned, the academic letters added to my name have held far less meaning for me than the empowering and continuing sacrament of my divorce experience.

An essential aspect of a positive divorce is a clear faith in one's God — perhaps not the God we were taught in our younger days, but the God who unconditionally loves each one who has been hurt, the God who is always with us. My doctoral research was based on the stages of faith development posited by James Fowler, and I have come to believe that each of us speaks, responds, and prays to our own often unique concept of God. My personal theology incorporates ten years of experience working with mothers of multi-handicapped children. Those women taught me much and led me to believe in a very special God: a God who loves us above all else and does not send suffering. My belief is in a God who shares our grief, who experiences pain each time we are hurt, a God who has the most feminine of qualities. In my belief, God is all-knowing (omniscient), all-loving ("omnagape") but, as Dorothee Sölle has suggested, not all-powerful (omnipotent). I believe that God, like a Good Mother, has chosen to give to each of us a unique, individual conscience, a conscience that deepens as our faith develops, a conscience with which to determine our own decisions in all moral matters.

An aspect integral to my belief is what Viktor Frankl has termed "the will to meaning." This is perhaps the most basic of inner motivations, more basic, Frankl says, than the need to eat or to sleep. I believe this "will to meaning" is what kept me progressing in a steadfast manner throughout the darker days of my separation and divorce experiences. By the time my divorce was final I was even more deeply aware that my life was one of particular worth. With God's grace, there was much for which I was grateful: my three daughters continued to be self-sufficient and loving young women. Despite their pain during initial phases of our divorce, they have achieved a new maturity. After nearly thirty years of being a parent, twenty-five of those years married to the same man, I reflect on a life that has provided me with a good deal of meaning, and that meaning has emerged from a mixed blessing of frustration, challenge, and ultimately contentment. For me, the experience of meaning and empathy with myself and others during the coping phases of divorce is a manifestation of spiritual grace and self-growth through the divorce process.

My divorce experience moved from profound sadness during the crisis phase to an acceptance that evolved during the initial and ongoing coping phases. The acceptance then added to a deepening sense of contentment with the new meaning that remains in my life now; my lived experience became a sacrament for me. A sacrament is a "funnel" for God's gift of grace, a sacred and mysterious symbol of spiritual growth. Our relationship with God is essential to my proposed concept of divorce as sacrament and determines the sacramental qualities of one's "call" in this process; the final acceptance of any life choice is a personal graced decision of commitment to God. Tad Guzie defines sacrament as a festive action in which Christians assemble to celebrate their lived experience and to call to heart their common story. This festive action is a symbol of God's care for us in Christ. Enacting the symbol brings us closer to one another in the church to the Lord who is there for us. And so the final step left to take in my journey toward a positive and empowering divorce was that of a ritualizing and liturgizing of the graced divorce experience.

When planning my celebration of divorce as grace and sacrament, I met with a former Benedictine nun who was trained in the richness of liturgy (and who has since become a notable, wonderfully effective elected member of the Boston city council). She helped me locate and decide upon the various readings and songs appropriate for what I had in mind. My closest friends and family were invited and several were part of the liturgical celebration. Liberation theology themes of forgiveness, joy, and transition permeated this celebration. The "Christa," a feminine representation of Christ, was a hand-wrought bronze symbol in the center of our gathering, and a liturgy was offered as a symbol of my new relationship with the community and as one contentedly single and "happily unmarried" in loving connection with her God. In the liturgy celebrating this sacrament I wished to express in a public and meaningful way my gratitude for the new meaning in my life and to "offer up" the loss of what Viorst called "impossible expectations": those expectations that are no longer necessary to one's growth but that are painful to let go of. It is in this letting go that one attains a true maturity and a deeper perspective and wisdom about life. Viorst wrote: "As for our losses and gains, we have seen how often they are inextricably mixed. There is plenty we have to give up in order to grow. For we cannot deeply love anything without becoming vulnerable to loss. And we cannot become separate people, responsible people, connected people, reflective people without some losing and leaving and letting go."

Matthew Fox has written: "Tragedy is not in vain... for from it a deeper beauty is formed. The Resurrection, after all, could not have happened without a crucifixion. There is no Easter without a Good Friday." Carolyn Osiek observes that the root of a woman's sinfulness is passivity and fear of acting, yet if a woman rejects this fear a likely result will be "the cross... [which] is the cost of acting rather than remaining passive. [The woman's] need for relatedness and connectedness must at times be sacrificed in order to allow independent action. Her need for security and approval must be sacrificed in order to dare new ways of acting that may not win enthusiastic acceptance by those who have something to lose by it. Her need to be cherished and valued must be sacrificed in order that she may come to cherish and value herself and what she stands for. This is cross enough."

Florence Vinger (Gaia), a Catholic Church administrator at the time, reflected on her views of divorce, and I offer this as a concluding prayer:

Divorce or remarriage is not a sin. The reverse is often true — that we come to live more in the presence of God with more adult faith lives than ever before. We may be ostracized or rebuffed by the ignorant or the heartless, but we are finding the courage to reject that rejection and to take our rightful place in the midst of our faith communities. We have much to teach our church — about sacraments, marriage, false images of God, being an Easter people, systemic divorce in culture and religion.... People remarry in the hope of building a new life together. They divorce because it is the only solution to an intolerable situation or because it was thrust on them.... Out of shattered lives and identities we are forming for ourselves a fuller human existence and a new richer Christian identity reconciled with self and to the mystery of life within.

Be not afraid! Amen.

AUTOBIOGRAPHICAL STATEMENT

Married before Betty Friedan published *The Feminine Mystique*, before Catholic couples went their own way on contraception, and before husbands attempted to become equal partners in raising children, my husband and I became parents of three daughters within thirty-three months. Our lives became full of child care and the efforts to earn a living and make a home.

When my children were in grade school, I returned to college and divinity school. My degrees are a master of education from Boston College, a master of divinity from Andover Newton Theological School, and a doctorate in counseling from Boston College. Simultaneously during these years I also supervised students of both Boston College and St. John's Seminary in a social outreach program. For several years I counseled battered women.

Ten years before beginning the Ph.D., I worked as counselor and program coordinator with mothers of multi-handicapped children within the Boston College Campus School for Multi-handicapped Children. The experience with the mothers and their handicapped children has carried through every other facet of work in which I have been involved since that time. Working and learning with these women led to my completing a challenging Ph.D. dissertation; most important of all my gains it provided an important insight into the depth of women's psychological, emotional, and mental needs, and was a turning point in my own life.

In 1989 I accepted the position of coordinator of the separated/divorced ministry with the Family Life Office in the Archdiocese of Boston. Currently my professional focus is on two levels. I work as a psychotherapist with Interfaith Counseling Service in Newton, Massachusetts. I have also attained a long-term goal, that of teaching at the college level: child development at Framington State College and adolescent psychology at Lasell College in Newton. I feel that I have achieved a meaningful life, and I cherish and enjoy my achievements and life plans. Above all I have a deep pride in my three daughters, who are well into their professional careers.

BACKGROUND INFORMATION

The Census Bureau reported that in the United States in 1982 there was one divorce for nearly every two marriages. On the basis of National Center for Health statistics data, it was projected that (1) of each one hundred first marriages, thirty-eight will end in divorce; (2) of those thirty-eight divorced couples, twenty-nine (75 percent) will remarry, (3) of those twenty-nine, thirteen (44 percent) will divorce again.[1] One of every five American children under eighteen lives with one parent, that is, about 12.6 million children, an increase of 53.9 percent from the 1970s. Approximately 90 percent of the children in one-parent families live with their mothers. These statistics increase each year.

Divorce is different from other life crises in that the anger inherent in most divorce experiences often erupts into physical and verbal violence, violence that can cause serious psychological and physical harm for many years, not only to the feuding couple, but to their children and even to the legal system: Wallerstein pointed out that "judges, lawyers and police are in more danger of being shot or killed by angry family members than by criminals."[2]

The following are from a research study that documented the negative effect of divorce on adults:

1. Car accidents occur three times more frequently for the divorced than for the married. These rates double during the six months before and the six months after the divorce.

2. Risk of death by homicide is higher for divorced people than for other groups.

3. Divorced and widowed individuals have higher age-adjusted death rates for all causes of death combined than married people of equivalent age, sex, and race. Death rate by disease is much higher for those who are divorced.[3]

As a final note, in marriage wives adapt and make more concessions and become more depressed and phobic than do husbands.[4] Marriage, divorce or no divorce, obviously does not provide as healthy an environment for women as for men.

NOTES

1. P. Glick, and A. Norton, "Marrying, Divorcing, and Living Together in the U.S. Today," *Population Bulletin* 32 (1979): 4–34.

2. Judith Wallerstein and Sandra Blakeslee, *Second Chances: Men, Women & Children a Decade after Divorce (Who Wins, Who Loses, and Why)* (New York: Ticknor & Fields, 1989).

3. B. L. Bloom, S. J. Asher, and S. W. White, "Marital Disruption as a Stressor: A Review and Analysis," *Psychological Bulletin* 85 (1978): 867–99.

4. Jessie Bernard, *The Future of Marriage* (New Haven: Yale University Press, 1982).

BIBLIOGRAPHY

Bernard, Jessie. *The Future of Marriage*. New Haven: Yale University Press, 1982.

Bloom, B. L., S. J. Asher, and S. W. White. "Marital Disruption as a Stressor: A Review and Analysis." *Psychological Bulletin* 85 (1978): 867–99.

Brunsman, Barry, O.F.M. *New Hope for Divorced Catholics*. San Francisco: Harper & Row, 1989.

Duncan, Darlene, and Roger Duncan. *You're Divorced, But Your Children Aren't*. Englewood Cliffs, N.J.: Prentice-Hall, 1979.

Fisher, Roger, and William Ury *Getting to Yes: Negotiating Agreement without Giving In*. New York: Penguin Books, 1983.

Fowler, James. *Stages of Faith: The Psychology of Human Development and the Quest for Meaning*. New York: Harper & Row, 1981.

Fox, Matthew. *Original Blessing: A Primer in Creation Spirituality*. Santa Fe: Bear & Co, 1983.

Frankl, Viktor E. *Man's Search for Meaning*. New York: Washington Square Press, 1963.

Friedman, James. *The Divorce Handbook: Your Basic Guide to Divorce*. New York: Random House, 1982.

Gilligan, Carol. *In a Different Voice: Psychological Theory and Women's Development*. Cambridge: Harvard University Press, 1982.

Glick, P., and A. Norton. "Marrying, Divorcing, and Living Together in the U.S. Today." *Population Bulletin* 32 (1979): 4–34.

Guzie, Tad. *The Book of Sacramental Basics*. New York: Paulist Press, 1981.

Hillary, Marcia A., and Joel T. Johnson. "Selection and Evaluation of Attorneys in Divorce." *Journal of Divorce* 9, no. 1 (Fall 1985).

Jordan, Judith V. "Empathy and Self-boundaries." *Work in Progress*. Wellesley, Mass.: Stone Center Working Papers Series, 1984.

Katz, Sanford. Interview in the *Boston College Biweekly*. September 24, 1987.

Kohlbenschlag, Madonna. *Lost in the Land of Oz: The Search for Identity and Community in American Life*. San Francisco: Harper & Row, 1988.

Kressel, Kenneth. *The Process of Divorce: How Professionals and Couples Negotiate Settlements*. New York: Basic Books, 1985.

Leary, Janice P. "The Relationship of Coping with Chronic Stress and Faith Development in Women: Mothers of Multihandicapped Children." Boston College doctoral dissertation, 1988.

Miller, Jean Baker. *Toward a New Psychology of Women.* Boston: Beacon Press, 1976, 1986.

Osiek, Carolyn. *Beyond Anger: On Being a Feminist in the Church.* New York: Paulist Press, 1986.

Ruether, Rosemary R. *Woman-Church: Theology and Practice of Feminist Liturgical Communities.* San Francisco: Harper & Row, 1985.

Schneider, Karen L., and Myles J. Schneider. *Divorce Mediation: The Constructive New Way to End a Marriage without Big Bills.* Washington: Acropolis Books, 1984.

Sidel, Ruth. *Women and Children Last: The Plight of Poor Women in Affluent America.* New York: Viking Press, 1986.

Stark, Elizabeth. "Friends through It All." *Psychology Today* (May 1986).

Sölle, Dorothee. "Mysticism, Liberation and the Names of God." *Christianity and Crisis*, June 22, 1981.

Trafford, Abigail. *Crazytime: Surviving Divorce.* New York: Harper & Row, 1982.

Vaughan, Diane. *Uncoupling: Turning Points in Intimate Relationships.* New York: Oxford University Press, 1986.

Vinger, Florence (Gaia). "Divorced May Remarry." *National Catholic Reporter*, March 14, 1986.

Viorst, Judith. *Necessary Losses: The Loves, Illusions, Dependencies and Impossible Expectations That All of Us Have to Give Up in Order to Grow.* New York: Fawcett, 1986.

Wallerstein, Judith, and Sandra Blakeslee. *Second Chances: Men, Women & Children a Decade after Divorce (Who Wins, Who Loses, and Why).* New York: Ticknor & Fields, 1989.

Weitzman, Lenore J. *The Divorce Revolution: The Unexpected Social and Economic Consequences for Women and Children.* New York: Free Press (Macmillan), 1985.

RESOURCES

1. Churches often have established groups for separated and divorced persons, led by individuals who have constructively learned from their divorce experiences. For example, the North American Conference of Separated and Divorced Catholics, Inc., 1100 S. Goodman Street, Rochester, NY 14620, is an excellent source of support and information. Almost every U.S. diocese has a coordinator for separated and divorced in their Family Life Office.

2. Family guidance centers (for example, Interfaith Counseling Service, 60 Highland Street, West Newton, MA 02165) offer guidance and support on a therapeutic professional level.

3. Local divorce centers (listed by the YWCA or the telephone directory) offer practical approaches to dealing with the realities of divorce.

4. Divorce mediation is an area to consider before formal legal negoti-ations; my work with individuals who have consulted mediators leads me to recommend mediation as a supplement to working solely with a lawyer (Schneider and Schneider, 1984; Kressel, 1985). The entire issue of the *Journal of Divorce* 8 (Spring/Summer 1985) has divorce mediation as its focus.

5. A recommended self-support for individuals in any phase of divorce is reflective journal writing, which allows an individual to gain insight into his or her own feelings and needs. This process was of ongoing help during the early phase of my divorce. (Jim Thuline, a counselor with Interfaith Counseling Service in Newton, Massachusetts, offers therapeutic and spiritual guidance in his presentations on the Progoff Journal Method.)

6. Examples of rituals to acknowledge and celebrate divorce are included in Rosemary Radford Ruether's *Woman-Church: Theology and Practice of Feminist Liturgical Communities* (1985).

7. Many Catholics still retain misconceptions about what is "allowed" by the Catholic Church hierarchy regarding divorce and remarriage. There remain Catholics who hold the misguided perceptions that divorced or sepa-rated Catholics may not participate in the sacraments, or even be sponsors at baptism or confirmation. This is *not* correct. And even today these misguided perceptions overlap into thinking about remarriage after divorce. Some in-dividuals have the perception that there is no option offered by the church with regard to remarriage other than going through the process of annulment. Annulment is the "declaration of nullity" of the marriage by Church hierar-chy. This declaration of annulment states that what seemed to be a marriage never was a true sacrament of marriage. But there is an option to enduring this process: the church-accepted principle of "internal forum" honors the personal good conscience of an individual and the honest appraisal of his or her unique life situation in marriage and divorce (Brunsman, 1989, p. 79). Canon lawyer-priests at any diocesan tribunal have information regarding the principle of internal forum in the Catholic Church.

8. The "prodder provision" in my final divorce agreement is an inter-esting example of what is possible when one does sufficient research. This concept was published in one brief sentence (Friedman, 1982, p. 129), which states that if the recipient of alimony were to remarry the alimony is reduced *by only half*. Divorce lawyers with whom I have spoken since my divorce say they have never heard of such a concept — but it is in my divorce agreement and for me is a symbol of what is possible when one does her "homework." It is well to remember that alimony represents the earnings from the marriage contract, and not "welfare" settlement from a provider's "beneficence."

9. A word processor was a very helpful tool that helped me gain a sense of confidence as I was preparing details of the divorce settlement. The Macintosh word processor was the conduit that allowed me the ability to communicate on a man's terms, or in Gilligan's concept (1982) with a man's "voice," while thinking and feeling very much as a woman. I was able to put the logistics of our financial situation in a form that both enabled me to better communicate with my almost ex-husband, and at the same time have

the information in print for my lawyer. The word processor saved money by keeping costly and inconvenient phone calls to my lawyer to a minimum, and the typed copies allowed her the opportunity to consider my financial concepts and questions at her convenience. Word processing courses and information are given, among other places, at local high school or college adult education evening courses.

16

The Hidden Christ: AIDS

Jennifer M. Phillips

SERMON

Come, O Blessed of my Father, inherit the kingdom prepared for you from the foundation of the world, for I was hungry and you gave me food....As you did it to one of the least of these my brothers and sisters, you did it to me.

—Matthew 25:31–46

As for you my flock, thus says the Lord God: Behold, I judge between sheep and sheep, rams and he-goats.

—Ezekiel 34:11–17

If you aren't trembling in your boots as you listen to today's lections, you're missing something. Both Jesus and Ezekiel are pouring their passion into words of judgment and command. Jesus speaks with the urgency of his last three days of life. If the disciples don't get the message loudly and clearly now, it will be too late. He doesn't mince words. There is judgment — discernment — to come at the throne of the returning Christ, and that judgment will be based not on intention, philosophy, or any aspect of the inner life. It will be based on action of the most fundamental kind: tending the human needs of the least among us. That judgment will focus not only on our individual action but on the justice of our human communities, for it is the *nations* that the Christ will gather and separate: the peoples of the earth.

We are hearing these words with Thanksgiving approaching, as many of us prepare to sit in the company of friends and family, to eat and drink well, and to entertain guests. These blessings soon to be enjoyed are exactly the fulfillment of the gospel message; they fill our human need. We know their value. They remind us of the bountiful hand of the Creator, the generous breasts of God at which we are nurtured daily. We encounter the God who blesses us through the simple bodily delights of the world: through food and drink, through shelter and clothing, through human contact especially in times of isolation

---

This sermon was preached in 1988 as a guest sermon at Christ Episcopal in Cambridge, Massachusetts, in conjunction with their AIDS education program.

and weakness. When we nourish the littlest ones among us — the poor, the sick, the lonely, the unlovely — then we are nourishing in our turn the God who nourishes us. When we fail to care for the little ones, we hide God from those in greatest need of God.

This is a powerful word: in the little ones, we encounter the hidden Christ in need of us and we will be judged according to how well we care for that Christ. As we seek and find and care for Christ among us, we make manifest the hidden Christ to those who have lost heart in the seeking. In the graphic scene Jesus describes, clearly neither the righteous nor the unrighteous could guess that those they met in time of need contained the concealed being of Christ. While those of us schooled on this text may be able to discern easily the face of Christ in the face of the homeless person at our church supper, or the face of a sick child, or the face of a lonely elder shut in her room, we may miss the face of Christ in places we do not expect: the faces of Sandinistas in Nicaragua, perhaps, or the face of a Soviet leader, the face of an IRS auditor, the face of a drag queen, or a Washington Street hooker, the neighbor whose dog fouls our lawn, or a Palestinian refugee; the list goes on. If Christ's face is hidden and if our responsibility before God is a responsibility to minister to Christ wherever Christ is hidden, then we must lay aside our prejudgments and expect that wherever we see a human being in need or distress we may be gazing into the eyes of God.

Mahatma Gandhi said it in a slightly different way: If you don't find God in the very next person you meet, it is a waste of time looking for God further!

The eyes of the faithful heart see Christ in each and every other, and seeing, our hands reach out to feed and clothe and comfort and touch. And for the one being touched, lo and behold, the toucher's hands are the hands of Christ and in the toucher's face — our face — Christ is glimpsed, the hidden Christ, in an intimate recognition. Christ meets Christ, and we encounter our profound interconnectedness with all others in Christ.

This week the face of Christ looked up at me through the eyes of a young man with AIDS. Like many others, he was infected at a time when the world knew nothing about AIDS, at a time when in first adulthood he was searching for affection and closeness as a gay man who had experienced little of either at any time in his life. He was a gifted man, a collector of lovely antiques, a chef, a singer of opera. As AIDS laid his immune system open to infection, he contracted salmonella, which the hospital could not cure, and it spread until his skin sloughed from head to toe, leaving him as raw as a massively burned person, until he let go of his spirit and died. At that time in which he no longer wanted food, could not stand the weight of the lightest covering on his body, ceased craving even ice chips, it was human presence he wanted: friends to sit at his bedside, speak to him when awake, watch while he slept so that he could feel less alone than he had during much of his life. Blessedly, friends were there for him.

What is it that keeps us from the kindly activity of care? Often, it is not the lack of good intention. For many of us, it is lack of time in the whirl of our world and the worry of work. For some of us it is the unloveliness of the least of God's little ones: the dirtiness, difference of color or sexuality or habit from ourselves, sickness, deformity, values divergent from our own. We would prefer to keep them at a distance. Here in Massachusetts one suburban community raised a petition that a home for the multiply handicapped being built within its boundaries have a dining hall redesigned without windows so that neighbors passing by on the street would not be distressed by the sight of the residents eating. Many of our communities are protesting plans to build drug rehabilitation centers in neighborhoods, as though those little ones in need come from some other place and belong elsewhere.

As AIDS spreads globally, our nation will face a challenge of charity in the same manner. We in the West with our relative prosperity will be the first to have treatments and vaccines and information as they are developed. By the time any of those remedies come, our health resources will be stretched thin. We will be running out of health care personnel, equipment, money, and hospital beds. Yet Africa, parts of the Caribbean and South America, and eventually the Far East face a more desperate plight with less of everything to go around. Will we share what we have when it is not enough even for us? Will we as individuals lobby for the establishment of a global network for AIDS relief? Will we see the hidden face of Christ in Africa? In Haiti?

Within our own borders, as AIDS decimates our inner-city populations of color, of the poorest of the poor, and of gay men and slowly spreads to rural areas, will we respond with kindness? Will we try to wall AIDS out of our neighborhood enclaves by guarding the gates with shotguns and legislation, barring people who look risky or different? Will we create internment colonies of the sick, the well but infected, or those we assess as being at risk and their caregivers? Will the fear of infection and death come to govern all our interpersonal relationships?

As a Christian I am filled with hope, even in the face of a very grim future scenario of AIDS. I see hope in the ability of people to learn and to change their behavior as they live together in community. I see hope in the tried and true networks of communication, education, and neighborly care that the church has developed over centuries around the world. Through those channels and through new conduits that we develop, we can share whatever respite comes our way and move beyond our ethnic and national boundaries. It is urgent that we turn the mission energies of our various denominations toward the task. In parishes we bring together skills of home nursing, bereavement support, nutrition, friendly visitation, addiction intervention, and all the ordinary tasks of life, which will be needed by those touched by AIDS. We can teach these skills to one another and create teams for home care of the sick when the available beds in our hospitals are exhausted, and when individuals have no family support. I see hope in the ability of church communities to take on ministries that might overwhelm individuals and families: adoption of an infant with AIDS or even a lone sick adult.

I see profound hope in the gospel that reveals to us the God who has defeated death and the fear of death by sharing its deepest suffering with us and who has given us the promise of eternal life. We are people of the Resurrection. We may not live as those who have no faith, paralyzed by our fears. We must overcome our modern embarrassment at speaking of heaven, for it is ours by promise. The world needs that Good News just as we need to hear it repeatedly from one another.

I see hope in the ability of our Christian tradition to embrace our bodiliness, just as God embraced flesh to come among us. The Incarnation gives us a mandate to love and enjoy and be wise stewards of our bodies, our health, our sexuality. We must talk and reflect theologically and experientially with one another about these godly aspects of our being. The God who nourishes us with the real food and drink of Christ's own body in the Eucharist made us flesh, not just spirit. Embracing our bodiliness means embracing our diversity, for our bodies have different shapes, colors, erotic predilections, and experiences of self. In this stuff of our being, Christ is hidden, not elsewhere. It is not ours to judge which of our brothers and sisters is fit for the reign of God, for God has made us all of one humanity.

I see hope also in the strength of prayer. AIDS adds a new urgency to the command to pray for one another as individuals and as liturgical communities seeking healing in many ways.

If we spend our energies trying to discern who is and who is not lit by the Divine spark, who is and who is not righteous, who is and who is not the little one needing our care, who is a sheep and who a goat, we will be wasting our precious resources and time and missing the hidden Christ who will always take us by surprise. The pain is deep and the need pressing all around us. If we begin with the very next person we meet, expecting to minister to the hidden Christ, then we will hear, when we are called to render our account, "Come, O

Blessed of my Father, inherit the kingdom prepared for you from the foundation of the world." Amen.

AUTOBIOGRAPHICAL STATEMENT

When the first patient with a diagnosis of AIDS was admitted to the Brigham and Women's Hospital in Boston where I worked as chaplain for five years, I had already been following the discovery of this new disease in the back columns of the newspapers for some time. In 1985 and 1986 the number of patients increased steadily, and for many first hospitalizations ended with death. Gowns, gloves, and scrupulous precautions were the norm at first when transmission routes were unclear.

In a short period, much information was gained about the HIV virus and the humane care of those affected. In the fall of 1985 the new Massachusetts Episcopal bishop coadjutor, David Johnson, convened a diocesan AIDS task force, which at once became ecumenical. I was elected to serve as chair through its first three years and became a co-chair of the Pastoral Concerns Committee of AIDS Action Committee, the major service provider for people with HIV infection in Eastern Massachusetts. I began speaking and teaching in religious congregations across the state, a natural development from my background several years previously as a family planning and health counselor and educator. For the past five years I have given care to about two hundred persons with AIDS and their loved ones.

In 1988 I left chaplaincy work and became the co-rector of the parish of St. John the Evangelist, an inclusive parish in the Anglo-Catholic tradition, in downtown Boston, and now my AIDS work has a community rather than hospital focus. I now serve on the AIDS Task Force of the Massachusetts Council of Churches.

I have had a lifetime interest in medicine, being the daughter of a nurse and a research scientist, and by the time I graduated with my B.A. from Wellesley College in 1973, it was clear that I was destined for a ministry related to health care. I studied at Kings College, London, and then completed my master of divinity and doctor of ministry degrees at Andover Newton Theological School in Massachusetts, by which time I already was working as a chaplain.

I envision AIDS work as a vital part of the ministry of every religious community, with the church forming a global network for the sharing of resources, information, and care, in concert with other faiths.

BACKGROUND INFORMATION

By July 1989, over 99,000 men, women, and children had been diagnosed with AIDS in the United States. The Acquired Immune Deficiency Syndrome is a diagnostic label for the activity of the Human Immunodeficiency Virus (HIV) in causing malfunction of the immune system and symptoms related to the presence of one or more of over a dozen infections unusual in persons with healthy immune systems ("opportunistic infections"), most commonly pneumocystic carinni pneumonia. Uncommon forms of cancer, tuberculosis, and invasive infections with common viruses and microorganisms such as candida (yeast) may also lead to a diagnosis of AIDS. A much larger population with HIV infection may experience other forms of infection and symptoms from minor to chronic and debilitating, which fall short of the formal diagnostic categories. The largest group by far, possibly a hundred times as large as the number of those with AIDS, consists of individuals infected with HIV with no clinical symptoms and no knowledge that they are unwell and able to pass the virus on to others. It is probable that many these asymptomatic carriers will over decades become ill and finally die of AIDS.

AIDS is a global killer already widespread in equatorial Africa and the Caribbean and parts of Central and South America as well as on the North American continent. There is every reason to suppose it will move gradually across geographic boundaries and affect Asia and Eastern Europe on the same scale. Some futurists predict that the HIV virus might eventually infect one fifth of the world's population. Already the virus and its associated diseases are creating a massive drain on health care resources, a growing loss of productivity as young adults are stricken at the height of their working and reproductive years along with their infants, and a challenge to global health education and prevention technologies.

In the United States, 58 percent of all people diagnosed with AIDS have died. Here where the most up-to-date treatments are available to those with health insurance, access to well-informed physicians, and good nutrition and health maintenance practices, many more people with AIDS are living for years with their HIV infection, able to fend off the secondary opportunistic infections. The poor, particularly people of color, foreign language speakers, women and children, and IV needle users continue to die rapidly and in disproportionate numbers of HIV-related illness. The virus has spread most rapidly in the United States among the population groups that were affected earliest: gay men and IV needle users. The virus itself does not discriminate: it infects those who engage in behaviors that carry a high risk of transmission regardless of age, color, gender, or sexual orientation.

There are three routes of HIV transmission and in over a decade of close monitoring these routes remain the only significant ones. HIV is a blood-borne virus that can travel only in the body fluids that carry white blood cells.

The first route of transmission is by injection with infected blood. Whenever a needle carrying blood cells from an infected person enters the bloodstream of an uninfected person there is a likelihood of transmission. Consequently, IV drug users are at very high risk if needles and blood-contaminated drug equipment ("works") are shared. In the early years of AIDS, infected blood donors unknowingly gave HIV-infected blood, which resulted in transmission through blood transfusion. Blood products used by hemophiliacs also caused infection among this population. By 1985 all blood banks began testing all donated blood and blood products for the presence of HIV, and in recent years the risk of contracting HIV infection from receiving a blood transfusion is very small, less than the risk to life and health of not having a needed transfusion. Donating blood continues to carry *no* risk of transmitting AIDS.

It is not only injectors of street drugs who need to be concerned about HIV transmission, but also people who share blood contaminated needles for other purposes such as tattooing, ear piercing, or injecting steroids for body building. Thoroughly cleaning needles and drug equipment by soaking in a 10 percent bleach solution greatly reduces but does not eliminate the risk of HIV transmission to needle users.

The second route of transmission is through sexual intercourse. Semen and vaginal secretions contain large amounts of HIV virus in many infected individuals. Where these fluids are passed from one person to another, or where blood (including menstrual blood) of an infected person enters the bloodstream or contacts the mucous membranes of an uninfected person, transmission is possible. Anal intercourse carries a particularly high risk because the delicate mucous membranes of the rectum are easily abraded and damaged allowing blood or semen to be passed into the bloodstream of a sexual partner. Vaginal intercourse is also highly risky to both male and female partners. Oral-penile intercourse carries some risk particularly if semen is swallowed, or if there are scrapes to the mouth or gums or penis, though to date HIV transmission has not been conclusively traced through this route. A larger number of exposures seems to increase risk of contracting HIV, but infection can occur with the first exposure.

Only refraining from sexual intercourse with infected persons provides complete protection from sexual transmission. Apparent good health or the absence of symptoms of illness is no guarantee that a partner does not carry HIV infection, and even a detailed sexual history does not preclude the possibility of undetected infection if either partner has been sexually active in the past. For assistance in assessing one's sexual history for AIDS risk, consult a well-informed physician, or an AIDS hotline through your local Department of Public Health, or an AIDS service provider agency.

A frequently asked question is whether deep kissing carries a risk of HIV transmission. Saliva, like urine and sweat and tears, may carry relatively minute amounts of HIV virus in an infected person, but there seems to be a substance in saliva that inactivates the virus for the most part. Deep kissing may not be perfectly safe but it carries very little risk.

The proper use of latex condoms during any form of sexual intercourse, from beginning to end, offers good but not complete protection against transmission. There is a small but real failure rate even when condoms are put on carefully, inspected for pinholes by holding up to the light, have some space left at the tip, and are held at the base when the penis is withdrawn from the partner. They must never be reused, should be stored away from heat, light, and pressure (not in a wallet in a back pocket), and used with adequate lubrication. No petroleum-based lubricants (such as Vaseline) should be used, as this damages the latex. Condoms give added HIV protection when used with a viricidal foam, but some of these products can cause allergic reactions in some individuals.

The third route of transmission of the HIV virus is from infected mother to infant, *in utero*, or in the process of childbirth. The virus can cross the placenta. Estimates vary, but possibly as many as 50 percent of babies born to infected mothers will also have HIV infection and most of these babies will die within a few years of birth.

The HIV virus is not passed by casual contact: by coughs or sneezes, by shared eating utensils or linen, by toilet seats or telephones, or by the common Communion cup in church. Though no case of infection has been traced to a shared razor or toothbrush, common sense dictates that people not share items contaminated with the blood of another person. An ordinary household disinfectant or 10 percent bleach solution will kill the virus on surfaces and can be used to clean up spills of body fluids.

While the level of AIDS awareness and education in this country is improving, the plight of many affected by AIDS is worsening. Available hospital beds for those with HIV infection and AIDS may run out before the first years of the next century. Gradually the virus will spread among heterosexual people, but first its rapid spread among the urban poor, particularly people of color, both by IV needle and sexual transmission will create ghettos of infection that will exacerbate the dynamics of racism already present. Even though the level of new infections among gay men seems to be reaching a plateau because of intensive educational efforts by that community, large numbers of men who have had sexual contact with men will become ill and die of infection already contracted, increasing fear of and violence toward gay and lesbian people.

As the number of AIDS deaths climbs, ironically, the mentality of the nation shifts from a crisis mode to a chronic problem mode and AIDS recedes from the attention of the news media. State by state, the approaches taken to disease prevention, treatment, and education vary widely. Some states like Massachusetts are spending at relatively high levels and passing legislation to protect the insurance, employment, housing, and nondiscrimination rights of those afflicted. Others are preparing punitive legislation to make testing for HIV mandatory among large groups of the population.

Mandatory mass testing is prohibitively expensive, can produce both false positive and false negative test results with devastating consequences, and carries no guarantee of changing the sexual or drug-sharing behaviors of those tested. As more treatments for HIV-related infections are developed and medications are found that may slow or prevent the first appearance of these infections, then being tested will confer more of a benefit than it does now. A person who is at risk and wishes to be tested is wise to find one of the many federal test centers where complete anonymity can be guaranteed and counseling is provided before and after testing. Testing done in a doctor's office, by a hospital, or at a merely "confidential" test center can result in identification of the testee to his or her insurer or to a variety of medical personnel. Whether a test is negative or positive, the same behaviors are recommended: avoid sharing drug needles and equipment; avoid sexual intercourse with possible infected individuals; bear in mind that most people with HIV infection do not know they are infected and look and feel well; always use a new latex condom during sexual intercourse of any kind; seek HIV counseling before starting a pregnancy if infection of oneself or one's partner is possible. These behaviors protect the HIV positive person from transmitting the virus and prevent the uninfected person from contracting HIV.

There is much that religious communities can do to prepare for the growing challenge of AIDS. Here are a few possibilities:

- add to youth and adult curricula AIDS information presented in the context of healthy human sexuality. AIDS should not be the first thing young people hear about sex in church or school!

- develop home care teams to teach congregation members skills of home nursing, nutrition, visiting the sick, and bereavement support so that those who become ill can be cared for in their homes.

- consider a community project to assist a family to give foster care to a child or adult with AIDS. This is very difficult for a family in isolation but becomes manageable with well-organized help.

- where resources allow, offer support groups to people with HIV infection or AIDS, and their loved ones, parents, caregivers.

- sponsor a blood drive with a few other congregations. Fear of HIV infection has reduced the number of blood donors.

- contribute money or volunteer labor to your local AIDS service organization.

- add petitions for those living with AIDS and for the fearful to the Sunday prayers of the people; observe a vigil or a day of special prayer.

- offer your sanctuary for funerals and memorial services for those who die of AIDS who have no church home or who have felt unwelcome in their own communities.

- become politically active and lobby legislators and candidates for adequate spending and nondiscrimination legislation.

- increase self-education about racism, homophobia, drug use. Ask for or present sermons on these subjects, as well as AIDS. Bear in mind that there may be people in the congregation who are infected or who have a loved one who is, unknown to you or their neighbors.

- work toward open dialogue about sensitive personal matters. In a congregation where people feel safe to speak about their unemployment, domestic violence, drug and alcohol use and abuse, marital strains, and ordinary illnesses, people will also likely feel free to speak about their HIV infection.

- Publish and post the National AIDS Hotline number: (800) 822-7422.

BIBLIOGRAPHY

Fortunato, John. *AIDS: The Spiritual Dilemma*. Minneapolis: Winston Seabury Press, 1986.
———. *Embracing the Exile*. Winston Seabury Press, 1982.
Nungessen, Lon G., *Epidemic of Courage: Facing AIDS in America*. New York: St. Martins Press, 1986.
Patton, Cindy. *Sex and Germs*. Boston: South End Press, 1986.
Peabody, Barbara. *The Screaming Room*. San Diego: Oak Tree Publishers, 1986.
Quackenbush, Marcia, and Pamela Sargent. *Teaching AIDS*. San Diego: CA Network Publications (P.O. Box 1830, Santa Cruz, CA 95061), 1986.

Selwyn, Peter A. "Aids: What Is Not Known." *Hospital Practice*, May 15, 1986, pp. 67–76 (Part 1), and June 15, 1986, pp. 127–64 (Part 2).

Shelp, Earl E., and Ronald Sunderland. *AIDS and the Church*. Philadelphia: Westminster Press, 1987.

Shelp, Earl E., Ronald Sunderland, and P. Marsell. *AIDS: Personal Stories in Pastoral Perspective*. New York: Pilgrim Press, 1986.

Shilts, Randy. *And the Band Played On*. New York: St. Martins Press, 1987.

Snow, John. *Mortal Fear: Meditations on Death and AIDS*. Cambridge, Mass.: Cowley Publications, 1987.

Tatchell, Peter. *AIDS: A Guide to Survival*. New York: Gay Men's Press, 1986.

VIDEO RESOURCES

The AIDS Crisis and the Church (two 30-minute tapes with study guide). Interviews Ryan White and Surgeon General Koop; a bit moralistic and homophobic. EcuFilms, 810 Twelfth Avenue, South, Nashville, TN 37203. $35 each.

Beyond Fear (three parts, each 20:00). Available through your local Red Cross. "The Virus," "The Individual," and "The Community." On loan only.

Doors Opening: A Positive Approach to AIDS (55:00). Hay House, 3029 Wilshire Blvd., Santa Monica, CA 90404. $35.

Dying, Yet Behold We Live. Shows a parish healing service. The Episcopal Church Center, 815 Second Avenue, New York, NY 10017.

Epidemic of Fear: AIDS in the Workplace (23:19). Comes with workbook and sample personnel policies. San Francisco AIDS Foundation, 333 Valencia Street, 4th Floor, San Francisco, CA 94103. $398.

The Human Face of AIDS (35:00). An interview with James E. Hurley. Contact Judith E. McBri, Connecticut College, Department of Philosophy, (203) 827-7632.

In the Midst of Life (28:00). Care for PWA's in San Francisco General AIDS ward. KRON-TV Films Incorporated, 5547 N. Ravenswood Avenue, Chicago, IL 60640.

Sex, Drugs and Aids (17:54). Aimed at junior and senior high school students. ODN Productions, 74 Varick Street, Suite 304, New York, NY 10013. $315.

Shanti Training Series (20 hours of training tapes with 28-minute preview tape available). Shows volunteers the complexity of working with people with AIDS. Shanti Project. (415) 558-9644.

The Subject Is AIDS (18:00). Similar to *Sex, Drugs and Aids*, but a better ethnic mix and more emphasis on abstinence and less on condoms. ODN Productions, 74 Varick Street, Suite 304, New York, NY 10013.

1986 and 1987 New England Episcopal Conference on AIDS. Complete video or audio tapes of these three-day conferences. Christ Church Tape Ministry, Red Hook, NY 12571.

17

Declaration of Interdependence: Good News in the Environmental Crisis

Kate Penfield

SERMON

When the dragon saw that he had been thrown down to the earth, he went in pursuit of the woman who had given birth to the male child. But she was given the wings of a mighty eagle, so that she could fly to her place in the wilderness where she was to be looked after for three and a half years, out of reach of the serpent. From his mouth the serpent spewed a flood of water after the woman to sweep her away with its spate. But the earth came to her rescue: it opened its mouth and drank up the river which the dragon spewed from his mouth. Furious with the woman, the dragon went off to wage war on the rest of her offspring, those who keep God's commandments and maintain their witness to Jesus.

—Revelation 12:13–17

In the summer of 1990, as we celebrate the Fourth of July and the Declaration of Independence, the contemporary world scene is alive with movements toward independence. Everywhere from the Soviet Union to China to Latin America to South Africa, there is ferment as people strive to attain rights inalienable as described in our revolutionary document of 1776. The achievement of independence is an essential step along the way of human development, but it must never be mistaken for the final goal. People need independence so that we can stand face to face and see one another as equals, so that we can live together in relationships that acknowledge and support our *inter*dependence. It is dependence that is the goal, even of independence.

The Bible *begins* in the book of Genesis with the premise that it is not good for a human being to be alone, that we are made to

---

This sermon was preached on July 1, 1990, at the First Baptist Church in America in Providence, Rhode Island.

be partners, face-to-face companions. The very goodness of creation consists in the harmony of all its parts, women and men together created in the image of God, living plants and creatures and the earth itself. Human beings are given the mandate and the privilege to have dominion over the rest of creation by taking care of it.

The Bible *ends* in the book of Revelation with a picture of the consummation of creation in heaven where human beings are circled around the throne of God, therefore standing side by side. By the very nature of a circle, the closer to God humanity moves, the closer to one another we stand. The language of heaven in Revelation is praise, and the singers are not just people but all created things together, things in heaven, on earth, under the earth, and in the sea. The origin from which we come and the goal toward which we move from start to finish draw all parts of creation into relationships of interdependence.

On the other hand, the systems of hierarchy operative in the world we know are based on the premise that some people must be at the bottom, resulting in an oppression that is considered legitimate, and indeed essential, to the basic order of things. How far this world is from God's dream of interdependence, this world of street people and violence in the schools, of unequal opportunity for some and overabundant opportunity for others. What is the source of this sin?

The source of this sin is dualism, the human tendency to see the other as alien. It is a system of either/or: either male or female, either black or white, either you or me. Never both/and. Dualism is incarnated in such "isms" as racism and classism.

Joan Chittister, prioress of the Benedictine Sisters in Erie, Pennsylvania, in speaking on one aspect of dualism clarifies the interconnection of all its aspects:

> What we're trying to say is that sexism — the notion that God built inferiority right into the human race, that women are somehow a lesser creation than men — validates violence against anyone. That's what I call the theology of domination. It says that some humans are more human than other humans and, therefore, have the right and the duty to control those lesser than themselves. If you accept that, if you buy the fact that God built inequality into the human race, if you believe that men are more finely developed creatures and more open to the grace of God — then you're a short step away from the extermination of red people or the lynching of black people or the napalming of yellow people or the gassing of the next generation of Jews. Some of us are in charge, and we know who we are.... But that's not the theology that is the vision of the gospel.

Dualism is the antithesis of interdependence. It leads to a reversal of the biblical vision of paradise — hell on earth. One would hope that the urgency to amend our ways would cry out to us from the horrors of the Holocaust, apartheid, abuse within families. One would expect that the burdens we ourselves bear when caught within systems that have marginalized us or expect us always to be stronger than possible would urge us to overthrow the status quo. Apparently these examples of human relationships gone awry are insufficient to prompt us to conversion, probably because conversion that demands such a radical inner revolution is desperately difficult.

What challenge will wrench us away from a theology that translates dominion as domination and prevents the recognition of our interdependence? The environmental crisis offers such an opportunity, perhaps the final one, to exchange our domineering, separatistic ways for interdependence. If, in our dualism, we persist in raping and pillaging the earth into silent submission, we shall lose not just mother earth but our home and even ourselves.

Wendell Berry, both a farmer and poet, has pointed out the similarity between behavior toward others and human behavior toward the earth: "It is impossible to care for each other more or differently than we care for the earth.... There is an uncanny *resemblance* between our behavior toward each other and our behavior toward the earth." If we can learn to respect the earth, perhaps we can transfer that to the human part of God's creation.

Revelation describes in vivid imagery the consummation of creation through the bizarre scenario of a woman in flight from a serpent that spews a flood of water to sweep her away. But the earth comes to her rescue and drinks up the flood. The serpent is symbolic of our ancient enemy, evil, intent on deceiving us into destructive behavior. We witness evil at work wherever the very goodness of creation is being destroyed: wars, poverty, pollution, a hole in the ozone layer. The list is endless. The woman pursued by the serpent and protected by the earth represents the people of God from every time and place, and that includes each one of us.

We hear such devastating news about the environment that we are tempted to despair of the earth's fate. How appropriate that within the book of the Bible written to assure us that, regardless of appearances to the contrary, God's will for the world shall prevail, there lies embedded this nugget of good news. *The earth is on our side.* The earth, abused by our inability to perceive the interdependence of all created things, is seeking to rescue us from our folly.

At the same time as independence movements spring up across the world, interdependence movements called Green are rallying increasing numbers of proponents. People everywhere are beginning to recognize and respond to the signals the earth is sending: that what is "other" is nevertheless also of God's creation and deserving of respect, and that now is not a moment too soon to right our relationship with the earth.

Here is the hope within the crisis. Perhaps if we can learn at last how to relate to the earth as God intends, we can also learn to relate lovingly to other human beings. Perhaps if we can unlearn a dualism that requires the suppression and oppression of anything and anyone different from us, human history can move nearer to the heavenly hope of interdependence. Perhaps women and men, Christians and Jews, red and yellow, black and white, citizens of the Soviet Union and citizens of the United States — people so very different but fundamentally far more alike than different — will begin to look at one another and see not competition for the top spot on the ladder but a sister or brother with whom to hold hands together around the throne of God.

African Christians in Malawi sing a hymn that we all might pray:

> Jesu, Jesu,
> Show us how to serve
> The neighbors we have from you.
>
> Neighbors are rich people and poor.
> Neighbors are black people and white.
> Neighbors are nearby and far away.
>
> Neighbors are animals and trees.
> Neighbors are mountains and grass.
> Neighbors are all creatures on earth.

Jesus Christ came to break down barriers, mend rifts, and teach us to be neighbors, so that God's dream of interdependence will become reality. To enter human life so full of tears, God must have yearned to show us the way to that dream.

There is a yearning in us also for that dream, an empty place that will be filled only when God is truly at the center of our lives so that our sisters and brothers are beside us and we them. Then side by side we will form a circle of interdependence with the whole created order.

Sometimes when I consider how things are in this world, I weep for God's dream, but then the works of God's hand, the green earth and the singing of birds outside my window, the sunshine and the endless stretches of sand and waves at the beach speak to my soul, and my heart echoes the lyrics of the old song about God who is Father and also Mother of us all:

> This is my Father's world,
> O let me ne'er forget
> That though the wrong seems oft so strong,
> God is the Ruler yet.

This is my Father's world;
The battle is not done;
Jesus who died shall be satisfied;
And earth and heaven be one.

Let us therefore ask God's help as we celebrate today the sacredness of this good earth on which we live our lives and through which we are so often awed by the presence of God. Let us acknowledge our sorrow for the wounding, scarring, and desecrating of the earth and the air and the sea that too frequently accompany our "progress." Let us pour out our gratitude and praise for all the good gifts that sustain and enrich our lives and reveal God's grace.

We pray that God will teach us how to live and reveal the secrets of being stewards in this world, of exercising dominion not as plunderers, but as caretakers of creation. As we are privileged to stand in all the holy places of our lives — on the ground that is sacred because it is God's, in relationships that are sacred because where even two or three are gathered God is there, in our own beings that are sacred because they mirror God's image — in all these holy places we pray that God will give us directions toward a new creation when all shall live together in harmony.

We seek the face of God in order that we might have such a life, yet we have already seen the face of God in the face of Jesus Christ, in whom lordship looks like love; through whom dominion is revealed as service; from whom we know that fullness of being comes only in self-emptying on behalf of the other, whether the other is sister or brother, someone very unlike us, or even the very ground on which we stand.

Let us bow our heads and lift our hearts to the Creator of everything that exists, as the one who called the cosmos into being and draws it toward a consummation more magnificent than we can imagine but about which we do know that all things and all people will be united. May the Divine enter our thinking and our feeling and our doing, turn our understanding upside down so that our power is used for service, and so shine forth from our faces that we see this world with the eyes of God and live our lives with the love of God. We ask God to heal us that we might be whole, and to heal our land that suffers because of us so that all that is sacred because God made it to be very good might shine with God's glory.

AUTOBIOGRAPHICAL STATEMENT

I entered seminary as a wife of a busy and successful professional husband and the mother of five children. At that time I had never seen a woman minister and was unsure about the vocation to which God was calling me. I am still the wife of that same husband and the mother of five children, at this writing from fifteen to twenty-five years in age. I have not only seen many women ministers but count some of them among my closest friends. Most days I am very sure about this vocation to which God has called me and which perfectly fits the woman God created me.

My academic background includes degrees from the State University of New York at Albany, the University of Cincinnati, and Andover Newton Theological School. Before entering seminary, I had been a high school teacher and an employment counselor.

My family moved to Rhode Island in the summer of 1976, carried on a wave of many prayers that we would go out from our last church as part of a river of living water to touch and transform the world. Once in Rhode Island, Gary went off to his work for which we had made the move, and I stayed at home cut off from my accustomed routine of church and community activities. I began to pray that God would reveal to me my own role in this new land.

By the autumn of 1977 I had an unclear and partial vision of the entry point to my new role. I enrolled in seminary with the intention of entering whatever doors God might open, until I encountered a door that would not open. Each time an obstacle presented itself a solution was provided: the Greenville Baptist Church paid the early installments of my seminary tuition; a friend volunteered quality child care in my home; a field education position in a Providence church opened up; a clinical pastoral education program was initiated in Rhode Island Hospital the summer I needed it. Even my firm conviction that I would never preach was overcome when a pastor invited me to preach twice in his absence and out of pride that would not let me admit that preaching was not something I intended to do, I did preach, and discovered a passion for preaching.

In rapid succession, from December 1980 through February 1981, I completed my master of divinity degree, underwent an ordination council, was ordained, became installed as the associate pastor of the church where I had been a field education student, and was launched in the career for which God began to call me in 1976, but for which God had been preparing me at least since my birth. My one regret was that my grandmother, always instrumental in the process of my becoming a woman of faith, died before my ordination. At least she knew that it was to be.

On May 3, 1987, I began my current pastorate at the First Baptist Church in America, in Providence, Rhode Island. This church was founded in 1638 by Roger Williams, who had also founded the city of Providence as a shelter for persons distressed of conscience. Roger

Williams was an ardent advocate of freedom of conscience for all people regardless of religion or gender. Among the body of believers who convinced him of the rightness of believer's baptism was Catherine Scott, sister of Anne Hutchinson. I sometimes wonder how the first pastor of this church would react to the news that the thirty-third pastor is a woman. I hope that he would be as delighted to have me follow in his footsteps as I am to do it.

BACKGROUND INFORMATION

By every measure, the twenty years since the first Earth Day celebration sought to rally environmental activism in 1970 have seen further deterioration. Partial progress is represented in the comeback of endangered species such as the American bald eagle and alligator, and here in Rhode Island the piping plover. Lake Erie has been cleaned up and now again supports a thriving fishing industry. Rivers such as the Potomac and the Cuyahoga are no longer considered threats to life. However, these are isolated instances in an overwhelmingly negative environmental picture.

The air bears contaminants from automobile and industrial pollutants. It is heating up at an alarming rate because of carbon dioxide emissions from fossil fuel burning and from the destruction of rain forests. Global warming threatens rising sea levels and more droughts and hurricanes. There are great holes ripped in the ozone layer that allow lethal amounts of the sun's rays to bombard the earth, with the consequence that malignant melanoma has increased 350 percent in men and 460 percent in women since 1963.

Water everywhere is being poisoned. Chemicals leaking from toxic waste dumps make their way into aquifers, source of much of our drinking water. Industrial wastes contaminate rivers. Medical wastes and oil spills threaten the oceans. Acid rain has killed numerous lakes.

The land on which we live, from which we grow our food, is being eroded at such a rate (four billion tons of topsoil lost each year in the United States alone) that if it continues unchecked, early in the next century fertile land will be depleted by one-third. Americans use an area of land the size of Indiana to grow grains just to feed the more than five billion chickens slaughtered for food annually; we cannot continue to produce chickens, meat, milk, and eggs to feed our population high on the food chain at the expense of the land. Recognized and unrecognized chemically poisoned sites have resulted in the doubling of birth defects worldwide in the last quarter century, along with escalating cancer rates.[1]

A Declaration of Interdependence is designed to echo two other declarations. In 1848 Elizabeth Cady Stanton and Lucretia Mott at the Seneca Falls Conference composed a Declaration of Sentiments modeled on the Declaration of Independence and claiming that women are entitled to the rights considered inalienable by men.[2]

In 1973 the Chicago Men's Gathering drafted a Declaration of Principles urging rights of men:

> To achieve our goals, we have come together in a non-hierarchical, non-elective community, devoted to the fostering of a new male identity....We deplore the rigid and destructive traditional masculine role which demands of us that we be tough, aggressive and competitive, that we suppress our emotions and become insensitive to the feelings of others, and that we "prove our manhood" by dominating and intimidating others, sometimes through violence. We are committed to freeing men from the destructive impact of this stereotyped role![3]

Since Christianity has traditionally imaged God as white and male, all who are other than white men have suffered the stigma of being considered less in the image of God, therefore subject to domination. Obviously most of the human and all the nonhuman portion of creation find themselves on the list as victims of dualism. At the same time, men promoted to the top by systems of dualism are also victimized by stereotypes that are just as restrictive as those that bind women and nonwhite men. While, on the face of it, dualism in a patriarchal culture appears to present a win-lose scenario, in fact the outcome is lose-lose, with those who would appear to be the big winners losing their right to be vulnerable and to share burdens.

At least we who are human have voices to protest and to negotiate with one another. The nonhuman part of creation is forced to remain mute as humanity carelessly abuses it. Animals are tortured and rain forests are destroyed and the earth is poisoned, but few hear their cries of pain as humanity imposes upon nature the same dynamic of dualism that has divided and oppressed us.

The time is at hand when we must begin to pay attention. Creation is keeping a record of the wounds that we inflict and is calling us to account with a now familiar litany of repercussions: global warming, depletion of the ozone layer, carcinogens in the air we breathe and the water we drink and the earth upon which we live. Now is the time, if it is not too late already, to come together for cooperative and dramatic actions to save the earth and perhaps in the process our very souls.

It is not just for the sake of humanity that we must save the earth;

it is for the sake of all living creatures facing the extermination of species and for the sake of the earth itself. Even if, as some people predict, it is too late to save our industrial society and perhaps even humanity itself, we have no right to kill the earth and its nonhuman inhabitants.

A spiritual awakening is needed to reverse our death-dealing tendencies by arresting our worship of the gods of progress and power that demand rape and pillage of the earth to satiate their appetites. My prayer is that such a spiritual awakening will heal the brokenness within and between and among all parts of God's good creation, to the end that we shall live together in interdependence.

NOTES

1. Diane MacEachern, *Save Our Planet* (New York: Dell, 1990).
2. Carol Gilligan, *In a Different Voice* (Cambridge, Mass.: Harvard University Press, 1982), p. 128.
3. Matthew Fox, *A Spirituality Named Compassion*, 2d ed. (San Francisco: Harper & Row, 1990), pp. 55–56.

BIBLIOGRAPHY

Fox, Matthew. *The Coming of the Cosmic Christ*. San Francisco: Harper & Row, 1988.

———. *Original Blessing*. Santa Fe, N.M.: Bear & Company, 1983.

———. *A Spirituality Named Compassion*. 2d ed. San Francisco: Harper & Row, 1990.

———. *Whee! We, Wee: All the Way Home*. Santa Fe, N.M.: Bear & Company, 1981.

Gilligan, Carol. *In a Different Voice*. Cambridge, Mass.: Harvard University Press, 1982.

Lovelock, James. *The Ages of Gaia: A Biography of Our Living Earth*. New York: Bantam Books, 1990.

McDaniel, Jay B. *Of God and Pelicans: A Theology of Reverence for Life*. Louisville: Westminster/John Knox Press, 1989.

O'Brien, William. "Joan Chittister: Model for Christian Feminism," *Other Side* (April 1986): 14.

Trible, Phyllis. *God and the Rhetoric of Sexuality*. Philadelphia: Fortress Press, 1978.

Walker, Alice. *The Color Purple*. New York: Harcourt Brace Jovanovich, 1982.

RESOURCES

The Earthworks Group. *50 Simple Things You Can Do to Save the Earth.* Berkeley, Calif.: Earthworks Press, 1989.

Diane MacEachern. *Save Our Planet.* New York: Dell, 1990.

Utne Reader, a bimonthly publication of the LENS Publishing Co., Fawkes Building, 1624 Harmon Place, Minneapolis, MN 55403.

Appalachian Mountain Club, Pinkham Notch, P.O. Box 298, Gorham, NH 03581; (603) 466-2727.

Sierra Club, 730 Polk Street, San Francisco, CA 94109; (415) 776-2211.

18

Sanctuary: Confronting Oppression

Darlene Nicgorski

SERMON

[Setting: sandals, candle, and woven pieces of cloth from Guatemala and a photo or painting of a Central American woman.]

Our first task in approaching another people, another culture, another religion, is to take off our shoes, for the place we are approaching is holy. Else we may find ourselves treading on another's dreams. More serious still, we may forget that God was there before our arrival.
(Source unknown)

At this point I want to remove my sandals and walk barefoot for two reasons. First, because I feel I'm walking on holy ground, in a sanctuary, a community of women that welcomes the word I speak — the only real word I can speak — the truth of my life. I believe that *acompañamiento* — walking with — may be the new kind of "spiritual exercise" relevant for today. It is not withdrawal but engagement — opening one's eyes to all in order to find the cause of systemic evil. And second, I remove my sandals because they are symbolic of journey and each of us has been on our own particular journey. Our Native American sisters and brothers have an expression that addresses with respect the uniqueness of our lives and journeys. Until we have walked in the sandals or moccasins of another, we cannot understand their lives. Come and walk with me awhile.

Alice Walker writes about the importance of naming our teachers. And so I begin my journey with reference to some of our foremothers who have gone before and given us the courage to pick up our own struggles. It was Joan Chittister, O.S.B., who I first heard refer to Moses' mother and Pharaoh's daughter as forgotten women. She named them the first two co-conspirators who defied every law and order of the male paternalistic system by refusing to be enemies. And

---

Although this exact sermon was never delivered, it was developed over several years and major portions of it have been preached to several congregations as well as at numerous sanctuary, women's, and student conferences and ecumenical prayer services.

in so doing, they not only saved a child but a nation and a race. They followed the truth they knew within themselves as women — life is valuable. They have given us an extraordinary example of solidarity that required both civil and ecclesial disobedience. They dissented by refusing to collaborate and contribute to death in order to protect some male political leader's ego.

Another scriptural story of two women, Ruth and Naomi, illustrates going beyond the expectations of law or custom in the bond of friendship. Ruth's story, long one of my favorites, is one of the best examples of *acompañamiento* or solidarity. Here is Naomi, a widow, left with no resources to sustain her in her society, and Ruth, who according to law and custom had fulfilled her duty to her dead husband. Ruth exemplifies faithfulness; she goes beyond common sense, beyond human horizons, beyond the human response of what is safe or legal. I think it is no mere coincidence that it is a woman, a foreigner, Ruth, who breaks down the barriers of societal custom. Like Moses' mother and Pharaoh's daughter, she does not meet destruction but rather opens the door to her own blessing.

In more recent history, there are the stories of Harriet Tubman and Sojourner Truth, who risked their own lives many times to lead other slaves to safety in the North in the 1850s. Many other examples of such women exist, too numerous to mention here. But to continue the personal remembering, let us stop for a moment of silence to remember a woman who by her courage in word or deed has been a foremother for us.

> Praise our choices, sisters, for each doorway open to us was taken by squads of fighting women who paid with their wombs, their sleep, their lives that we might walk through these gates upright. Doorways are sacred to women for we are the doorways of life and we must choose what goes out. Freedom is our real abundance.
>
> (Marge Piercy, *The Moon Is Always Female*)

In this tradition women have also been in the forefront of the national sanctuary movement. The underground railroad that transported Central American refugees from the desert of Arizona to the sisters' house of prayer in Kansas was sustained primarily by women. For the most part it was women who were feeding, transporting, housing, and clothing the Central Americans. Legal representation for the refugees, whether in Phoenix, Harlingen, or Los Angeles, was a response by women attorneys who worked long hours with little success for small salaries. The indictment against sanctuary workers in January of 1985 in Phoenix accused sixteen of conspiracy. Eleven of us were women.

These phenomena reflect the witness of our Latin American sisters. One contemporary example is the Mothers of the Plaza in Argentina, who for eight years faithfully gathered every Thursday to protest the disappearances of children and husbands; these women are now being vindicated as the new government investigates the crimes they exposed. In Guatemala, GAM (Grupo Apoyo Mutuo), the Mutual Support Group, was formed during 1984 by the wives and mothers of students abducted from San Carlos National University in the first half of 1984. According to the *New York Times*, part of the inspiration for GAM came from a tape made by the "Mothers of the Disappeared in El Salvador." This group has been active for years in raising a voice on behalf of the disappeared.

I remember too the witness of the lives and assassinations of the four North American churchwomen in December of 1980. I was preparing to leave for Guatemala to assist my congregation, the School Sisters of St. Francis, in setting up a pre-school when I saw the news reports of their brutal rape and assassination. The graphic film footage on TV of American Ambassador Robert White and Maryknoll sisters — watching as the bodies of the four women were dug from the shallow graves — led me to wonder what was ahead for me. I became more confused and angry as I watched the official reports from the state department: Alexander Haig, then secretary of state, called the murdered women "gun-runners" and explained that "maybe they were caught in the cross-fire." Jeanne Kirkpatrick, U.S. ambassador to the U.N., stated publicly: "They were not ordinary nuns." Ernest Lefever, the defeated Reagan nominee for undersecretary of state for human rights, suggested that "their concern for the poor had exceeded the bounds of their religious calling."

My own journey had begun before my first trip to Guatemala. Sometime in the mid-1970s I left Milwaukee, birthplace and headquarters of my religious congregation, for a new territory in rural Mississippi. I was going to a new people — a people I didn't know — southern, rural, and black. I encountered blatant racism both around me and within me. I saw women cooking cornbread over open fires in black iron skillets. The sociological term "the feminization of poverty" took on new meaning for me. Living, working, and praying with these people gave new challenges to my own life. I left Mississippi after five years to work in a low-income housing project in Omaha. Again my work with women and children opened my eyes to the systematized oppression that exerts its heaviest burden upon women.

My budding consciousness of the interconnectedness of oppression was exponentially propelled when I responded to a request by the Guatemalan religious community to help them set up a pre-school in 1980. I came with little analysis of the social, economic, or political realities of the region. After less than six months in the country

I was enmeshed in the reality when on July 1, 1981, our pastor was assassinated returning from Mass. Our entire congregation left the country within days when warnings came to us that we would be next if we didn't leave. No longer was I accompanying — "walking with others." I was either being dragged along, not sure why or where to, or running for my life — mere survival.

I began slowly to peel back the layers of my life until I reached the core where I painfully and anxiously examined the premises upon which I had built my life. Each experience — the eight months of exile in southern Mexico and work with the diocesan refugee committee responding to the needs of the Guatemalan refugees; the capture and kidnapping of Albertina, the religious worker with whom I was to begin work in El Tesoro refugee camp, Honduras — left me more vulnerable. Through those months I came to understand the challenge of *life* in the daily experiences of Central Americans. Although I had made my vows as a Catholic sister here in the U.S., the experiences of accompanying our Guatemalan sisters clearly brought home to me the cost of that commitment. I examined my own courage, fidelity, and trust in a God that I had proclaimed from childhood. Having walked with our Guatemalan sisters, living those months of fear, terror, and hope with them, I came a little closer to experiencing what horror repressive military dictatorships exert upon their citizens.

I left Mexico and returned to the U.S., where I worked in Arizona with Central American refugees and later the sanctuary movement. During these first years back in the U.S., I began to feel the anger and guilt of realizing that within myself exists both oppressor and oppressed. There was no way to get around the fact that I was privileged as white, middle-class, well educated, and part of the institutional church in the United States. I live off the privileges of this U.S. society that are usually gained at the expense of poor Third World peoples. I also became increasingly impatient with my own oppression as a woman and my second-class status in this society and this church. There was a sense of power growing in me as I began to claim this reality.

What I saw in the sanctuary movement was not only an opportunity to respond out of compassion for those in need but an occasion to act in solidarity by giving up the privileged status of "legal" when others are declared "illegal." By giving the refugees public platforms in communities of faith and love where they could speak the truth of their lives, I sensed growing within me the urgency to say out loud my own truth. This power was growing within because I thought I could make a difference. I believed that if more people knew the reality of Central America, we could make a difference. We would say *"Basta," "Enough,"* to the policies and money exported from the White House that maintain the war machines that create the refugees.

As a result of my work in sanctuary, I was indicted for conspiracy to violate immigration laws in January of 1985 and my home was searched by agents of the Immigration and Naturalization Service. The public trial that dragged on for almost seven months forced me to confront two of the most patriarchal institutions, the legal system and the institutional church. I saw the truth compromised in so many ways. I saw how those in power and with money often manipulate the truth and control the media to serve their own ends. And so it was no great surprise when on May 1, 1986, eight of us were convicted because the court had never allowed the jury to hear the truth nor advised them of their right to acquit regardless of the evidence. At that time I faced a possible twenty-five-year prison sentence, having been convicted of five felonies.

The next two months I tried to prepare myself for the prospect of prison, however one does that. Prison is supposed to be the ultimate unfreedom, the worst curse of society. What I experienced was a sense of great inner freedom that I had never known before. Following my conscience, my own inner light and truth, had become more important than preparing for prison. I knew I wanted to speak my truth in the courtroom to Judge Carroll and the public before he would sentence me. In a moment I realized that was the best and probably only preparation I could really do. I sensed a liberation. There was really nothing Judge Carroll could do to hurt me because I had already said yes to prison rather than sell my conscience or sense of integrity. Speaking the truth became more important and in the risk my power grew — a power that had nothing to do with locks, bars, and guards, but a great deal to do with breaking down inner barriers, speaking the truth one knows within.

On July 1, 1986, the fifth anniversary of the assassination of Tullio, our pastor in Guatemala, I spoke my forty-five-minute prepared statement to Judge Carroll. This was the only time I was allowed to speak publicly in that courtroom. No one could take this right from me for there was nothing left to fear — except my life, and that was mine to give. Judge Carroll sentenced me to a suspended sentence and five years' probation, much to the relief of my family and religious congregation. The journey deepened me in many ways, although I have never spent a day in prison. I had made a choice for truth and conscience over the expectations of society and could not retreat. My sanctuary actions flowed from my anger and guilt as I experienced myself as a North American, responsible for the actions of this government and society relative to policies in Central America. I sensed that I had to begin to deal with my own oppression — I needed to pick up my own struggle.

Knowing my need to deal with my own oppression and knowing the importance of a community of supportive women to make these connections, I moved to Womancenter in Plainville, Massachusetts, in November of 1986. It was from this center that I continued speaking and writing about sanctuary. And it was in the safe womanspace of Womancenter, with the words of many women who dared to live their lives and write the truth of their journeys, that I timidly picked up my sandals to carry on the struggle.

> It is ironic. Sanctuary is about living dangerously. Sanctuary is about taking risks beyond the ordinary. Risks of class security or race security. Risks of the heart. Physical risks. Taking risks has allowed me to be the person I always wanted to be.
> (Judith McDaniel, *Sanctuary: A Journey*)

In June 1987 after six months of serious discernment, I took the risk of seeking dispensation from canonical vows. It was the only way I could unlock the prison that the relationship of "Sister" to the institutional patriarchal church had become for me. I loved my sisters and valued being a part of a community of women concerned for justice issues, who had backed me all the way through the public trial when most of the hierarchy stood back cautiously. But speaking publicly about justice issues while injustice became more blatant in my own church made it impossible for me to continue. Tearfully, I wrote: "The relationship of 'Sister' with the institutional church has become personally oppressive to me. I cannot accept or teach directly or indirectly by my institutional association the church's dogmatic and repressive stance against women, its teachings regarding sex and procreation, and its oppression of lesbians and gays. I cannot continue to grow in the structures of a canonical religious congregation bound to the patriarchal organization. I must go where I am called to life and growth."

My journey does not end here, for one step leads us along a path until we must take another step. We rarely know where that first step will take us, but we know we must go for another — for a cause, but ultimately for ourselves. But what is important is that I have been changed by the experience. I can no longer go back to being the person I was before. And so I continue the walk — *acompañamiento* — that our foremothers began. I find the support to keep walking from my sisters. Knowing the struggle of so many around the globe, I pick up my sandals and go on.

Asking the questions and doing the analysis is what makes it possible to go on. There are those who had asked at the end of the long and expensive trial: Who won? The INS? Sanctuary? The refugees? With the eyes of faith, it is the wrong question. The important question is not whether what we advocate is effective, acceptable, or even "lawful" but *is it faithful?* Is that not what Ruth asked? We are in for the long haul. Faithfulness is the virtue of the day — the faithfulness of walking alongside, following, whatever the costs. And in the process *we will experience ourselves changing.* This is what is important, that we experience ourselves changing, coming into our own power. And as we change we see ourselves in a new relationship to the basic institutions of our society. We can no longer ignore the causes of death in our world, death to the environment, death to our children, death to ourselves because our spirit of hope has been killed. If we no longer believe that we can make a difference, we are already dead. We must change the structures of power and dominance that allow dollars allocated in a military budget to determine our security. U.S. military and economic aid to the counterinsurgency forces in Central America and the Nicaraguan Contras is a form of institutionalized violence. It attempts to kill not only the body but the spirit as well.

Ultimately the most important challenge of sanctuary is not to the U.S. government but to ourselves. When we encounter masked refugees telling stories of persecution, we are invited to remove our own masks of security and power that often keep us one from another. We are asked to begin to question a government that calls itself democratic and yet allows a band of military officers to decide foreign policy in the basement of the White House. We are asked to question why a Stacey Merkt, sanctuary worker from Texas, served time in prison for her acts of compassion to Central American refugees while an Ollie North, who sold weapons to a terrorist country that holds hostages, used the profits to get weapons to the Contras, and in the process allowed drug smuggling into the U.S., was called an "American hero" by President Reagan. The message of terrorism and hostages and guns is clear: until no one needs to ask for refuge, wear a mask, watch their children starve to death, or die in the streets from cocaine-bought bullets, none of us is free.

Our greatest security lies in our ability to see the connections we have one to another as human beings. Guatemalan refugee Elena Excot sees to the heart of the matter:

> As long as there are people in misery, exploited, oppressed and massacred, none of us can pretend to be truly Christian without suffering too, without being in solidarity with their struggles and their desire for the resurrection. Solidarity is to practice Christian Communion because when one member suffers all suffer with that member, and when one receives an honor everyone receives that honor. *Hoy por mí, mañana por tí.*

In her statement to U.S. District Judge Filemon Vela at her June 1984 sentencing in Brownsville, Texas, Stacey Merkt reiterated this sense of connectedness we feel as women:

> I stand before you because twelve persons after seventeen hours finally decided that I broke the law....I am here...because I see that we have lost our connection to one another — person to person. We have lost sight of the fact that when any one of our sisters or brothers is hurting, we are hurting. I see that and I have to respond. I can't not respond....I am here to make those connections one to another...I am no celebrity and I am no martyr and I am no felon. First, I am a woman with a heart and a mind. My faith commitment connects me to people and to justice. I am a worker. You and I, we are the co-creators right now of this earth inasmuch as we accept that responsibility to work and to transform.

Let us go forward, not always sure where but clear that together across fences and barriers, we, the faithful women following in the footsteps of our often forgotten foremothers, can co-create a world in which we see and live our connectedness one to another. Help me, sisters, to continue the struggle, to keep on walking — *acompañamiento* — until there are no more doors to closet the truth, no more fences to imprison our differences, no more borders to make for war, and no more hierarchies to sanctify domination, but only a sister circle of equals creating justice. *Peregrina, no hay camino, que el camino se hace al andar.* Pilgrim, there is no road, the road is made in the walking.

AUTOBIOGRAPHICAL STATEMENT

I came to feel very much like a refugee myself — always on the move and often being displaced without consent or time to say good-bye. While in Arizona recovering from surgery and beginning to work with refugees, I kept repeating, "I can't say good-bye — no more good-byes." And yet there would be another wrenching leaving. My quest for truth and honesty led me to integrate the connections that I had made between the oppression of Central Americans and my own struggle as a woman in the church. This led me to speak my need for dispensation from canonical status in the Roman Catholic Church after more than twenty years as a School Sister of St. Francis. I tried to make my position clear — I didn't want to be separated from a community of justice-seeking women but could no longer continue to be publicly affiliated with the institutional, hierarchical, and patriarchal church. As the years go on the pain heals and I do what I can to stay connected to the friends that have always been there for me.

Today I live in Somerville, Massachusetts, where I am making a home with Christine Blackburn. She has been a friend and *compañera* in the struggle for truth and justice. That sense of rootedness or at-homeness has become very important to me. I struggle to find the ways to have "a room of my own," as Virginia Woolf describes this sense of at-homeness while working and living in a community and world that I have helped make to be a place to live. I ask you, the community of women who have helped me to become who I am, to keep me honest as I carry on the struggle. I sustain myself through teaching and counseling in ESL (English as a Second Language) programs.

July 1, 1990, ended my five years of probation. I'm hoping to organize a women's tour of Central America. (The judge had not allowed me to visit Mexico or Central America during this probationary period.) I continue to count on the support of women in the struggle through participating as a board member in NARW (National Assembly of Religious Women). I'd love to share my faith in words as I have through this sermon, but right now I'll have to do it through writing. I hope to finish a book I began about my journey as I learned through the sisters in the struggle.

BACKGROUND INFORMATION

> If we had wings we'd fly and denounce these atrocities; yet nobody listens to our cries. You were sent to be the carriers of our voice. Carry the message for us.
>
> (Salvadoran women — 1986 Cambridge–
> El Salvador Sister City Project)[1]

The Sanctuary movement of the 1980s was a national religious response to the suffering of refugees from El Salvador and Guatemala and the treatment they received from the U.S. government. It grew out of the mass exodus of Salvadoran refugees fleeing the escalated killings and terror that began in the spring of 1980 and resulted in at least 18,000–20,000 being murdered or "disappeared" in that year alone. Today human rights organizations list the number of civilian deaths at more than 60,000, with at least one-fourth of the population displaced. Beginning in the fall of 1981, the killing of hundreds of Indians in the highlands of Guatemala led to a similar exodus into Mexico. Unofficial estimates put the number of disappeared in Guatemala at over 38,000, with 100,000 killed. The massacres of civilians in the army's counterinsurgency war operations in 1982–83 destroyed 440 villages, making orphans of 120,000 children.[2]

Most of the Guatemalan refugees remain in Mexico, which has an estimated refugee population of 125,000. Mexico, with its own economic and political problems, is not able to provide a safe haven for the majority of refugees. The New York–based human rights group Americas Watch, in its study of Guatemalan refugees in Mexico from 1980 through 1984, concluded that Guatemalan refugees in Mexico face "severe legal, subsistence and security problems. Political asylum as it now stands in Mexico is not benefiting the Guatemalan refugees."[3]

Conservative estimates place the number of refugees in Central America at 2.3 million, or about 15 percent of the population of the entire region. Within El Salvador only about 10 percent of internal refugees are sheltered in church-owned camps. The vast majority of persons displaced by bombings are crowded into rapidly expanding slums on edges of major cities. Estimates in 1986, when dislocation was at its highest, put the number at 700,000 for the city of San Salvador alone. Another equally large group of refugees displaced by bombs in Salvador are outside their country: in Honduras (estimated 70,000); Mexico (15,000); Belize, Costa Rica, Nicaragua, and Panama each with smaller estimates.

Seeking safe haven under the flag of democracy and opportunities to support themselves and their families left in Central America, an estimated 500,000 Salvadorans have found their way to the United States. A smaller number of Guatemalans followed in their paths. In the beginning most of these refugees entered Texas and southern California, but later many arrived in Arizona and New Mexico. The rate of Salvadoran and Guatemalan refugees entering Los Angeles jumped from 5,000–10,000 annually before 1980, to 20,000–30,000 thereafter.

In May 1980, twenty-six Salvadoran refugees were abandoned by their "coyote" guides in the Ajo desert of California. This act made national headlines when half died and the other half in need of medical attention and emotional aid were brought to Phoenix and Tucson where INS officials asked the churches to help in meeting the crisis. What INS did not anticipate was the awakening of the community of faith to the refugees' plight. As INS arrested the survivors and prepared to return them to their countries, the churches learned of the systematized injustices in INS policies, such as detention, bonding, and deportations. The reality of one thousand deportations a month urged the churches to organize ecumenical task forces in both Tucson and Phoenix to counter these injustices. At the height of the Sanctuary movement while the government was investigating us, less than 3 percent of Salvadorans and less than 1 percent of Guatemalans who applied for political asylum under the Refugee Act ever received it.[4]

Arthur Helton in an article in Harvard's *Civil Liberties Law Review* writes:

> Ideological and foreign policy considerations continue to influence asylum determinations, resulting in ready asylum grants for applicants fleeing communist regimes. Far less generous grants are given to those fleeing regimes with which the United States has good relations, irrespective of their human rights records. For example, in 1985, 73 percent of the Libyan, 59 percent of the Romanian, 57 percent of the Czechoslovakian, and 46 percent of the Russian cases received political asylum. On the other hand, asylum was granted in less than 15 percent of the Pakistani, 1 percent of the Haitian, 1 percent of the Guatemalan and 3 percent of the Salvadoran cases.[5]

Helton further explains how El Salvador is a prime example of this discriminatory process of political asylum application, a process that is documented in INS's own 1982 internal report.

After their churches were nearly bankrupted by putting up bond money to bail the Central Americans out of detention, several refugee workers, frustrated by the system and experiencing its futility, looked for ways to bring this issue to the public's attention. On March 24, 1982, Southside Presbyterian Church in Tucson, Arizona, pastored by Reverend John Fife, declared itself a public witness sanctuary. On the same day five churches in the Bay Area — in common covenant — declared sanctuary. Through the efforts of the Chicago Religious Task Force on Central America, on July 24, 1982, the Wellington Avenue United Church of Christ in Chicago declared itself a sanctuary and received a young Salvadoran. Some eighty-five churches in the Chicago area endorsed the Wellington action. What had been a response by concerned people living in the Mexico/U.S. border states to victims of torture became a national ecumenical movement confronting the government's policy, which had politicized the granting of refugee status to desperate people.[6]

Thus a new "underground railroad" was born and the 1980s version drew on a rich and courageous history. The Chicago Religious Task Force's materials for educating congregations to these realities quickly spread the call to conscience throughout the country. In one of the organizing booklets, *Sanctuary: A Justice Ministry*, the history of sanctuary is explored. It is worth reading this religious and political history to understand its roots.

What began as a humanitarian act for some soon became a politicizing and radicalizing act. Congregations that received refugees, men, women, and children fleeing deportation and return to possible imprisonment or death, found themselves forced to confront U.S. foreign policy. Middle Americans, mainline Protestant, Catholic, and

Jewish congregations, began to question this country's foreign policy in Central America because of the Sanctuary movement and the refugee testimonies they had heard.

NOTES

1. Poster from the Cambridge–El Salvador Sister City Project, 1986.
2. Gary MacEoin, *Sanctuary: A Resource Guide for Understanding and Participating in the Central American Refugees' Struggle* (New York: Harper & Row, 1985). A good background source on the beginnings of the movement.
3. Americas Watch Committee, "Guatemalan Refugees in Mexico 1980–1984," September 1984.
4. *Salvadorans in the United States: The Case for Extended Voluntary Departure*, National Immigration and Alien Rights Project, Report No. 1, American Civil Liberties Union. There is much documentation included here on numbers of arrivals and deportations.
5. "Ecumenical, Municipal and Legal Challenges to United States Refugee Policy," *Harvard Civil Rights Civil Liberties Law Review* 21, no. 2 (Summer 1986): 497.
6. Renny Golden and Michael McConnell, *Sanctuary: The New Underground Railroad* (Maryknoll, N.Y.: Orbis Books, 1984). An excellent book that gives the story from the religious and political viewpoint of the Central Americans and North Americans who risked to make it happen.

BIBLIOGRAPHY

Americas Watch Committee, "Guatemalan Refugees in Mexico 1980 — 1984," September 1984.

Chittister, Joan, O.S.B. Presentation at Women in the Church Conference: "Sexism in the Church: Agenda for the 90s," October 10–12, 1986.

Golden, Renny, and Michael McConnell. *Sanctuary: The New Underground Railroad.* Maryknoll, N.Y.: Orbis Books, 1984.

"Ecumenical, Municipal and Legal Challenges to United States Refugee Policy." *Harvard Civil Rights Civil Liberties Law Review* 21, no. 2 (Summer 1986): 497.

Loder, Ted. *No One but Us: Personal Reflections on Public Sanctuary.* San Diego: Lura Media, 1986.

MacEoin, Gary. *Sanctuary: A Resource Guide for Understanding and Participating in the Central American Refugees' Struggle.* New York: Harper & Row, 1985.

McDaniel, Judith. *Sanctuary: A Journey.* Ithaca, N.Y.: Firebrand Books, 1987.

Piercy, Marge. *The Moon Is Always Female.* New York: Alfred A. Knopf, 1980.

RESOURCES

The list of resources about sanctuary is a book in itself. This page is meant to give a few starting points for further information. Almost every major denomination, except Catholics, has created its own study guide or resource packet around sanctuary and Central American refugees. Additionally many cities have Sanctuary Coordinating Committees or a Central American Task Force. Most major cities have at least one publicly declared sanctuary congregation. Sanctuary does not have nor has it ever had a national organizing office. Since 1986 the level of public sanctuary activity has dwindled because of changed conditions in Central America, the United States population, and the kinds of refugees. The following organizing bodies would be helpful to anyone pursuing further information.

The Chicago Religious Task Force on Central America
59 E. Van Buren, Suite 1400
Chicago, IL 60605
(312) 663-4398
    Organizing booklets, materials, national contacts, etc.

CUECOS, Champaign-Urbana Ecumenical Committee on Sanctuary
P.O. Box 2600, Station A
Champaign, IL 61820
(217) 352-3347
    Publishes 61-page bibliography on sanctuary.

The Valley Religious Task Force on Central America
37 E. Indian School Road
Phoenix, AZ 85012
(602) 265-9800
    Involved early in the movement and continues to work directly with refugees.

Tucson Ecumenical Task Force for Central America
317 W. 23rd Street
Tucson, AZ 75241
(602) 628-7525
    Continues refugee work today.

PART SIX

Dealing with Difference

19

Beyond Inclusivity?:
A White Feminist Reflects on Racism

Anne Scheibner

SERMON

Why would you or I or any white women be concerned with the oppression of people of color? From a liberal point of view, the answers are obvious. White women concerned with the struggle of women for equality believe in civil rights for all and want the system to be open to everyone. Our God is a God of justice. We are co-workers with God in wanting to see an end to all systems of discrimination. We are, or at least try to be, inclusive of our African American, Hispanic, Asian, and Native American sisters in all our work whenever they are interested.

But in that idea of inclusion lies the snare for us as white women who have been taught not to think of ourselves as racist. Racists, we think, are violent wielders of power like Bull Connor and people who claim superiority on the basis of skin color. In spite of our struggle to understand the structural nature of sexism and the unearned privileges that accrue to men simply by virtue of their being men, we resist seeing that the same analysis makes any white woman the recipient of unearned privileges and power.

In her paper "White Privilege and Male Privilege: A Personal Account of Coming to See Correspondences through Work in Women's Studies," Peggy McIntosh, associate director of the Wellesley College Center for Research on Women, discusses her own struggle:

> After I realized, through faculty development work in Women's Studies, the extent to which men work from a base of unacknowledged privilege, I understood that much of their oppressiveness is unconscious. Then I remembered the frequent charges from women of color that white women whom they encounter are oppressive. I began to understand why we are justly seen as oppressive, even

---

A sermon for white, middle-class women who feel connected to the women's movement but who are unclear about the connection of the women's movement to the issue of racism.

when we don't see ourselves that way. At the very least, oblivious-
ness of one's privileged state can make a person or group irritating
to be with. I began to count the ways in which I enjoy unearned
skin privilege and have been conditioned into oblivion about its existence, unable to see that it put me "ahead" in any way, or put my
people ahead, overrewarding us and yet also paradoxically damaging
us, or that it could or should be changed.

It requires concentrated effort for white women to recognize our
unearned privileges. In her paper, McIntosh lists forty-six examples.
We assume, for instance, that white neighbors or co-workers will tend
to like us and that what we say in a group will be taken as a personal
statement and not as representing "our race." In groups white women
like to think of ourselves as using nonhierarchical, renewed forms of
organization. Therefore it is hard for us to recognize that we put
women of color in the same difficult position that women are put
in so often in predominantly male groups. For example, if one or
two women of color are part of an otherwise white group they are
not usually there as delegates from a larger group of women of color
or mixed gender group. Regardless of how competent they may be as
individuals they are nevertheless seen on some level as "representing"
their race, thereby proving the nonracist legitimacy of that particular
white women's organization. The priorities and budget are set and
implemented by the majority group according to white women's race
and class interests.

Does this sound like a hard word? Well, it is hard. But I hope you
will resist the impulse to "kill the messenger" even if we are all at
different stages of hearing the message. What would Jesus say to us
in this situation? Listen:

A white woman came up to Jesus and asked, "Good teacher, what
shall I do to inherit eternal life?" And he said to her, "Why do you
call me good? No one is good but God alone. You know the commandments. Do not commit adultery, Do not kill, Do not steal, Do
not bear false witness, Honor your father and mother." And she said,
"All these have I observed from my youth. And when Jesus heard it,
he said to her, "One thing you still lack. Give up trying to make it
as an individual in the system and you will have treasure in heaven;
and come, follow me." But when she heard this she became sad because she had many connections. Jesus looking at her said, "How
hard it is for those who have connections to enter into the reign of
God! For it is easier for a camel to go through the eye of a needle than for a white woman to be part of the reign of God." Those
who heard it said, "Then who can be saved?" But he said, "What is
impossible for mortals is possible with God." (Adapted from Luke
18:18–27)

It is rare for white women to acknowledge our unearned advantages, our access to resources, and our connections. It is painful for us to recognize the power that we have by virtue of being the daughters, mothers, wives or sisters, friends and neighbors of white men in positions of power. It means that there are very real differences between us and women of color in dealing with the principalities and powers. To speak of "patriarchy" abstracts the difficulty when we consider whose fathers we are really talking about.

Let me share an example of how our blindness to our privilege and our resulting dominance plays itself out. In the early 1980s I participated in a national conference sponsored by my denomination's Task Force on Women. In the morning, a panel on "The Black Women's Agenda" featured several nationally prominent black Episcopal women. They spoke of the struggle for survival facing the men, women, and children of the black community. They spoke of police violence, lack of drug treatment facilities, inadequate educational and employment opportunities. Although they did not deny the realities of sexism, they did point out that issues of the deployment of clergywomen and inclusive language simply could not be priorities for them. One speaker stated the positive value in the black community of having positive male images.

I remember how confused and afraid I felt at the gulf I saw these differences creating between me and those black women with whom I had worked in the urban caucus and elsewhere. The reactions of other white women in the almost exclusively white audience were a mixture of confusion and hostility. "We supported you in the civil rights movement. Why can't you see that your interests are with us now?" was a dominant theme. The white women resisted the suggestion of the panelists to break into small groups with other white women to discuss the issues presented. Our discussion centered on why black women were so angry and alienated!

That afternoon I was on the all-white panel on "Women Claiming Our Power." There was no discussion of the implications of the morning session and total denial of our real relationships with white men. We did not acknowledge the likelihood that we, rather than women of color, would achieve positions of power. As middle-class white women we thought of those positions as our birthright. Power was the concern of the white women; community was the concern of the black women. As white women we avoided and denied difference because we were afraid to acknowledge that there were different and in fact competing agenda. We did not want to acknowledge that with limited time, budget, and resources, choices and priorities are necessary. We lost a valuable opportunity to learn and possibly even to cooperate. So white women continued to control the church's various "women's" caucuses, task forces, councils — and to shake our heads over the difficulty of "including" women of color.

Toward the end of the 1980s, I thought I had achieved greater clarity about my own and my white sisters' racist behavior. I initiated an attempt to organize a conference on how white women and women of color could work together. In spite of my careful balancing of the committee (there were four women of color and three white women), several conference calls, one subcommittee meeting, and my detailed memos, the initial overnight face-to-face planning meeting of the entire group foundered; one woman of color and the three white women came. My feelings of frustration, anger, and rejection were immense. But since all my feelings were, I thought, inappropriate in dealing with women of color (after all that *would* be racist!), I sat on the feelings.

It was over a year before one of the black women who had not come bumped into me coming out of the ladies' room at another conference and said, "Let's talk about what happened." We did talk. And the basic issue from her side was trust. Given my typically liberal, racist behavior in the women's caucus and urban caucus over the past ten years, there was mistrust that I was somehow trying to use women of color and even the agenda of doing a mutually agreed upon conference to further my own ends. Probably the only reason we could finally have this conversation was that I had not sought "more responsive" women of color and gone ahead with the conference. I had taken what happened as a sign that something was very wrong in spite of my good intentions and carefully designed process of inclusion.

Many white Episcopal women were bitterly disappointed over the election of the Rt. Rev. Barbara Harris as the first Anglican woman bishop. She had no college degree. She wasn't seminary trained. She had little parish experience. It's too bad she couldn't have been more qualified. The fact that she is a gifted preacher, pastor, and advocate with decades of experience as a lay leader in the (black) Church of the Advocate in Philadelphia was discounted. When I heard of Bishop Harris's election, I was overjoyed because it was such a departure from the usual climbing the ladder of success through serving large, white congregations. At the joyous consecration service in Boston, the preacher, the Rev. Paul Washington, pointed out that if we had just come to see a woman consecrated bishop then we were missing the point. "We cannot," he said, "and we must not, overlook the fact that this woman who is being consecrated today is not just an American woman. She is a black woman." He emphasized that like Mary before her, Bishop Harris represents the despised and marginalized women whom God has chosen to do a mighty work.

It took quite a while after the consecration for the meaning of those words to sink in. I had thought that Bishop Harris would represent the need for a renewed antiracism effort from all of us. How else could we be in unity with her, as our tradition understands the role of the bishop? But I now see a deeper meaning in the consecration of this African American woman. It means the opportunity to let go of the myth of equality in an unjust social, political, and economic order. White women wanted a white woman they could identify with to be elected bishop. But Jesus understood that equality was not a thing to be grasped; he himself modelled taking the form of a servant and emptying himself even unto death, even death on a cross (Phil. 2:5–8). This is not the kind of equality that various liberation movements in the United States have talked about. No one wants to be equal with the homeless. We want to be included at the top of the pyramid without having to think about the unearned privilege of those at the top and the unearned disadvantages for those who are somehow not equal.

So what does this all mean for the reign of God and for us as white women? Perhaps we are being called to consider whether we are serious about community — a diverse, heterogeneous community in which real power is shared. White women and gay men and lesbians have appropriated the black community's model of struggle from the 1960s and called ourselves "communities." But that usage obscures real differences. Communities are made up of men, women, and children who are interdependent within some kind of social, political, and economic framework. During the years of segregation this was true for black people in this country. It is still true to varying degrees for African Americans, Asians, Hispanics, and Native Americans and various European ethnic groups. But people who share a common viewpoint or who gather in single sex or single sexual reference groups for sanity and refreshment do not thereby constitute a community. There are serious limits to single-issue and single-constituency politics if we want to engage in a genuine and risk-filled struggle to transform our society. Are white women really interested in community or just in being with like-minded women and enjoying the benefits of inclusion in a social structure that excludes people on the basis of race and class?

Why do I — why should we — bother with racism? We don't have to. That is one of the racist facts of white life in this society. And grappling with the effects of racism is often very anxiety provoking! I don't like it. I don't like thinking of myself as participating in a fallen and broken world. I don't like having to acknowledge my need for God's — and my neighbors' — mercy and forgiveness. But the struggle with racism is a call to all God's people for wholeness and holiness. It is a struggle for justice or right relationship one with another and among nations. We are in a time when the East-West split is being replaced with a North-South split, and race will be a dominant if unacknowledged factor shaping new international power relationships.

Even though I often resist the knowledge, I need to know that I am part of a baptized community made up of brothers and sisters who are African American, Hispanic, Asian, Native American, and, yes, European American. We are called to build up a community in which God reigns. We therefore engage in this struggle for justice, for life together. For with God all things are possible.

AUTOBIOGRAPHICAL STATEMENT

I was born in Westerly, Rhode Island, and grew up as a white, upper-middle-class woman in Stonington, Connecticut, a small New England town. My father's family were German immigrants who came to work in the local textile plant. My mother's father was rector of the local Episcopal church and her family could trace our Dutch/English roots to colonial times.

In the summer of 1968 I was a sophomore in college and volunteered to work with the summer youth program of an Episcopal church in New Haven, Connecticut. It was my first experience of working in a city with the church and in a multiracial situation since all the teenagers in the program were African American. Fortunately for my formation as an adult Christian, the Rev. Canon Edward Rodman was the patient and gifted African American priest in charge of that program. My work with him and knowing his family that summer was the first step in my becoming part of an ongoing community of hope and struggle.

Canon Rodman, the Hon. Byron Rushing, now state assemblyman in Massachusetts, and I were among the staff of the Urban Bishops Coalition 1978 hearings on the role of the church in the city. Annmarie Marvel, the now Rt. Rev. Barbara Harris, the Rev. Butch Naters-Gamarra, Mattie Hopkins, the Rt. Revs. John Burgess and John Walker, and many others were among the founders of the Episcopal Urban Caucus in 1980. I was elected to the national caucus board with the support of an informal women's caucus within the EUC and saw myself representing "women." During the decade of the 1980s the caucus served as a multiracial microcosm of the church and society at large. The discernment of a vision and working style by the caucus as a genuine community and not as a coalition of interest groups has been part of my learning over the past decade.

I have had a base for doing antiracism work through my participation in the National Council of Churches Faith and Order

Commission. Dr. Randall C. Bailey of the Interdenominational Theological Center in Atlanta and I co-chair the Unity of the Church and
Renewal of Human Community Study Group. This multiracial ecumenical group is currently working on examining the ways in which
race has been both church-dividing and church-uniting — that is, exploring both the current and historical experience of denominations
including those that split during the Civil War over slavery and the
experience of African American churches.

BACKGROUND INFORMATION (by Linda Powell)

As an African American feminist reflects upon the state of race relations in our country today, three powerful and dangerous myths
become apparent.

Myth One: The historic pattern of racial violence — and oppression enforced by the threat of violence — against people of color is
a thing of the past.

United States Department of Justice statistics suggest that racial
violence may be increasing. Many of these racist acts include the
crossburnings and firebombings with which we are (unfortunately)
familiar. But others display eerie twists on the age-old pattern of
racist violence. In particular, many of these terrorist acts are "family
affairs," in which children and adults share in a ritual humiliation
of African Americans. And while these statistics are complex and
difficult to decode, it is clear that racist violence is a continuing
phenomenon that does not respect class, region, or color.

And so this myth goes against the facts. But this myth is protective and comforting. Perhaps we can all become complacent in our
concerns for justice; we refuse to see escalating patterns of racist-
inspired terrorism. Instead, we simply perceive isolated "incidents,"
which are less frightening.

The feminist analysis of violence against women helps us to understand this phenomenon. We know that not all men rape or abuse
women. However, the existence of that violence shapes and imprints
women's psyches and affects all of our relationships with men. We in-
tuitively understand a relationship between rape, sexual harassment,
pornography, and woman-hating jokes. We also recognize how difficult it can be for even the most supportive men to join in the political
fight to end violence against women: to do so may bring them into
direct confrontation with their friends, colleagues, and families.

In a parallel process, we can see how the legacy of racial violence — and its constant *possibility* — shapes the relationships of
people across color lines. And we can imagine how demanding it is
for whites, perhaps especially white women, to struggle against white

racism: to do so is likely to bring them into direct conflict with those closest to them.

Myth Two: Racism is overt and obvious.

This myth obscures the reality of modern life, especially in religious or progressive circles. Racism is not just the ugly epithet or the frank refusal of service (although these, too, continue). As our culture has appropriated the language and ethos (if not the substance) of liberation, these overt behaviors are not the sole carrier of racist intent. Today there is the comment "I've never really thought of you as black (Hispanic, Asian, Native American, etc.). You're just a person." This comment is often offered as a compliment. Or racism comes in the form that intellectual prowess, long-term marriages, or avoidance of athletics must be "unusual" in your culture. Or the classic example of the woman of color who is an economist with a specialty in Eastern Europe who is invited to speak for twenty minutes on African American culture!

While these examples may seem slight, they form a litany of common experiences for many women of color. And these examples betray an important pattern of "thoughtlessness" among whites: that which is related to people of color is trivial, marginal, and not worthy of serious thought or effort.

Today racist actions are often a complex outcome of many factors. They can be discerned in group process — who is included and listened to, whose issues are considered central and whose are marginal. This distinction is at the heart of difficulties with concepts like "inclusiveness." The subtlety of the power differential when white women define the domain of feminist issues and "invite" interested women of color to join is a good example.

White racism is often shrouded in the white complaint, "We *tried* but we just couldn't find a woman of color to write for our anthology/join our collective/take the job." Rarely, if ever, is this complaint followed by serious examination of the underlying dynamics of the task. The real question is, how has the editorial process of a publication, or the politics of a collective, or the hiring process of an organization harbored "white is right" suppositions that have never been examined.

Myth Three: The natural subject matter for any consideration of racism is the culture and history of people of color.

While this myth may seem nonsensical, it captures a common experience. Imagine the following scenario: A white group has become concerned about racism, *and they invite a black woman to come and consult with them.* This myth is dangerous at two levels. First, it perpetuates the idea of "mandatory presence," the concept that for race to be discussed, a person of color must be involved. At its worst, this idea legitimizes blindness to issues of racial justice if the required minority person isn't present. We then carry the sole responsibility for fairness and justice. It implies that the solutions to racial problems lie magically with people of color, as though whites have no racial identity to grapple with and no ability (or no need) to think for themselves about these matters.

But the most crucial danger of this myth is the powerful way it obscures the locus of the problem of racism; fundamentally, racism lies with and in white Americans, and they must deal with it in themselves, their families, and their communities. White women need to trust that they have the courage and the stamina to undertake an examination of their attitudes for the purposes of healing and empowerment. There is a crucial ministry here that — at this historic juncture — only whites can perform for other whites.

One way out of this quandary is a return to the early enthusiasm about feminism and its promise as a way of knowing and community-building for both women and men. Second-wave feminists believed they had found not simply a specific set of politics, but a powerful new way of seeing the world and understanding power. If the "personal was political," vast areas of human functioning and relationship were opened for inspection and — ultimately — transformation. Somewhere, we may have lost our way and settled instead for tactics and issues. The conference described by Anne Scheibner provides an excellent example of this confusion. The alleged stalemate between black women's issues (men, children, and community) and white women's issues (inclusivity and jobs) describes a dichotomy that we can and must overcome. First, the bridge must be built between women of color and white women through a willingness of white women to deal with their individual and collective racism. It is not impossible to establish trust: just difficult. Second, we must become willing to make contributions to *each other's* work, not just insist that everyone sign on for ours. Surely there is such a thing as *feminist* analysis of social problems: Is there no contribution that feminist theory can make to questions of family and community? Is there nothing about inclusiveness that wouldn't be enriched by contributions of African American women?

Finally, we must agree to be empowered by our visions of what is right, not what seems convenient or possible. We must move in light of our commitments and be willing to live with the consequences of them. Faith tells me that there are links that we cannot see until we begin to work on them. Feminist analysis offers something valuable and unique to all women and men who are committed to change and justice. If we settle for less, we are reduced to defending various turfs, which will continue to be narrowly defined by our race and class interests.

Linda C. Powell is a consultant and black feminist social critic. In the mid-1970s, she served on the staff of the Ecumenical Women's Center in Chicago and later with the Division of Church and Society of the National Council of Churches. Her work has appeared in *Home Girls: A Black Feminist Anthology* (Kitchen Table: Women of Color Press, 1983) and *Conditions*, a feminist literary magazine. A graduate of Northwestern University, she is currently enrolled in the doctoral program in clinical psychology at George Washington University. Rooted in the African American church tradition, she is a member of Metropolitan Baptist Church in Washington, D.C. Her interests in psychology and theology come together in her current work on a research documentary focusing on African American fathers and daughters.

BIBLIOGRAPHY

Understanding Difference

Andolsen, Barbara H., Christine E. Gudorf, Mary D. Pellauer, eds. *Women's Consciousness, Women's Conscience: A Reader in Feminist Ethics*. New York: Harper & Row, 1985.
Eisenstein, Hester, and Alice Jardine, eds. *The Future of Difference*. Boston: G. K. Hall & Company, 1980.
Joseph, Gloria I., and Jill Lewis. *Common Differences: Conflicts in Black and White Feminist Perspectives*. Garden City, N.Y.: Anchor Books/Doubleday, 1981.
May, Melanie. *Bonds of Unity*. Atlanta: Scholars Press of Georgia, 1989.
The Mud Flower Collective (Katie G. Cannon, Beverly W. Harrison, Carter Heyward, Ada Maria Isasi-Diaz, Bess B. Johnson, Mary D. Pellauer, Nancy D. Richardson). *God's Fierce Whimsy: Christian Feminism and Theological Education*. New York: Pilgrim Press, 1985.
Russell, Letty M., et al. *Inheriting Our Mothers' Gardens: Feminist Theology in Third World Perspective*. Philadelphia: Westminster, 1988.

Understanding Racism from a White Perspective

Andolsen, Barbara H. *Daughters of Jefferson, Daughters of Bootblacks: Racism and American Feminism*. Macon, Ga.: Mercer University Press, 1986.
Bulkin, Elly, Minnie Bruce Pratt, and Barbara Smith. *Yours in the Struggle: Three Feminist Perspectives on Anti-Semitism and Racism*. Ithaca, N.Y.: Firebrand Press, 1984.
McIntosh, Peggy. "White Privilege and Male Privilege: A Personal Account of Coming to See Correspondences through Work in Women's Stud-

ies." Wellesley College Center for Research on Women, Working Paper no. 189, 1988.

Smith, Lillian. *Killers of the Dream.* New York: W. W. Norton, 1949.

Thistlethwaite, Susan Brooks. *Sex, Race and God: Christian Feminism in Black and White.* New York: Crossroad, 1989.

Understanding Racism from a Black Perspective

Davis, Angela. *Women, Race and Class.* New York: Random House, 1981; Vintage, 1983.

Grant, Jacquelyn. *White Women's Christ and Black Women's Jesus: Feminist Christology and Womanist Response.* Atlanta: Scholars Press, 1989.

Hooks, Bell. *Feminist Theory: From Margin to Center.* Boston, Mass.: South End Press, 1984.

Women of Color Studies: A Sampling

Anzaldua, Gloria, ed. *Making Face, Making Soul = Haciendo Caras: Creative and Critical Perspectives by Women of Color.* San Francisco: An Aunt Lute Foundation Book, 1990.

Fabella, Virginia, M.M., and Mercy Amba Oduyoye. *With Passion and Compassion: Third World Women Doing Theology.* Maryknoll, N.Y.: Orbis Books, 1988.

Hull, Gloria, Patricia Bell Scott, and Barbara Smith. *All the Women Are White, All the Blacks Are Men, But Some of Us Are Brave: Black Women's Studies.* Old Westbury, N.Y.: Feminist Press, 1982.

Isasi-Diaz, Ada Maria, and Yolanda Tarango. *Hispanic Women: Prophetic Voice in the Church.* San Francisco: Harper & Row, 1988.

Moraga, Cherrie, and Gloria Anzaldua, eds. *This Bridge Called My Back: Writings by Radical Women of Color.* New York: Kitchen Table: Women of Color Press, 1981, 1983.

Smith, Barbara, ed. *Home Girls: A Black Feminist Anthology.* New York: Kitchen Table: Women of Color Press, 1983.

RESOURCES

"White Privilege and Male Privilege: A Personal Account of Coming to See Correspondences through Work in Women's Studies," Working Paper no. 189, 1988, by Peggy McIntosh, Associate Director, Wellesley College Center for Research on Women, Wellesley College, Wellesley, MA 02181. The paper is available for $3.50 from the Center.

Southern Poverty Law Center — Klan-Watch Project
P.O. Box 548
Montgomery, AL 36195

Religious Network for Equality for Women (RNEW)
475 Riverside Drive, Room 830A
New York, NY 10115

Women's Theological Center
555 Amory Street
Jamaica Plain, MA 02130

20

Wonderfully Made:
Preaching Physical Self-Affirmation

Chandra Taylor Smith

SERMON

For you created my inmost being; you knit me together in my mother's womb. I praise you because I am fearfully and wonderfully made; your works are wonderful, I know that full well.
—Psalm 139:13–14, Oxford NIV Scofield Study Bible

Oh Lord, when we learn to truly see ourselves, we are able to see thee more clearly. . . . You are our maker and you have made each of us in your image. Help us to see our beauty, dear Lord. Heal our spirits and our eyes. We are beautiful because we are your children. The beauty we possess is of you. . . . I thank you God, for creating and using me. Amen.

Racism is a physically, spiritually, and mentally consuming disease. Many a sermon has been preached, to both black and white people, naming and rebuking this disease that lingers in epidemic proportions in our society. It is not the sermon about racial injustice that is seldom heard. The voices, words, concerns of Mahatma Gandhi, Martin Luther King, Jr., John F. Kennedy, Desmond Tutu, Jesse Jackson, and so on ring loud and clear from pulpits all across the country every Sunday. Thus, statistics about the poverty rate, illiteracy, joblessness, teenage pregnancies, the low birth-weight rates and shorter life spans among blacks are not what is seldom heard. Sermons that cry out about the slow progress of black people in America, the drug and alcohol problems, the numbers of black men in jail are not seldom heard. These sermons are being preached more and more, and must continue to be preached.

Since everything that lives experiences pain in its own intimate way, so do black people experience the pain from the symptoms of the disease of racism. The sermons seldom heard are those that bring

---

I preach the concepts in this sermon in my ministry with grassroots young women and men in the Roxbury communities, Boston, Massachusetts.

244 · Chandra Taylor Smith

voice and healing to the blinding aches and soreness that black men and women feel, sermons they need to hear to bear up under the illness of racism.

We black women often feel unhappy with the way we look, with the textures and color of our hair, the curves and shapes of our bodies, which we are constantly trying to change. What is so wrong with the way we look, the way we are, that way that God has made us?

Granted we must often diet and exercise for health purposes. Many types of cosmetics available are supposedly to enhance our natural beauty. But we black women often change ourselves blindly. We change the color and texture of our hair and our skin; we try to accentuate certain parts of our body and minimize other features because we have not truly seen our natural image. The blinding glare of racism obstructs our vision of the beauty of our natural selves.

What I mean by natural physical beauty is the way we are as God has made us, unaltered by any fashionable image. For many changes we put our bodies through are just that: attempts to mirror what is in vogue. What is "in" does not always affirm our natural physical beauty that is of God. The normative Western ideal of beauty has been historically designed by a racist as well as a sexist standard.

Since slavery, we black women have contended with the dual denigration of our bodies from relentless racial and sexual oppression. Many sociological, historical, and anthropological studies reveal how black people have been made to feel inferior because of their bodies. Joseph R. Washington, Jr. traces the negative image of black people back to the mythology of the "curse of Ham," in Genesis, chapter 9. He describes how English biblical scholars and their lay followers once claimed African peoples were the descendents of Ham through Canaan, which is why they have "...red eyes, because Ham looked upon the nakedness of his father; they have misshapen lips, because Ham spoke with lips about the unseemly condition of his father; they have twisted hair, because Ham turned and twisted his head around to see the nakedness of his father; and they go about naked, because Ham did not cover the nakedness of his father...."

This insidious prejudice prevails today in the overt exclusion of our indigenous dark lineaments among images of the physical standards of beauty in America. Professor Margaret Miles succinctly describes the contemporary countenance of this racism in her book *Images as Insight*. She describes the defined images in our society for beautiful physical being as, "young, wealthy, slim, sexually attractive Anglo-Saxon women and men." It is this reality that brings W. H. Grier and P. M. Cobbs to their poignant conclusion in *Black Rage*: "The Negro woman's Black face, African features and kinky hair are physical attributes which place her far from the American ideal of beauty and make her in reference to the American ideal, ugly."

Black women are made to feel unhappy about our physical appearance, bombarded as we are daily by the glamorization of the white woman's physical features. Think back to the last time you were at the grocery store and grabbed one the popular fashion magazines to thumb through while you were waiting in the check-out line. Many a time I have leaned attentively on the back bars of my grocery cart and become engrossed with the new seasonal color forecast for lips, eyes, cheeks, and nails. In *Mademoiselle, Vogue, Glamour, Self, Cosmopolitan*, and *Woman's Day*, the colors, suggestive and sensuous, are exciting and irresistible on page after page of perfect models. Images of pinks, lavenders and emerald greens complement hazel and blue eyes. The deep reds on deliberately pouting lips accentuate rosy rouges on smooth ivory cheeks. Long, white, slender fingers with brilliant lacquered tips are often delicately poised on Caucasian, sculptured chins or point deliberately at what they demand or command. Dark and curly brunettes define a certain sexiness. And billowing, golden tresses of carefree, sun-streaked locks becrown every other pretty head.

We can turn to magazines like *Essence, Ebony, Blacktress*, but many of the models and images in these magazines for black men and women do not seem to authenticate the natural beauty of the black body. They are colored copies of the images we see in the general magazines. If you are standing in a line where the store does not have a large black clientele, you won't even find these specialty magazines.

Thus, we have become so accustomed to seeing the images of white women as the standard of beauty in magazines, in our morning newspapers, and on the television that many of us have become numb to how unrelated these images are to what we look like. Not unlike the way America has become desensitized to images of violence, famine, and death in the media, my Sisters, we have become anesthetized to the violence, denial, and death of the beauty of our black female bodies. As a result, to feel accepted, to feel beautiful, we find ourselves challenged to recreate ourselves according to images that esthetically disaffirm many of our unique features. This disaffirmation is not simply that models typically portray what is archetypically beautiful as the young, skinny, and white woman, but that the myriad textures and indigenous curves, shapes, and above all colors of our bodies are rarely celebrated as beauty in our society.

Many black women have lost sight of our natural beauty because we have spent much energy trying to achieve the standard of physical beauty that merely imitates the natural features of white women.

Unless we are born with certain features akin to white women, we can never authentically emulate these alienating measures of beauty. Therefore, we make incessant trips to the beauty parlor and go through daily routines of creams and buffers. Some of our cosmetic routines to recreate ourselves have become as automatic as eating. We do it without thinking. This constant, rather unconscious changing of ourselves ultimately batters our self-esteem. In the words of James Nelson, author of *Embodiment:* "The greatest dehumanization occurs when a person of a rejected body group internalizes the judgment made by others and becomes convinced of his or her own bodily (and thus personal) inferiority." In our internalized inferiority we become spiritually disconnected from ourselves and above all from God who has made us. As a result, we are vulnerable to sexual and mental abuse as we look to others for love and physical self affirmation.

We see this happening every day to many of our beautiful little black girls who are having babies when they themselves are still only babies. For they too are blind to their beauty, worth, and physical dignity. Many of our girls don't even know that God made them, that they are God's children. In their struggle to feel good about themselves, to feel pretty, they search for love and self-affirmation through sexuality.

It is precisely for our daughters that we must begin to see ourselves today, black women, to heal the cataracts of racism that blind our eyes so that we cannot see our beauty and God. We need to cleanse our veins of the poison of racism that numbs us. For racism has eclipsed God's beauty by substituting a white supremacist gauge for beauty. But the Lord's standard of beauty takes precedence over the bigoted criterion that has been established and is revered in this world. God created beauty in each of us. You, I, all of us are God's expression. The fact that we are toasty yellows, honey browns, creamy chocolates, and ebony blacks, with thick and curly, tight and wooly, straight and shiny, short and long hair reveals the multiplicity of God's beauty. For beauty is as God. God is beauty.

The Psalmist in Psalm 139:1–14 articulates the profundity of this beauty and the God who has made us. Many scholars have described this portion of the passage as a lament, a hymn expressing grief. But, my Sisters, when we read it more closely we know that it is a song of praise and affirmation. The poet is glorifying the knowledge of God who created him as he exclaims in verse 13:

> You created my inmost being:
> You knit me together
> in my mother's womb.

And I dare suggest that the Psalmist could have been a poetess standing before a mirror as she sang out in verse 14:

> I praise you because I am fearfully
> and wonderfully made;
> Your works are wonderful,
> I know that full well.

The poetess's testimony here is an affirmation of her physical being and the One who has made her. The Psalmist feels good about herself and is praising God for it. What she sees, her body, is fearfully and wonderfully made. And her understanding is not a self-indulging admiration because she knows that God has created her flesh inside and outside. It is comforting that God knows her so well, knows her thoughts hidden deep in her mind; God's right hand will hold her tight and be her constant guide. She delights in the self-affirmation that God's works are wonderful. A racist standard of being that would denigrate her body is not logical, does not make sense, cannot exist in the encompassing reality of God in her life.

This God the Psalmist praises, we serve. This God created you, loves you, and made you beautiful. It is this God in whom you will find consolation and delight when you go home, Sisters, and look in the mirror and take a good look at what God has made. Know God's works are wonderful and know it full well! For as you look at yourself say out loud, "I am fearfully and wonderfully made!" Touch the rich and natural texture of your hair and then say, "My hair is fearfully and wonderfully made!" Observe the deep, natural color of your eyes and your skin and say, "The color of my body is fearfully and wonderfully made!" As you examine your elegant features, smile as you behold your lips, discern the delicate lines of your cheeks and the natural contours of your nose. Then again, in humble admiration of God's work, say, "Every feature of my face is fearfully and wonderfully made!" And you'll know it full well when you stand before the mirror and see the naked truth: the natural shape of your breasts, the curves of your hips, your legs and your feet are all fearfully and wonderfully made. God has made your body, in all of its natural textures, colors, and curves beautiful to behold.

In Toni Morrison's novel *Beloved* I like the way Baby Suggs preaches the self-affirmation of our bodies. Having been a slave and living in a time when racism was flagrantly inflicted on black people, she preached:

> In this here place, we flesh; flesh that weeps, laughs; flesh that dances
> on bare feet in grass. Love it. Love it hard. Yonder they do not love
> your flesh. They despise it. They don't love your eyes; they'd just
> as soon pick em out. No more do they love the skin on your back.

Yonder they flay it. And O my people they do not love your hands. Those they only use, tie, bind, chop off and leave empty. Love your hands! Love them. Raise them up and kiss them.

Touch others with them, pat them together, stroke them on your face 'cause they don't love that either. You got to love it. You!

Then she goes on to proclaim loving your mouth, feet, neck, your insides and heart. She is acknowledging that we are fearfully and wonderfully made and we should know it, we must know it full well.

Learn to praise the Lord when you adorn your body. Embellish yourself because you are already beautiful, not because you are trying to make yourself beautiful. Like the elegant trees in a forest in autumn or the myriad flowers in a garden, the colors that you wear complement the colors that are in you. The jewelry, make-up, and creams, the coiffures and raiment that you choose should say something different from the fashion statements made by black women and girls who are blinded by racist standards of beauty. Their appearance suggests that they emulate the latest fashion for white women to the best of their ability. The most beautiful fashion statement you can make says, "I am God's standard of beauty myself, look at me and see God's wonderful works."

When we know that we are fearfully and wonderfully made, we will keep our spirits and our bodies in shape. Eating right and exercising daily is not a fad but is done to keep God's works wonderful. When we see our bodies and love them because we know that God has made them fearful and wonderful, our daughters will be able to see what they themselves truly look like and will be able to stand up in self-affirmation demanding that every man and woman, white and black, love and respect their bodies because God has made them.

Black women, the Lord's beauty is already stamped on us. Know it and know it as the Psalmist does full well. Love how you look because God made you and God loves you. Do not let anything make you not love yourself and deny your beauty. Be as God has made you to be.

Be
Fearfully
and
Wonderfully
Made!

Praise God and be naturally beautiful, my Sisters, I love you! Amen.

AUTOBIOGRAPHICAL STATEMENT

I graduated from Vanderbilt University with a B.A. in philosophy, religion, and fine arts. Recognizing my call to preach to grassroots young women and men of low self-esteem caused by their economic and social situation, I returned to school. I received my master's of divinity from Harvard in 1988. Presently I serve as development officer for Harvard Divinity School, where I am also assistant for ministerial studies.

My husband, Benny, whom I married in 1986, is also a minister and works with me for Comprehensive Health Center in Cambridge. He also serves on the board of Casa Myrna Vasquez, a shelter for battered Hispanic and black women.

On December 10, 1989, I was ordained to the Baptist ministry by my minister father of the Second Baptist Church, in Evanston, Illinois. I now minister to Baptist churches in Roxbury, Massachusetts.

My desire is one day to complete my doctorate in theology and to serve as president of a black educational institution. My goals include becoming a good steward of my many gifts and talents: singing, dancing, and ballet.

BACKGROUND INFORMATION

"Wonderfully Made" is a sermon that is seldom heard because the excruciating pain of racism that alienates black women from the standard of beauty in this country is numbing. Many black women are not aware that one of the debilitating effects of this disease is that we have been blind to our natural beauty. Its torment attacks the physical, spiritual, and mental immune systems. This experience of racism is profoundly personal, so when it is spoken it can only be expressed in general terms. It is not statistical. Without being able to articulate feelings about these traits of racism and without being able to recognize the physical denigration of our bodies that it imposes, this present experience of racism is seldom heard. But when black women begin to name how the disease of racism is making them particularly sick, they can then begin their healing process toward wholeness.

Sermons that name the intimate pains of racism for black women are seldom heard, yet, they are not never heard. Many voices of black women who have preached about the anguishing experience of racism on their bodies like Baby Suggs, in Toni Morrison's novel *Beloved*, can be heard throughout history. But sensitivity to black women's personal experience of racism is necessary to recognize the cry. For the passionate, rhetorical question, "Ain't I a Woman?" was proclaimed through the shivering lips of a tall, gangly black woman, bearing the undeniable lineaments of her African features. Study a picture of Sojourner Truth, then hear her message. Never is a black woman's experience seen as generic, separate, and distinct from the present fact of her physical existence, the blackness of her body.

Deep in Sojourner's universal voice, as she proclaimed liberation for all women and minorities, there are personal inflections of her painful struggle toward a positive physical image of herself. Sojourner's own desires to feel good and beautiful about her physical self were the kindling that ignited the fire in her timeless voice. History records how the overt racism that tried to cripple Sojourner's physical self-esteem was once publicly injected by a doctor who raised doubts about her femininity and chided her to submit to an inspection of her body. Mustering every immunity that she physically and spiritually possessed to ward off this racist poison that would tear her body down because she was black, Sojourner cried out in a sermon of great physical self-affirmation:

> "My breasts have suckled many a white babe, even when they should have been suckling my own." She stabs a bony finger. "Some of those white babes are now grown men and even though they have suckled my Negro breast, they are in my opinion far more manly than any of you appear to be." Suddenly without warning, she rips open the front of the dress. "I will show my breast," she says to the entire congregation. "It's not my shame but yours. Here then see for yourself." Her eyes lock on the face of the doubting doctor and she says quietly, "Do you wish also to suck?"[1]

The black woman's history is rich with stories of mothers, grandmothers, great grandmothers, sisters, and aunts like Sojourner Truth who have had to stand in lonely defiance in the face of racism. But every black woman who is able to recognize and fight the disease of racism that would have her feel ugly knows who she is in relationship with God. Black women know that God created them and has made them beautiful.

To know full well that we are fearfully and wonderfully made and that God's works are wonderful is the balm that black women must rub on their wounds from racism. I reach to rub myself down with this healing salve daily. As long as I feel the pains of racism, I will continue to preach sermons about self-affirmation until all my sisters are healed from this plague of racism on our beautiful, colorful bodies.

NOTE

1. Lerone Bennett, Jr., *Before the Mayflower: A History of the Negro in American 1619–1964* (Baltimore: Penguin, 1966).

BIBLIOGRAPHY

Bennett, Lerone, Jr. *Before the Mayflower: A History of the Negro in America 1619–1964.* Baltimore: Penguin, 1966.

Cannon, Katie G., et al. *Inheriting Our Mothers' Gardens.* Ed. Letty Russell. Philadelphia: Westminster Press, 1988.

Grier, W. H., and P. M. Cobbs. *Black Rage.* New York: Basic Books, 1968.

Jones, Major J. *The Color of God: The Concept of God in Afro-American Thought.* Macon, Ga.: Mercer University Press, 1987.

Lerner, Gerda. *Black Women in White America.* New York: Vintage Books, 1973.

Miles, Margaret. *Images as Insight: Visual Understanding in Western Christianity and Secular Culture.* Boston: Beacon Press, 1985.

Morrison, Toni. *Beloved.* New York: Knopf, Random House, 1987.

Nelson, James B. *Embodiment: An Approach to Sexuality and Christian Theology.* Minneapolis: Augsburg, 1979.

Washington, Joseph R., Jr. *Anti-Blackness in English Religion.* New York: E. Mellen Press, 1984.

Washington, Mary Helen. *Invented Lives.* New York: Doubleday, 1987.

West, Cornel. *Prophesy Deliverance: An Afro-American Christianity.* Philadelphia: Westminster Press, 1982.

RESOURCES

Resources for physical self-affirmation of black women include:

Group work, above all with the many who lack self-esteem. Some of the best group work includes literacy programs, parent-child classes in neighborhood/housing areas, and classes on health issues.

Black women's written works are pouring into the mainstream. Of particular value are books by Alice Walker, Toni Morrison, Zora Neale Hurston, Katie Cannon, Maya Angelou, and Ntozake Shange.

The black church has always been a community for black women, enabling civic, religious, political, and social bonding. Today, black women, who comprise 75 percent of their churches' membership, must strive to attain an equal role in leadership. Attaining this leadership will be a resource for empowerment of women in church and society.

21

Anti-Semitism:
Looking beyond Hostility

S. Tamar Kamionkowski

SERMON

Justice, justice shall you pursue....
—Deuteronomy 16:20

In Brooklyn a man is murdered for protesting the swastikas painted on his front door. Robert Cooley, a leader of the anti-choice movement, remarks that "affluence and comfort lead to abortion" and that "the majority of abortionists are Jewish." Upon hearing of these things, who among us would not express at least disapproval, if not outright rage? A synagogue is burned — Jews and Christians alike condemn the act. Verbal slurs are made — we jump in to challenge the remark. For far too long, anti-Semitism, expressed as hostility toward Jews as a religious and/or ethnic minority, has been a significant part of the history of Christianity. Many Christians today recognize the evil of anti-Semitism and are actually working against it; and yet, once we address the stereotypes, the discrimination, and the violence, can we say that the battle against anti-Semitism is over? Is anti-Semitism simply about hostility toward Jews?

As a Jewish woman who has been actively involved in interfaith dialogue, particularly among feminists, I am sad to say that anti-Semitism is very much alive in even the most progressive white Christian communities. It is a form of anti-Semitism that is not expressed as overt hostility, but that stems from a Christian tendency to ignore Jewish experience. This ignorance parallels and ultimately undergirds classic patterns of Christian anti-Semitism.

Ignorance lies at the root of prejudice, stereotyping, and the dehumanization of entire populations. It is this dehumanization, this creation of "other"-ness, that inevitably results in the dismissal of

---

This sermon is addressed to progressive white Christian communities, particularly to those involved in the women's movement. It is especially appropriate for the Easter season or conferences or workshops on interfaith issues.

a group's existence. Christian anti-Semitism is rooted in this phenomenon of ignorance, dehumanization, and dismissal; furthermore, this phenomenon is built into the structure of Christianity itself. The actions or attitudes that develop as a result of this dehumanization fall along a very broad spectrum. In the Middle Ages, dehumanization meant turning Jews into demons, blood-suckers, and baby killers; in a modern progressive world, it means ignoring and thus devaluing the differences between Jew and Christian and negating the distinctiveness of Judaism. The manifestations of anti-Semitism are different, but the roots are much the same.

The roots of anti-Semitism came with the birth of Christianity and its negation of its parent religion, Judaism. One of the outstanding analyses of this early dynamic can be found in the work of Rosemary Radford Ruether, in her book *Faith and Fratricide*. Ruether noted that embedded within the New Testament and the writings of the early Church Fathers is an attitude of triumphalism; the covenant with Israel was to be completely superseded by a new covenant for the community of believers in Jesus. With the arrival of the Messiah, the Holy Scriptures became obsolete; the only purpose of the Old Testament was to serve as a proof for the claims of the young Christian community's beliefs. There was no place in this belief system for those who did not participate in it. Early Christians did not understand how it could be possible that people could still find meaning in their religion without accepting Jesus as the savior. Hostility toward Jews, who "missed the boat," became a necessity in maintaining the veracity of Christianity. This hostility, and the early church's confused relationship with its parent religion, set up dynamics that have filtered down the centuries and into all areas of Jewish-Christian relations. Even Christians today who take such an active stand against anti-Semitism unconsciously perpetuate some of the old patterns.

Ruether's observations have forced theologians to re-examine the nature of Christian theology and to ask: "Is Christianity inherently anti-Semitic?" The debates regarding this question could easily serve as the basis for an entire series of sermons; regardless of the answer to this very critical question, the fact is that the continued viability of Judaism has troubled Christians, and their response to this confusion has resulted in the dismissal of Judaism.

Let me begin with an example. Some years ago, while I was a student at Harvard Divinity School, a Protestant friend shared a guidebook for his denomination's education of grade-school children with me. The booklet had a section on Jewish history and was thus considered to be progressive by my friend. The outline for the lesson began with the life of Abraham and moved through biblical history to the Maccabean revolt and Roman conquest. The history of Judaism ended with Jesus. I found this lesson plan extremely distressing for a number of reasons. First, Jesus is not a significant part of Jewish history. Other figures like Hillel, Yochanan ben Zakkai, and Simeon bar Kokhba had a greater role in Jewish development during that period. Second, Jewish history does not end with the life of Jesus. In many ways, it does not begin until the development of rabbinic law, which essentially postdates Jesus. Why were the development of the Mishnah and the Talmud, the contributions of Maimonides and Rashi, the impact of the Chasidic movement, the ideology of Haskalah, the history of Zionism, and the development of Reform, Conservative, and Orthodox Judaism all absent from the curriculum?

Christians' inability to cope with the viability of Judaism after Jesus has led to a general ignorance about the religion and the culture. The Jewish experience has been negated in order to raise the status of the gospel. And as Ruether states: "This very suppression of Jewish history and experience from Christian consciousness is tacitly genocidal. What it says, in effect, is that the Jews have no further right to exist after Jesus."

This longstanding negation of Judaism's existence as a living and prospering tradition still lives on today even within progressive Christian communities. It has become fashionable, in our times, to speak of a Judeo-Christian tradition. This notion reflects an attempt to look to our shared roots and common beliefs, to make connections and to bond in mutuality. Rather than completely dissociating from Judaism, the parent religion is embraced. On one level, this attempt is admirable; but on a deeper level, it is disturbing. The first clue to the problem is in the term itself. In its hyphenated form, "Judeo" simply modifies the primary concern: Christianity. Judaism, as its own entity apart from Christianity, is invalidated by this expression. As Arthur Cohen, author of *The Myth of the Judeo-Christian Tradition*, points out, the term "Judeo-Christian" was first coined in nineteenth-century German Protestant scholarship to account somehow for the Jewish element within Christian society.

In addition to analyzing the origins of the term, we also need to ask what it is that we, Jews and Christians, really share. What is common to both traditions? Our so-called shared Scripture is the most obvious point of contact; but do we actually share the same Scripture? Our canons are different, the languages with which we read the texts are distinct, and our methods of interpretation are disparate. We do share similar notions of God, monotheism, and moral values; but we understand these things differently. So what of significance remains in common?

Another problem with the idea of a "Judeo-Christian" tradition, is that it masks the hatred with which Christians have treated Jews for centuries. As Arthur Cohen asserts: "We can learn much from the history of Jewish-Christian relations, but the one thing we cannot make of it is a discourse of community, fellowship, and understanding. How, then, do we make of it a tradition?" This modern notion of a "Judeo-Christian" tradition, in fact, merely perpetuates the negation of Judaism as an independent, thriving religion. By looking to the similarities before recognizing and fully acknowledging the differences, the integrity of Judaism is essentially negated.

This negation of Judaism is one of the primary forms of anti-Semitism among many progressive Christian communities. This form of anti-Semitism is not hostile nor is it consciously perpetuated; but it is dangerous and harmful. Specifically within white Christian feminist circles, there has been a tendency to group Jewish and Christian women together and to deny the unique experiences of Jewish women. For example, since the growth of neo-pagan feminist movements in recent years, an apparent split has developed between those who retain the Bible as their primary source of inspiration, and those who reject the Bible and look to other sources. Many people choose to define themselves as either biblical feminists or Goddess feminists. However, this dichotomy stems from Christianity and is not necessarily valid for Jewish feminists. Postbiblical sources and teachings inform my spiritual identity and my practice more significantly than do direct biblical readings. The question for a Jew is not: "Should I adhere to the Bible or move toward the Goddess?" but rather: "Which sources should I draw from in creating a Jewish life for myself?" Jewish women's interactions with Goddess movements will naturally raise unique issues that cannot be subsumed under Christian categories. The assumption that Jewish and Christian women's similarities are greater than their differences renders Jewish women's experiences invisible under the umbrella of Christianity. This is a form of anti-Semitism.

To give you another example: For a number of years, I participated in a women's spiritual group. Although I was the only Jew in a group of Christians and post-Christians, we all felt connected by our desire to explore feminine images of the divine and woman-centered rituals. In those years, we grew together through our explorations and adventures. However, I also discovered how greatly Christian assumptions permeate much of the new women's spirituality movements. I realized that much of the language we used was not my own, but rather Christian language. In addition, our attitudes about ritual were different. Whereas ritual was an old friend to me, it was a new and uncertain guest for those raised in a Christian world. Consequently, I felt excluded or misunderstood all too often, even though we had all expected to bond through our similar visions and concerns. I was disturbed not because my fellow group members did not know more about my tradition, but rather because they took their Christian assumptions for granted.

Even when Christians have a perfect opportunity to learn more about Judaism, they find a way to avoid it. The integrity of Judaism is not only denied by subsuming Jewish experience under the domain of Christianity, but it is also denied by Christian appropriation of Judaism. Two thousand years ago, the Holy Books of the Jewish people were reinterpreted, reordered, and translated (thereby rewritten) by Christians. A Jewish work was stripped of its essence and altogether changed. Christians have not recognized this and have instead spoken of the Old Testament as a common book between us; however the Christian Old Testament is not the Bible of Jews.

Similarly, today a new trend has developed by which Jewish traditions are again appropriated. Seen in a positive light, this move reflects the attempt to reclaim the Jewish roots of Christianity. In reality, however, the integrity of the Jewish tradition is undermined. In recent years, it has become popular for Protestant Churches to have a Seder around the time of Easter. The Seder's theme of liberation from oppression, the timeliness of the holiday around Easter, and the opportunity to interact with Judaism draws progressive Christians to the ritual. But the appropriation of the Passover Seder simply repeats old anti-Semitic dynamics. The holiday is not simply about general oppression and liberation, but rather about a specific historical event — the Exodus of the Jews from their slavery in Egypt. One of the most distinctive marks of Jewish holidays is their rootedness in specific historical events. This holiday provides a time for remembering the oppression of Jews and their ability to endure persecution and to survive. The format of the Seder is also specifically rooted in a particular Jewish context. To take the Seder out of its larger framework is to misuse it and to destroy it. Moreover, when Christians, who have been the persecutors of Jews for centuries, misappropriate the skeleton of the holiday without acknowledging their own role as the oppressors of Jews, then they perpetuate denial and a continuing inability to take responsibility.

Anti-Semitism is still very prevalent in the world today; much more awareness is necessary. Just two generations ago, my grandmother, as a teenager, had to leave her family and escape from her home in Europe. Even today my family is forcibly separated by a Soviet government that maintains openly anti-Semitic policies. Christian oppression of Jews is still very alive today; it is not to be relegated to the history books. Given this unfortunate fact, perhaps it would be more appropriate for Christians to use Passover as a time to reflect on their role as the oppressors, rather than universalizing the evil of general oppression. Maybe this holiday season could be used to consider the anti-Semitic aspects of Easter. This time of year could also provide an excellent opportunity to learn more about current Jewish practices and the real significance of the Passover Seder.

My Christian fellow seekers of justice continue to make assumptions about my experience while remaining ignorant of my religion and culture; they discuss common bonds and similarities and celebrate them with an impatience that ignores the vast differences, and they misappropriate the Seder and other Jewish rituals and language. As long as all these dynamics still operate, I must walk cautiously among those with whom I do share so much. We all hope for peace and justice in this world, yet I see old patterns lying unchallenged.

The compilers of the history of Judaism section for Sunday school education, Christian participants in church Seders, and my Christian sisters in the feminist movement all unconsciously participate in the continuation of anti-Semitism by rendering the Jewish experience invisible. It was a parallel ignorance and dehumanization of Jews, although much more extreme, that led to massacres and humiliation through the centuries. How can anti-Semitism be eradicated in our day as long as Christians remain ignorant of Judaism? Overt acts of discrimination and subtle negations of Jewish existence have the same roots — a disregard for the integrity of Judaism. How can Jews and Christians come together for dialogue when the oppressors still continue to dismiss the viability of Judaism and fail to recognize that Christianity may be built upon a negation of Judaism?

The eradication of anti-Semitism does not simply require the end of malicious actions and statements; it demands a complete transformation of Christianity's triumphalistic basis. It entails a total rethinking of the way that Christianity operates in a pluralistic society. In the words of Martire and Clark, who conducted a study of anti-Semitism in the United States in the early 1980s: "The study of anti-Semitism must be understood, then, not simply as the study of attitudes toward one small minority group but rather as the study of the character of the culture itself."

Anti-Semitism has caused insufferable pain to Jews, but ultimately it is a Christian problem and not a Jewish one. Anti-Semitism cannot be fully overcome simply by becoming more sensitive to our differences, but only by turning inward and exploring why it has been so difficult to acknowledge these differences. How can one begin to follow the precept "Love your neighbor as yourself" without first knowing who that neighbor really is?

AUTOBIOGRAPHICAL STATEMENT

As a child, I remember hearing many stories about anti-Semitism in my family history. Each one of my grandparents had a story about escaping from Eastern Europe, being divided permanently from their families, and somehow making it to Argentina. I remember hearing about relatives who had been murdered by the Nazis. I will never forget the intensity of emotion in my mother's voice when she received a phone call from relatives in the Soviet Union that we did not even know were alive.

All these family stories taught me, at an early age, that there were people who hated me just because I was Jewish; but at the same time, I never experienced that type of anti-Semitism personally. I was raised in an upper-middle-class, well-integrated suburb outside Cleveland. My friends were both Jewish and Christian; some of us went to synagogues and some of us attended churches. My parents' stories did not quite fit into my personal experiences. I concluded that anti-Semitism did not exist within integrated, progressive communities.

I was stunned by another reality upon my matriculation at Harvard Divinity School in the mid-1980s. I met generally well informed, highly educated Christians who exhibited a great gap in their learning when it came to matters concerning Judaism. These were people trained in religious studies, entering the ministry or pursuing advanced degrees, who held extremely simplistic views about Judaism. I observed doctoral students in one of the most liberal divinity schools in the country equating Judaism with the religion of the Hebrew Bible, as if there had been no development of a religion in over two thousand years. I noticed students of religion using the terms "Israelite," "Hebrew," and "Jew" interchangeably. Feminists, upon discovering that I was Jewish, would ask me how I could cope with the patriarchal and violent religion of the Hebrew Bible, as if Judaism had not gone through its own internal growth over the past millennia.

The incongruence of such well-educated people holding such simplistic and ignorant notions of Judaism was very troubling to me. In response to my experiences, I began to explore anti-Semitism in its nonviolent manifestations. Some of the results of my thought are reflected in the sermon.

BACKGROUND INFORMATION

Hostility toward Judaism has a long and complex history, whose roots are traceable to the birth of Christianity. What began as religious hatred developed over the centuries into an economically and racially based phenomenon. Unfortunately, any account of the history of anti-Semitism cannot include a conclusion, because it still permeates societies throughout the world in various ways. I would like to present a very brief and oversimplified summary of the history of anti-Semitism. Those interested in more detailed studies are referred to any of the basic overviews listed in the bibliography.

Brief History: Antiquity to the Twentieth Century. Although Jews suffered persecution before the birth of Christianity, it was only with the inception of the new religion that Jews were condemned simply on the basis of their religion. The gospel writers blamed Jews for the death of Jesus, minimized Rome's role in the crucifixion, and displayed antagonism toward Pharisaism, one of the rival Jewish sects of the period. The early competition that Christians felt with Judaism created a tension that developed into full-blown animosity by the period of the early Church Fathers.

After Christianity became the official state religion, this hatred was translated into anti-Jewish policies. Christians were prohibited from interacting with Jews, and the rights of the latter were greatly restricted. Political and church leaders actively encouraged enmity. St. John Chrysostom (344–407) wrote:

> The Jews are the most worthless of all men — they are lecherous, greedy, rapacious — they are perfidious murderers of Christians, they worship the devil, their religion is a sickness. The Jews are the odious assassins of Christ and for killing God there is no expiation possible, no indulgence or pardon. Christians may never cease vengeance, and the Jew must live in servitude forever. God always hated the Jews....It is incumbent upon all Christians to hate the Jews.[1]

Similarly, Augustine claimed that the existence of Jews in a state of humiliation served as a constant witness to the triumph of Christianity.[2]

The first large-scale exhibition of violence against Jews was the First Crusade in 1096. Leaders who called for the extermination of the enemies of Christ oversaw the brutal massacre of thousands of Jews throughout Europe and the Middle East. In the name of their Lord, Christians from all segments of society pillaged, raped, and murdered their Jewish neighbors.

By the twelfth century, anti-Semitism began to make its first transition from a strictly theological phenomenon to an economic one. The church forbade Christians to loan money at interest, but allowed Jews to practice this trade. Since Jews were forced out of almost all guilds and many professions, they had no choice but to enter the world of finances. With this, the stereotype of Jews as greedy money-lenders originated.

Around this time in history, deep-rooted superstitions began to play a more critical role in attitudes toward Jews. Rumors started to circulate accusing Jews of stealing the Host and torturing the wafers to renew Jesus' suffering. In 1671, for example, when a consecrated Host was missing from a Church in Lisbon, the entire Jewish community was accused of stealing it and was banished from the region.[3] It was also believed that Jews murdered Gentiles to obtain blood for a Passover ritual and for other demonic purposes. Tales about Jews stealing children, torturing them, and crucifying them in hatred of Jesus were commonly circulated. These superstitions have survived into the modern period, and were eventually used by the Nazis.

The Fourth Lateran Council of 1215 established several provisions regarding Jews: Jews were forbidden to appear in public during the Easter season; they were barred from public office; and all Jews were required to wear badges on their garments to separate them from Christians.[4] In each country, these regulations were enforced in different ways; and so, for example, in 1397, Queen Maria of Spain ordered that all Jews wear only pale green clothing.[5] In 1418 in Germany a council required Jewish women to wear bells so that Christian men could be warned of their approach.[6]

By the thirteenth century, as international finance developed, Jews were no longer indispensable in society as loan providers. Mass expulsions had begun as early as 250 in Carthage; but by the twelfth century they occurred with more frequency. From 1290 on, there were expulsions from England, France, Spain, Portugal, and Germany. These were not only motivated by religious factors, but also by economic ones because expulsion meant that Christians could confiscate land and personal property. (This was also common during World War II.) The stereotype of the Wandering Jew, condemned to roam and belonging nowhere, began with these expulsions.

In the 1400s, the Spanish Inquisition began. Jews were subjected to forced conversions or expulsion. However, even after converting, new Christians were still subjected to discrimination, oppression, and the torture of the Inquisition. Jews who had converted were still viewed suspiciously by virtue of their birth. This phenomenon marks another shift in anti-Semitism, from theological and economic to racial.

The Reformation did not much improve the lot of Jews in Christian territories, although on the whole, life was easier in Protestant countries than in those under the domain of the Catholic Church.

By the onset of the modern period, Jews were given formal equality through the emancipation. With this formal equality also came the expectation that Jews would assimilate completely into Christian culture. As long as Jews maintained a separate identity, they were viewed suspiciously.

The general attitude toward Jews in this period is reflected in the work of Wilhelm Marr, a journalist, who first coined the term "anti-Semitism" in 1879. He maintained that it was crazy to blame Jews for the crucifixion and that religious persecution should not be tolerated; but he did believe that Jews were to blame for the corruption of German government and the lowering of German standards. Marr believed that Jews, by nature, were power-hungry and corrupt, and could not be changed because their flaws were racially determined.[7]

In Eastern Europe, Christians instituted pogroms, that is, outbursts of murdering, pillaging, and raping with the support of the governments. Boycotts and limitations of the numbers of Jews in professions or societies were also standard, as was a forced twenty-five-year military service in Russia.

The extermination of six million Jews during the Holocaust was the most systematic and brutal exhibition of anti-Semitism. Most of the propaganda that the Nazis used was taken from centuries of Christian superstitions, oppression, and ignorance. Nazis did not invent their ideas; they simply systematized age-old beliefs and actions on a mass scale.

The Present. The post–World War II era has seen the declaration on non-Christian religions (*Nostra Aetate*) of the Second Vatican Council, sincere dialogue between Christians and Jews, a grappling with the anti-Semitic nature of Christianity, and strivings for mutual understanding. The United States, not without its history of discriminatory practices against Jews, has provided a good atmosphere for Jewish and Christian dialogue.

But even in the United States, problems still exist today. In 1989, 1,432 anti-Semitic incidents were recorded by the Anti-Defamation League; this is the highest figure of the 1980s.[8] In the week of November 6–13, 1989, on the fiftieth anniversary of Kristallnacht, over sixty incidents were reported — four times the weekly average.[9] Although incidents include murder, assault, and threats, most anti-Semitic actions in the United States are against property — swastikas, arson, bombings, and cemetery desecrations.

Apart from anti-Semitic acts, dangerous statements and attitudes abound both from the Right and the Left in this country. On the Right, anti-choice rhetoric is filled with anti-Semitic comments. Extremists like Lyndon LaRouche guilefully claim that the Holocaust is a hoax, that the Jews killed Jesus, and that Zionism is racism. The Ku Klux Klan and skinhead organizations continue to increase their membership from year to year.

On the Left, criticisms of the state of Israel reveal anti-Semitic attitudes. As Ellen Umansky points out: "Critiques of Israeli policy become critiques of Jews. Those who equate Zionism with racism not only deny legitimate Jewish aspirations for a national homeland but also falsely equate the Zionist dream with the particular objectives of the current Israeli government."[10] The same activists who honor the self-determination of other peoples repudiate this right for Jews.

Even within the women's movement there has been blatant anti-Semitism. The oppression of Jews has existed from the days of Elizabeth Cady Stanton's *The Woman's Bible*,[11] in which Jews were blamed for the patriarchal elements of the Bible, to the refusal of the Women's Joint Congressional Committee to take a stand against the persecution of Jews in Europe during World War II.[12] As recently as 1980, at the United Nations Women's Conference in Copenhagen, Letty Cottin Pogrebin documented a shocking number of anti-Semitic remarks.[13] In the past couple of decades anti-Semitism has made its way into liberation and new feminist Christian theologies.[14] Also, in the rewriting of prehistory and early history, Jews have recently been accused of creating patriarchy and killing the Goddess.[15]

Whether overt or covert, hostile or unintentional, it is imperative that anti-Semitism continue to be challenged in all its manifestations. This problem has gone far beyond the church today, but it is within local church communities that so much can be done.

NOTES

1. Dagobert D. Runes, *The Jew and the Cross* (New York: Philosophical Library, 1965), pp. 61–62.

2. *Anti-Semitism*, Israel Pocket Library (Jerusalem: Keter Publishing House Jerusalem, 1974), p. 13.

3. Ibid., p. 103.

4. Paul E. Grosser and Edwin G. Halperin, *The Causes and Effects of Anti-Semitism: The Dimensions of a Prejudice* (New York: Philosophical Library, 1975), p. 110.

5. *Anti-Semitism*, p. 87.

6. Ibid., p. 93.

7. Paul W. Massing, *Rehearsal for Destruction* (New York: Howard Fertig, 1967), pp. 6–9.

8. "Anti-Semitic Incidents during 1989 in the United States," *Patterns of Prejudice* (Winter 1989–90): 49.

9. "Anti-Semitic Incidents during 1989 in the United States," *Patterns of Prejudice* (Spring 1989): 52.

10. Ellen Umansky, "Racism, Classism, and Sexism: A Jewish Woman's Perspective," in *Women of Faith in Dialogue*, ed. Virginia Ramey Mollenkott (New York: Crossroad, 1987), p. 117.

11. Elizabeth Cady Stanton, *The Woman's Bible* (New York: European Publishing Co., 1898).

12. Elinor Lerner, "American Feminism and the Jewish Question," in *Anti-Semitism in American History*, ed. David A. Gerber (Urbana: University of Illinois Press, 1986), p. 3

13. Letty Cottin Pogrebin, "Anti-Semitism in the Women's Movement," *Moment* (July/August 1982): 28–34, 49–53.

14. Judith Plaskow, "Blaming Jews for Inventing Patriarchy," *Lilith: The Magazine for Jewish Women* 7 (1980): 11–12.

15. Annette Daum, "Blaming Jews for the Death of the Goddess," *Lilith: The Magazine for Jewish Women* 7 (1980): 12–13.

BIBLIOGRAPHY

Cohen, Arthur A. *The Myth of the Judeo-Christian Tradition.* New York: Harper & Row, 1970.

Daum, Annette. "Blaming Jews for the Death of the Goddess." *Lilith: The Magazine for Jewish Women* 7 (1980): 12–13.

Eckstein, Yechiel. *What Christians Should Know about Jews and Judaism.* Chicago: Word Books, 1984.

Flannery, Edward H. *The Anguish of the Jews: Twenty-Three Centuries of Anti-Semitism.* New York/Mahwah, N.J.: Paulist Press, 1985.

Heschel, Susannah. "Anti-Judaism in Christian Feminist Theology." *Tikkun: A Bimonthly Jewish Critique of Politics, Culture & Society* (May/June 1990): 25–28, 95–97.

McCauley, Deborah, and Annette Daum. "Jewish-Christian Feminist Dialogue: A Wholistic Vision." *Union Seminary Quarterly Review* 38 (1983): 147–190.

Martire, Gregory, and Ruth Clark. *Anti-Semitism in the United States: A Study of Prejudice in the 1980s.* New York: Praeger Publishers, 1982.

Plaskow, Judith. "Blaming Jews for Inventing Patriarchy." *Lilith: The Magazine for Jewish Women* 7 (1980): 11–12.

Ruether, Rosemary Radford. *Faith and Fratricide: The Theological Roots of Anti-Semitism.* Minneapolis: Seabury Press, 1974.

Schneider, Susan Weldman. "The Anti-Choice Movement: Bad News for Jews." *Lilith: The Magazine for Jewish Women* 15 (1990): 8–11.

Talmage, F. E., ed. *Disputation and Dialogue: Readings in the Jewish Christian Encounter.* New York: KTAV Publishing House, 1975.

RESOURCES

Shermis, Michael. *Jewish-Christian Relations: An Annotated Bibliography and Resource Guide.* Bloomington: Indiana University Press, 1988. This book includes an extensive bibliography on a wide range of issues as well as listings of media resources, speakers, service groups, and journals, and tips for new interfaith dialogue groups.

American Jewish Committee
Institute of Human Relations
165 East 56th Street
New York, NY 10022

Anti-Defamation League of B'nai Brith
National Office
823 United Nations Plaza
New York, NY 10017

National Conference of Christians and Jews
National Office
71 Fifth Avenue, Suite 1100
New York, NY 10003

Religious Network for Equality for Women
475 Riverside Drive, Room 830A
New York, NY 10115